BUSINESS AS USUAL

POSSIBLE FUTURES SERIES

Series Editor: Craig Calhoun

In 2008, the World Public Forum convened a group of researchers and statesmen in Vienna to take stock of major global challenges. The magnitude of the global financial crisis was only just becoming clear, but the neoliberalism and market fundamentalism of the post-Cold War years had already taken a toll of their own.

Austrian Prime Minister Alfred Gusenbauer opened the meeting with a call to make sure the urgent attention the financial crisis demanded was not just short-term and superficial but included consideration of deeper geopolitical issues and governance challenges facing the global community.

In this spirit, several of the researchers present envisioned a project to bring together the analyses of leading scholars from a range of different countries, assessing not only the financial crisis but shifts in relations among major powers, trends in political economy, and the possible futures these opened. The group sought insight into emerging issues; it did not indulge the fantasy that the future could be predicted in detail.

The World Public Forum, created to facilitate a dialogue of civilizations rather than a clash, saw value in bringing high quality research to bear on public issues and possible futures. It provided financial support to the project including opportunities for many of the researchers to gather at its annual meetings on the island of Rhodes. This initial support was crucial to inaugurating the present important series of books.

VOLUME I

Business as Usual: The Roots of the Global Financial Meltdown

Edited by Craig Calhoun and Georgi Derluguian

VOLUME II

The Deepening Crisis: Governance Challenges after Neoliberalism

Edited by Craig Calhoun and Georgi Derluguian

VOLUME III

Aftermath: A New Global Economic Order?

Edited by Craig Calhoun and Georgi Derluguian

ALSO IN THE POSSIBLE FUTURES SERIES

Russia: The Challenges of Transformation

Edited by Piotr Dutkiewicz and Dmitri Trenin

Business as Usual

The Roots of the Global Financial Meltdown

Edited by Craig Calhoun and Georgi Derluguian

A joint publication of the Social Science Research Council
and New York University Press

NEW YORK UNIVERSITY PRESS

New York and London

www.nyupress.org

© 2011 by Social Science Research Council

All rights reserved

Text Design: Debra Yoo

Library of Congress Cataloging-in-Publication Data

Business as usual : the roots of the global financial meltdown / edited by Craig
Calhoun and Georgi Derluguian.

    p. cm. -- (Possible futures series ; v. 1)

    "A co-publication with the Social Science Research Council."

    Includes bibliographical references and index.

    ISBN 978-0-8147-7277-5 (cl : alk. paper) -- ISBN 978-0-8147-7278-2 (pb
: alk. paper) -- ISBN 978-0-8147-7279-9 (e-book : alk. paper) 1. Financial
crises. 2. Capitalism. 3. Global Financial Crisis, 2008-2009. 4. Consumption
(Economics) I. Calhoun, Craig J., 1952- II. Derluguian, Georgi M.

HB3722.B867 2011

330.9'0511--dc22   2010052308

New York University Press books are printed on acid-free paper,
and their binding materials are chosen for strength and durability.

Printed in the United States of America

c 10 9 8 7 6 5 4 3 2 1

p 10 9 8 7 6 5 4 3 2 1

References to Internet websites (URLs) were accurate at the time of writing.
Neither the author nor New York University Press is responsible for URLs that
may have expired or changed since the manuscript was prepared.

Contents

Series Acknowledgments   7

Series Introduction: From the Current Crisis to
Possible Futures   9
Craig Calhoun

Introduction   43
Craig Calhoun and Georgi Derluguian

1   The End of the Long Twentieth Century   53
        Beverly J. Silver and Giovanni Arrighi

2   Dynamics of (Unresolved) Global Crisis   69
        Immanuel Wallerstein

3   The Enigma of Capital and the Crisis This Time   89
        David Harvey

4   A Turning Point or Business as Usual?   113
        Daniel Chirot

5   Marketization, Social Protection, Emancipation:
        Toward a Neo-Polanyian Conception of Capitalist
        Crisis   137
        Nancy Fraser

6   Crisis, Underconsumption, and Social Policy   159
        Caglar Keyder

7   The Crisis of Global Capitalism:
     Toward a New Economic Culture?   185
     Manuel Castells

8   The Convolution of Capitalism   211
     Gopal Balakrishnan

9   The Future in Question: History and Utopia in
     Latin America (1989–2010)   231
     Fernando Coronil

     Notes   265

     About the Contributors   293

     Index   297

Series Acknowledgments

The volumes in this series have their roots in discussions at the World Public Forum, Dialogue of Civilizations. At a 2008 meeting in Vienna, the WPF honored former Austrian chancellor Alfred Gusenbauer for his leadership in global affairs and assembled a "high-level summit of experts" to join him and WPF president Vladimir Yakunin in discussion of the financial crisis then unfolding and its implications. Several contributors to these volumes were among the participants in that discussion, and the larger Possible Futures project was initiated. We are grateful to the WPF and especially to President Yakunin for this initial launch, for subsequent intellectual discussions, and for leadership in assembling a range of international scholars to address key public issues. Dr. Yakunin has himself written with distinction on these matters; without his initiative this project would not have taken place.

We also want to thank the World Public Forum more generally for providing crucial financial support and the occasions for subsequent discussions in Rhodes and Yerevan. Colleagues at each of these meetings made valuable suggestions that improved different chapters. Dr. Vladimir Kulikov provided valuable administrative support. We are also grateful to Professor Piotr Dutkiewicz of Carleton University, who played a crucial role in formulating and carrying out plans for the meetings and subsequent volumes. With Dmitri Trenin, Professor Dutkiewicz has edited a volume on the future of Russia that is an important companion to the Possible Futures series: *Russia: The Challenges of Transformation*.

The Editorial Department of the Social Science Research Council provided excellent support. We thank especially Paul Price and Alyson Metzger. Sara Maria Acosta provided administrative support at the SSRC with efficiency and aplomb. Likewise, our editor at NYU Press, Ilene Kalish, led a special effort to bring these books out quickly so they could inform continuing discussions. We are pleased by NYU Press's embrace of the idea of "real-time social science."

From the Current Crisis to Possible Futures

Craig Calhoun

The phrase "global financial crisis" has been repeated ten million times since March 2008. The rich countries of the twentieth century have been plunged into the worst recession since the Great Depression. Even after massive infusions of taxpayers' money, financial institutions remain shaky. Major banks have failed; sovereign states in Europe face bankruptcy with unpredictable consequences for the European Union. Recovery remains elusive, and perhaps "recovery" is not the right word, for this crisis may mark a dramatic moment in a more basic shift of economic momentum and political power from the rich countries of the twentieth century— especially in Europe and North America—to more rapidly developing countries in what had long been capitalism's semi-periphery. The crisis should focus our attention not just on the immediate events that precipitated it but also on the potential for deeper transformation. A recovery to something like the patterns in place before 2008 is only one of the possible futures open now, and not the most likely.

The word "crisis" can easily be abused. It carries a sense of urgency belied by the willingness of politicians, investment bank managers, oil-rig supervisors, and many of the rest of us to put off decisive action. It suggests the necessary climax to a natural process, like the turning point in a disease. When a high fever breaks, if a patient hasn't been killed, he or she usually recovers. Yet when a social problem is called a crisis, neither the turning point nor where we turn is likely to be so clear. Crises call attention to social problems, but they open a variety of possible futures. A return to business as usual may be one of those possibilities, but not necessarily the most likely.

Indeed using the word crisis is commonly a way to try to get people to take action, to indicate that we have no choice *but* to do *something*. It is performative, not merely descriptive. It is a call to action. And so the very naming of a crisis—and the repeating of the name in a million newspaper articles, political speeches, and dinner-table conversations—actually helps to constitute it. The definitions that gain currency focus attention, suggest what courses of action are appropriate, and even invoke different pre-crisis histories. They accordingly demand critical examination.

Focusing on the suddenness with which the financial crisis became acute may be deceptive. To be sure, few people were prepared for the news of bank collapses and stock market crashes like the startling one that began March 7, 2008. The suddenness came from a tipping point, when long-term factors produced a discontinuous drop in market values and set off a chain reaction. In fact, warning signs had been accumulating since at least 2005 or 2006—and a few prominent analysts had issued actual warnings.[1] The housing-and-mortgage bubble itself peaked in 2006, though it took a further eighteen months for the implications to become fully manifest. More basically, the 2008 crisis was one in a long recurring pattern of financial crises shaped both by contradictory pressures in the financial system and the recurring illusion that "this time growth is different" and growth can be sustained without crisis.[2] There was the Asian financial crisis of 1997; there was the end of the dot-com bubble in 2000. This series of financial crises is part of the general tendency of capitalism to crises but also specific to an era shaped by "financialization"—a large-scale turn away from industrial production toward finance as a source of profit in the world's richer countries (and a consequent decline in manufacturing employment and a rise in service jobs, though this never quite made up for the loss).

A "financial crisis" mattered much more after thirty-five years in which the financial sector grew dramatically both in absolute terms and as a proportion of the economy of rich countries. It mattered for capital accumulation, but also for the well-being of people who had mortgaged their homes, invested their retirement savings, or taken jobs in highly leveraged and vulnerable businesses. Analyzing the crisis through the conceptual framework that shaped financialization itself encouraged government responses centered on the financial sector and specifically banks. These were initially dominant, securing the stability of markets—and the fortunes of the wealthy—through contributions from the taxes of all. There was much less substantial effort to secure the finances of the poor and the middle class. This was a matter not just of class bias—though it was that—but also of analytic frameworks that focused on financial wealth rather than material production or human well-being.

The version of financial thinking that was predominant in response to the crisis was that which grew with massive expansion of financial markets in the preceding decades. It emphasized immediate liquidity for markets and the role of large firms. So there was less help for individual homeowners faced with possible foreclosure as their mortgage payments escalated. The same focus on finance extends into austerity programs designed to reduce government deficits and reassure bond markets, not least in Europe. To be sure, the US government and some others have also taken up financial stimulus packages, including investments in infrastructure and support for nonfinancial industries. These have been neither immediate nor ubiquitous. But the point is less about the detail of government responses than about the extent to which they were organized by the ideas central to expanding financialization.

The financial crisis is frequently described as "global," but here too one has to think past the most immediate senses of the term. It is undeniable that financial upheaval transcends national markets, linking Wall Street and the City of London to Greek sovereign debt and Russia's investments of the profits from its oil industry. But it is not equally a crisis everywhere. China has kept on growing right through it, even if its export markets contracted for a time and its heavy investment in US debt caused worry. The national economies of Brazil and India are also flourishing. The phrase "global financial crisis" rolls off the tongue and is not false. But saying "global" can obscure both the unequal impact of financial crisis and the extent to which it is a moment of acceleration in a broader, longer-term shift of economic momentum from West to East, and perhaps somewhat from North to South.

And of course it is absolutely true that the crisis involved greed and theft, fraud by firms and individuals, failures of management, and failures of regulation. It was shaped by the prestige and profitability of traders, which allowed them to evade the scrutiny of less prestigious risk managers. It was shaped by successful campaigns to make sure that government didn't regulate the financial industry more or demand open, transparent accounting for its practices. It involved the development of new business practices and new financial instruments. But though all of these are important, none of them explains the crisis. And none of them enables us to look clearly at the options open for action now.

The crisis is all too real. Saying it can be understood in different ways, more superficial or more penetrating, does not mean it can be wished away. But in order to think well about the possible futures that are open, it is necessary to have a deeper understanding of the crisis that brought us here. Much too widely, it is discussed as though its causes were just short-term aberrations. Much too often, questions about the future are limited to asking when things will return to "normal." But the crisis is more than just a brief hiccup in business as usual. And the possible futures are more diverse and potentially more transformative than simply a resumption of economic growth.

In the first three volumes of this series, some thirty-six of the world's leading social scientists analyze the crisis in historical context and with broad comparative attention to different parts of the world. They address the connections between financial upheaval and a range of other social issues, and they consider the ways that both past history and current challenges shape possible futures. Volume 1, *Business as Usual: The Roots of the Global Financial Meltdown*, looks at the crisis itself, situates it in historical context and asks how it might influence transformations of global economic and political relations and whether this upheaval in older economic relations reveals patterns of new possibility. Volume 2, *The Deepening Crisis: Governance Challenges after Neoliberalism*, connects the financial crisis to a variety of other issues. These include challenges of global governance and financial regulation, of environment, conflict, and security, and also the ways religion, ethnicity, nationalism, and media shape each. Finally, volume 3, *Aftermath: A New Global Economic Order?*, focuses on the different ways in which future economic growth may take place, how this will shift balances among different parts of the world, who is likely to win and who will lose, and how this will relate to prospects for a new and perhaps more multilateral world order.

In the remainder of this introduction to the series, I offer a view of the financial crisis itself, of its relationship to the previous crises of the 1970s and to the long bubble that connects the 1970s to the present. While this is shaped by my own interpretation, it is also intended as background to the discussions that different contributors offer of longer-term views, views shaped by implications for other crises, views from other continents, and views of future challenges. It is important both to see the crisis from different perspectives and to see the connections among these different views. It should be clear that this is only a proximate history; some contributors would stress much longer-term patterns. But it is important at least to connect the very immediate crisis in American credit markets to broader patterns and implications.

There are manifestly many themes that I cannot address in detail here, like the return of geopolitics to international relations and the restructuring of world regions or the tensions between multilateral cooperation and multipolar competition as efforts are made to stabilize global political economy. I don't propose to summarize the contents of these three powerful and provocative volumes but rather to suggest one possible thread that may help to integrate their contents—and the different histories and challenges that connect the current crisis to possible futures.

The Financial Crisis

In early 2008, shares on the New York Stock Exchange fell with alarming speed. Business reporters wrote about a "subprime-lending crisis." Readers learned that billions of dollars' worth of mortgages were not being repaid. Many of these had been made to borrowers who didn't have the kinds of assets or incomes that predict a good chance of repayment.

This happened partly because a number of banks discovered a route to rapid—if unsustainable, dangerous, and possibly criminal—profits.[3] Rather than simply lending money prudently and deriving profit from the interest paid, they would write as many mortgages as they could and sell them off as fast as they could. Most of this was done in private markets, but the process was aided by government programs designed to help less well-off Americans get mortgages.[4] The now-infamous Fannie Mae and Freddie Mac bought enough mortgages to maintain liquidity in the market and helped repackage them as tradable securities.[5] Securitization was crucial. Historically, a specific bank might lend money to a specific homebuyer, who would repay that bank over a period of years. Securitization broke this connection between making the original loan and its long-term ownership and repayment. It meant essentially bundling many mortgages together and selling shares in that pool of debt and rights to repayment. Mortgages made to those with good credit histories and high capacity to repay were bundled together with mortgages to people who might previously have been considered too risky to get a loan. Companies issuing mortgages had an incentive to make as many loans as possible, so their employees became more like aggressive salesmen than circumspect bank officers. In some cases, they even went door to door offering mortgages to people who already owned their homes. More and more mortgages were written with less and less scrutiny of the capacity of borrowers to pay. Mortgage-writing speed came to be rewarded more than prudence, for the practice of ignoring once-significant standards of prudence seems to have become habitual for many banks and companies that specialized in marketing "subprime"—that is, especially risky—mortgages.

In principle, the securities that combined many mortgages spread the risk. But much depended on the assumptions that housing prices would keep rising and defaults would be relatively few. When housing prices began to trend down, the mortgage-backed securities became toxic, and it was hard to sort out the good from the bad. The issue would resurface when banks set out to foreclose on mortgages not being repaid: many found they lacked crucial documentation. But once again, the old business virtue of prudence was not much in evidence. Major lenders, such as Bank of America and Chase, assigned low-level clerks to initiate foreclosure proceedings without fully reviewing documentation. Many of these were "robosigners" who processed hundreds or even thousands of mortgage foreclosures a day, predictably producing numerous errors.

Issuing so many shaky mortgages would have harmed many under almost all circumstances, but the effect was made more severe by the role these securities played in the larger financial system. Historically, mortgages have been a relatively solid asset, and so these new securities were treated as firm enough to count as collateral on the balance sheets of investment banks and insurance companies. Accounting practices

It's not just that there are multiple short-term causal factors to weigh—mortgage-backed securities, credit-default swaps, proprietary trading. It is also that different empirical accounts of this crisis—different stories—reflect distinct underlying concepts of capitalism, of finance, and of crisis itself and distinct ideas about whether to focus more on financial markets as such or more on the lives of ordinary people. Each analysis informs a particular vision of possible futures and policy or public actions. Is this just one more of the crises to which capitalism is prone? This would suggest that recovery is likely and business as usual will be restored. This would reveal crisis to be just a phase in the business cycle. But it is also possible that there will be a transformation—for example, an accelerated shift in economic momentum from West to East and North to South. Is the crisis a sign of the exhaustion of a particular hegemonic structure within capitalism that might be renewed with new leadership? This would suggest that the era of US dominance in the world economy may be over and that countries developing rapidly today, like China, India, and Brazil, may play bigger roles in the future. This could just mean new leaders for continued capitalist expansion, or perhaps the crisis is a sign that capitalism is reaching the end of its road. Perhaps the world economy may not be able to restore productivity growth, or perhaps limits to development have been reached. Or is the crisis a stimulus to move a long-gestating new economic culture from the margins to center stage? This might point to a future of vitality from smaller-scale businesses, greater environmental concern, and efforts to organize economic activity on bases other than capital accumulation.[11]

In sum, the contemporary crisis is large-scale and deep. There is a good chance that it will be part of a transformation in basic social and economic institutions. But the crisis is a historical event, not an event in some natural system (no matter how commonly the economy is discussed as though it were a natural system). It was made by human actions and will be made worse or better by other actions, including those of governments. What it means historically will depend in part on what is done now. And what we do will depend on how we understand the crisis.

The Pivotal 1970s

To understand the current crisis—all the intersecting current crises—it is indispensable to attend to roots in the 1970s. The specific responses made then to earlier crises shaped both intervening years and the crisis today. The 1970s saw the deepest recession between the 1930s and the present day. This came at the end of a remarkable postwar boom that brought expanding demand through the 1960s. The 1970s crises can be understood partly as a matter of business cycles, thus, but at the same time, they reveal the limits of that understanding. The postwar expansion was much more than just an economic expansion. To reduce it to a single indicator of growth in any aggregate economic measure is to miss the shift from a phase in which material production and distribution was ascendant to one in which finance was ascendant.[12] There have been previous phases of financialization over the history of global capitalism, and there may be more to come, but the one that took off in the 1970s is the largest and most transformative so far.

During the postwar boom, there was an enormous expansion in both state provision of services—like education and health care—and private-market provision of consumer goods. The middle class grew in numbers in Europe, America, and elsewhere, while, at the same time, middle-class consumption rose as cars, refrigerators, and televisions—and, for that matter, college degrees—became increasingly standard. Pressures for more egalitarian, or at least wider, distribution of wealth were prominent. There was an expansion not just in government services but also in the proportion of the population covered by private pensions and provisions for long-term corporate employment.

Decolonization was a central feature of international affairs during this period. This was of course marked by conflict—in Congo, in Algeria, and in Vietnam, where Americans took over when French colonial power failed in the 1950s. But decolonization also brought high hopes and substantial growth in some colonial and postcolonial economies. Colonial powers sometimes adopted pro-development strategies anticipating the transition away from colonial rule. After independence, a variety of the world's richer countries mounted substantial efforts to help postcolonial countries grow. Such efforts had both idealistic dimensions as part of a project of global modernization and more cynical motivations as expanding markets offered supplies of valued resources, potential consumers for the products of industrialized countries, and (at least in theory) bulwarks against the spread of communism.

Unilinear models of development in fact proved problematic, not least because newly independent countries struggled to make their way in a world where richer and more powerful countries dominated many markets. The Cold War itself was expensive with its demand for military hardware, even if this yielded economically productive spinoffs. Residual empire became a significant economic cost. Military engagements lost their patina of glory. Retaining colonies became a challenge to political self-understanding as participatory democracy became more clearly normative. Though America's Vietnam War was neo-imperialist rather than directly colonial like France's, it fits a similar model. It was enormously expensive and paid for largely by debt. It was costly in lives and undermined national solidarity and self-confidence for decades.[13]

By the 1960s, there was substantial and open discontent. A variety of social movements challenged the legitimacy of the institutional arrangements that had reconciled capitalism, democracy, and the Cold War in wealthy Western countries. Children raised amid consumerist expansion expressed discontent with the institutional arrangements, the cultural conformity, and the channeling of personal desire that supported it. The radicalism of the 1960s was sometimes Marxist and redistributionist, sometimes neo-Romantic and focused on self-expression. But in each case, it took not just corporate capitalism but the existing state to be an authoritarian enemy. So basic have right-wing attacks on the welfare state become that it takes an effort now to recall that many earlier criticisms came from the left.

This set the context for crisis in the 1970s.[14] The decade began amid a peaking of the so-called 1960s protest, linking the counterculture of rich countries to broader anti-imperialism.[15] In one of the most symbolically resonant episodes, Chile elected Salvador Allende and a largely socialist coalition government in 1970. Its policies of nationalization and other economic reforms brought sharp US opposition, intervention, and eventually a coup. Post-coup Chile would actually provide a setting for experimenting with neoliberal government as the famous "Chicago Boys" designed policies to maximize reliance on markets and private property rather than public delivery of social services. The Chilean experiments informed the later and larger projects of Margaret Thatcher and Ronald Reagan. That they were aided by a military government is a reminder of the extent to which neoliberalism generally has been imposed by government action even when leaders declared themselves hostile to government economic intervention.

Simultaneously, there was turmoil in exchange rates after the United States pulled out of the Bretton Woods Accord in 1971. Among its many effects, this caused the dollar to depreciate and revenues of oil producers to decline. It thus helped to pave the way for OPEC production controls and spiking oil prices—the most immediate cause of the 1973–75 recession. But then so did the Yom Kippur War of 1973, an inflection point in the ongoing entanglement of energy prices in politics and a reminder of the impossibility of separating economics from politics more generally.

The Vietnam War dragged on expensively, financed more by debt than explicit budget allocations even as it became more unpopular. Britain fought Argentina in a war over its continued colonial control of the Malvinas, or Falkland, Islands. International tensions perhaps peaked with the Iranian Revolution of 1979. Particularly severe in the United Kingdom and the United States, the 1973–75 recession brought drops of several percentage points in GDP and double-digit unemployment in many industrial countries—even while inflation soared—and left growth rates low for several years.

The disillusionment born from these factors helped bring Margaret Thatcher and then Ronald Reagan to power and usher in the era of neoliberalism. Whether in Chile or Britain or America, neoliberalism meant an effort to assert the primacy of private property against public regulation and as the sole basis for distributing goods and services, rejecting most state support. Privatization of government assets played a role in some countries (like the United Kingdom), as it would again in the former Soviet Union. There was also a concerted effort to break trade-union power.

A long campaign by followers of Friedrich von Hayek and Milton Friedman began to bear fruit in shifting public opinion as well as government policy. By 1986, the arbitrageur Ivan Boesky was able to give a speech at Berkeley praising greed.[16] Before long, Boesky was in prison, convicted of insider trading. But his huge if ill-gotten wealth as well as his view that greed was good became part of popular culture—along with similar views and behavior by the "junk-bond king" Michael Milken (who also went to prison after Boesky informed on him) and the corporate raider Carl Icahn. The three informed the fictional character of Gordon Gekko from the 1987 movie *Wall Street*, which at once popularized and satirized the phrase "greed is good."[17] Over the next twenty years, both the manifestations of greed and the size of the fortunes acquired would become even more dramatic.

The era of neoliberal ascendancy was also an era of increasing reliance on finance as the source of profits in the capitalist world.[18] This affected international markets as well as domestic capitalism. Lending to developing countries helped to precipitate its own crisis of sovereign debt and brutal "structural adjustment" by the 1980s. State debt played an important role in richer countries as well, but so did the less commonly emphasized massive increase of private debt. Rates of leverage went up on all sorts of assets. And the development of new financial instruments and accounting practices took off. In 1973, Fischer Black and Myron Scholes published their famous approach to pricing derivatives.[19] Aided by Robert C. Merton's improvement of the mathematics, this initiated a wave of expansion in hedge funds, derivatives trading, and the use of algorithms for more or less automated trading—all key factors in the eventual crisis of 2008 (and also foreshadowed in earlier crises).[20]

The turn to finance had partly to do with declining profits in manufacturing. In a range of industries, corporations responded by demanding that workers take cuts in compensation, introducing new technologies, insisting that governments provide tax breaks or outright subsidies, and/ or relocating manufacturing to other countries. Sometimes relocation came even after corporations had benefited from subsidies and wage cuts, in defiance of commitments to stay put. Neoliberal governments aided corporations in breaking the power of unions to resist these changes.

These are among the reasons why this era of financialization was one of intensified inequality in many countries. In the United States, the share of income going to the top 10 percent of the population fell dramatically during World War II and stayed relatively low (less than 35 percent) until the late 1970s, when it started climbing again, reaching prewar levels by the 1990s and just before the 2008 crash matching the level it had touched before the 1929 crash. Of course other factors were also at work, including not least dramatically increased rewards to investors, top executives, and other beneficiaries of financialization—like the investment bank employees who scandalized many with their annual bonuses of tens or hundreds of millions of dollars, even after their firms needed government bailouts.[21]

Corporations were pushed along in their pursuit of short-term profits by raiders like Icahn who insisted that corporations had no purpose other than delivering increasing value to their shareholders. In other words, they owed nothing to local or national communities, workers or managers, suppliers or customers. These were not legitimate stakeholders, the apostles of shareholder value argued, but rather simply means for delivering shareholders higher returns on their investments. When returns were not high enough fast enough, the corporation could be made the object of an internal fight for control or an external purchase. The profitability of corporations was judged on ever-shorter time frames. They were subject to constant control by capital markets—if they weren't bought and sold outright or broken up to realize greater profits from selling their pieces, they were nonetheless threatened by the potential that capital for their operations would become more expensive if their stock price dropped or their bond rating dipped. Many began to eliminate pensions even while they took to paying their top executives more in bonuses tied to short-term indicators of profit than they did in actual salary.

Bigger profits began to be made in trading than in making things. The trade could be currency arbitrage, or loans at high interest rates (like junk bonds, but also personal credit cards), or speculation in capital markets. But the key was that lending and generally moving money around supplanted investments in long-term production as a source of profits for many in rich countries. A partial exception to this was the role of venture capital in financing new technological developments and product innovations—most prominently in microelectronics, computing, and communications. Here (as in biotechnology and a few other cases) the availability of large amounts of capital did facilitate the creation of very valuable new technologies. But this was not a rational process driven straightforwardly by proven technological promise. It was dependent on the potential for financial profits *before* companies proved themselves profitable. A venture capitalist or a speculator invested not just on the basis of a good business plan but on the expectation that he could sell his stake at a profit before the business was really tested by the market.

This is why, despite the genuine achievements of the micro-electronics and IT industries, there was a dot-com bubble at the end of the last century. Venture capitalists backed start-ups with varying degrees of genuine promise. Together with investment banks, they helped these raise capital through offering stock to a wider range of investors (generally through initial public offerings—IPOs). Some of these investors were in fact speculators who bid up the stock on its first offering only to dump it later. And when too much pumping up and too much dumping happened too fast—as in 2000—the bubble burst. The NASDAQ composite index of high-tech and growth stocks peaked at $5,048 in March 2000, only to fall to a little over $1,000 by 2002. In some cases, the very bubble helped companies—and technologies—get off the ground that might never have made it were investing more rational.[22] But for every Google that became enduringly profitable, there were hundreds of other corporations that existed only fleetingly.

Bubbles are characteristic features of finance-driven markets, and since the 1970s, finance has been very much ascendant. Essentially a bubble means rapid growth in the value of financial assets without strong foundations in the underlying economy or actual business performance. Bubbles can finance technological innovation. But this is precisely because they mobilize capital beyond what is "rational" in terms of medium-term productivity growth or sustainable profits. Bubbles typically involve speculation, dangerous debt leverage, and accordingly, as the metaphor suggests, a propensity to burst.

The Long Bubble

Finance was already important in the 1960s, of course, but it really became dominant as recovery from the 1970s recession was based on financing growth with credit and extracting profits through financial instruments and speculation rather than material production.[23] Inside the world's rich countries, it involved growth in wealth without major increases in material production. It involved heightened inequality as that wealth was heavily concentrated and there was a decline in middle- and working-class shares of economic proceeds. It also involved cutbacks in a range of public services—especially in recurrent crises, but also even while growth continued, often in the name of "competitiveness." A "good business environment" came to mean one where taxes were low (and more and more often where governments exempted businesses from taxes). This meant that while aggregate financial statistics frequently suggested growth during the bubble years, there was actually a widespread pattern of underconsumption and underfunding of "social reproduction" (education, health, and in general, the conditions of life for future generations and thus also of labor for future capitalist enterprise).[24]

At the same time, finance was more and more globally integrated. While movements of workers and goods are important to globalization, it is in fact movements of money that became most instantaneous and friction-free. The results were sometimes disastrous for developing countries—as in the 1997 currency crisis, especially in Southeast Asia. But this also created the conditions for some of the world's poorer countries to parlay low-cost manufacturing, low levels of domestic consumption, and high savings or re-investment rates into sustained growth—and growth based on material production, not only finance.

In a sense, finance-driven growth since the 1970s has been one long bubble, with several smaller bubbles along the way. Kevin Philips calls this a "multibubble" since, of course, it was not simply a long smooth trend, but repeated cycles of boom and bust.[25] The United States saw three speculative binges, in 1984–89, 1996–2000, and 2003–7. Each created its own specific patterns of excess, corruption, and misjudgment and gave way to sharp "corrections" in financial markets. In each case, the Federal Reserve stepped in to cut interest rates close to zero, reinflating the depressed markets to the advantage of some individuals and firms but not of either the majority of the population nor the economy as a whole. Temporal patterns and institutional specifics differed in other countries, though in general, both the bubbles and the crises grew more tightly integrated as trade generally and financial flows specifically intensified interconnections in the global economy.

The long bubble was shaped by massive expansions both of personal and public debt and of consumption financed by this debt, especially in the twentieth century's rich countries. It was shaped also by extension of markets to a global scale, including formerly communist countries, by projects of privatization of state assets and deregulation of private economic activity, and by an intensification of inequality, both within the world's richer countries and globally. And it was shaped also by a long neoliberal campaign against government regulation, trade unions, public scrutiny of business practices, and broader views of corporations as having multiple stakeholders from employees to local communities (as well as customers, suppliers, and the "public"). The campaign favored free exercise of private-property rights against all restrictions, a theme manifested not just in resistance to regulation but in the reduction of the business corporation itself to a commodity to be bought and sold in pursuit of short-term "shareholder value."

Obviously there is much more to this story. The termination of the Soviet Union ended the Cold War, giving freer reign to capitalist globalization and introducing new sources of energy and cash into the capitalist world system. This was linked to a Westward reorientation in most of eastern Europe.[26] Joining the EU brought uneven benefits, especially as rapid growth shifted to financial crisis, but countries with significant manufacturing capacity fared relatively well. The period saw not just accelerated trade and financialization but huge flows of migrants (many of them not simply moving one way but relying on easier travel and communications to maintain strong connections within global diasporas).[27] The information technology and communications revolution that helped make this possible was influential in countless other ways.[28] And of course, not only were there "internal" crises within this finance-driven expansion, there were "exogenous" shocks, not least the attacks of September 11, 2001. These in turn brought new wars as a response and new borrowing to finance them.[29] And manifestly, politics and economics were not the whole story. For example, the September 11 attacks brought attention to an international renewal of politicized religion that had in fact long been underway.[30] The very economic bubble had encouraged a rosier view of continuous and continuously benign globalization than was warranted.

The dynamics of bubbles, and more generally boom-bust cycles, are well-enough known that at one level each new instance shouldn't be a surprise. In retrospect, we can see that there were advance warnings. This is certainly true in the case of the market meltdown of the last few years. So what's puzzling isn't that there are bubbles but why people are recurrently taken in by the notion that "now things are different."[31] Or again, how could neoclassical and some other versions of economics persist so long in models based on representative rational actors, smooth curves, and anticipations of unproblematic long-term growth? And were traders and managers on Wall Street really convinced by all the hype about new capacities to manage risk, or did they actually know the crash was coming but get taken in by the notion that they were so smart they could time getting out better than most did? Certainly one feature of the bubble years was drawing an array of the brightest students at top universities to work in investment banking, enculturating them in a world of playing late-night poker games, celebrating risk, denigrating risk management and regulation, and perpetuating the satisfying notion that they were not only brainy enough to deserve absurd fortunes for minimally productive activity but bright enough to know when to get out of the Ponzi scheme.[32]

Then there is also the question of why democratic governments ostensibly concerned about the welfare of their citizens and the vitality of national economies did not intervene directly to support either but instead to bail out the investment industry. This is a matter partly of the success of the long campaign to make neoliberalism common sense and partly of the campaign donations and other forms of pressure exerted by financial interests. Throughout the twenty years leading up to 2008, for example, the finance industry spent millions and worked hard to get politicians to reduce regulation.

The long bubble of the last thirty-five years also wove together deepening structural problems in rich economies and impressive growth enabling some of the world's poorer and previously "semi-peripheral" countries to move into positions of sustained economic growth and growing global leverage. Thus the US combination of massive borrowing, disinvestment from materially productive industry at home, and industrial investment where labor costs were cheaper (and environmental and other regulations less demanding) helped create the conditions for China to transform its economy, enjoy double-digit economic growth, and sell its goods to America and other rich economies, financing their purchases by buying their debt. Europe became a large-scale net borrower somewhat later than the United States, but with similar effects. And if those effects were overwhelmingly negative in the countries living beyond their means and securing profits in finance rather than industry, the picture was different in Brazil, China, India, and other countries, which had the chance to begin their own equivalents to the West's postwar boom, with cars, refrigerators, televisions, and higher education again becoming standard.

China is the most spectacular of several stories of countries previously in marginal positions in global capitalism enjoying impressive growth. At the beginning of the bubble years, attention was focused on Japan, which became a global investment force before itself entering into a long period of stagnation, its so-called lost decade. Brazil, India, and South Korea have long been semi-peripheral in the world economy but now may be moving into core positions. Indonesia, Malaysia, Mexico, Turkey, and others are not far behind. One central feature of this pattern is that these countries have flourished by flouting the so-called Washington Consensus of mainstream economists and advisors from rich countries and global institutions like the World Bank. Notably, although their rise is part of capitalist globalization, it has been shaped by strong state leadership and often by a combination of state financing and tariff barriers quite at odds with neoliberal economic ideology.[33] It has also generally included an emphasis on material production precisely at a time when many rich countries were reducing their industrial capacity.[34] This very success joins with the financial crisis to challenge dominant perspectives on economic growth and development.[35]

Not least among the views needing challenge is the notion that new technologies have ushered in a postindustrial era. Along with the idea of a "knowledge society," this helped to frame an image of benign transition in Europe or America away from manufacturing industries with their pollution and manual labor toward a future of office and service work in which intellectual capacities would be critical.[36] Not only did this underestimate deskilling and productivity pressures in office and service work, it overstated the ease of transition. Control of knowledge was indeed important, but abandoning industrial production proved deeply problematic. The citizens of rich countries didn't stop wanting physical goods, after all. They just stopped making them. This exported economic leverage to developing countries, eliminated large classes of jobs for Americans and Europeans, and became a basis for growing debt. Since many of these were unionized and well-paid jobs, this offered advantages to capital. But it was a strategy pursued in the era of financial ascendancy, not a simple response to technological change. And it had a range of problematic repercussions, including increasing dependence on fossil fuel as goods were shipped around the world and the undermining of local communities that lost their economic bases, career structures that enabled people to take long-term perspectives on their lives, and social solidarity generally.

From Economic Globalization to Geopolitics

The bubble years thus transformed not just economies but global power relations. The United States gradually lost the ability to maintain global economic and political order (though many were slow to see this, partly because, even while it was overstretched, it became the world's one superpower with the demise of the USSR). Though the United States remains the world's strongest political and economic power, it has lost a good deal of its hegemony.[37] It is severely economically indebted and militarily overstretched. But no other global power has stepped up to replace the United States (and the genuinely remarkable growth in China still does not support the notion that it is close to doing so).[38] There may yet be a renewal of US growth and creative energy—though this depends on not just meeting global challenges but overcoming domestic obstacles, like political gridlock, financial troubles at every level of government, and a dispiriting lack of a sense of public purpose. In any case, as a declining hegemon, the United States has choices about whether to be belligerent or to play a more constructive role in shaping a new, more multilateral world order.

This reorganization of global power relations is a reflection not just of economic change, of course, but also of the instability introduced into world affairs by the crisis and the end of the Soviet Union, which shook one major world region deeply and affected states and struggles around the globe. It eliminated the only large-scale competitor to the global expansion of capitalism. And it was not unrelated to the long bubble, driven as it was partly by an arms race itself dependent on massive spending by the American government under Ronald Reagan and supported by one of the boom cycles in the multibubble (the one that ended with the Savings and Loan crisis that started in 1986). The collapse of the USSR created the occasion for the privatization of state assets at prices that amounted to near theft—or more directly by actual theft. It also brought Russian natural resources, especially energy resources, into the global economy, mitigating high energy costs. Much Russian capital was invested abroad, further inflating bubbles of the last twenty years. Yet Russia itself may or may not achieve the industrial and technology-driven growth necessary to escape the status of regional power and supplier of natural resources to the global economy.[39] And Russia has become a leading example of the disconnection between accumulation of capital and wealth and projects of national development, leading a worldwide trend toward use of offshore investments and shelters to protect capital from absorption in the very countries where it is produced.[40]

Global instability was increased by the combination of assertions of Islamic militancy, sometimes with terrorist tactics, and the choice of the United States and a few allies to respond with war. The decision by President Bush to brand the attacks of September 11, 2001, acts of war and to respond with a "war on terror" actually dignified the terrorist action more than it deserved. Previously, terrorist actions were generally treated as crimes, and the leaders of groups (or networks) like al Qaeda were not treated as though they were heads of states, even rogue states. But it is true that non-state conflicts have been growing, especially since the end of the Cold War. And in any case, the United States and a handful of allies responded to the 9/11 attacks with an invasion of Afghanistan and an outright war of regime change and occupation in Iraq. This added to instability by increasing anti-American and radical Islamist mobilizations, by undermining American credibility (both because it emerged that the US administration had used deceit to justify its invasion of Iraq and because the United States managed the war and occupation badly), and by driving the US economy much deeper into debt.

In any case, it seems clear that we are entering a period with many major powers, none fully dominant. In addition to the United States, Europe clearly belongs on the list (though it is hard to say with what balance between individual European countries and EU cohesion).[41] China and India are major rising powers, the former much stronger than the latter. Russia remains a significant player on the world stage as well as a dominant one in its region. And a range of other countries may be among the central participants in global power sharing; Brazil, Iran, South Africa, and Turkey have among the best prospects. But this doesn't tell us to what extent global power will be organized in multilateral cooperation or how much in multipolar rivalry. Nor does it indicate how much will be organized globally and how much regionally. Global institutions remain important, though criticism of the World Bank and the IMF is widespread—even after they have undertaken some reform—and the United Nations is in a weakened condition in much need of reform, clarification of its mission, and more consistent support from member states.

Regional blocs are significant. Contrary to crude images of globalization as breaking down all differentiation of the world, it has actually encouraged regional integration—most prominently in the European Union, but in different ways in other parts of the world. The African Union is proving more effective than its predecessor, and economic integration in that region is growing, though with South Africa as a budding regional hegemon. The Arab League has had only modest successes, but Al Jazeera television has shaped a shared political consciousness throughout the Arab world (to the regret of several dictators). Latin American integration is challenged by tensions between more "liberal" and more "socialist" governments but is nonetheless growing. There are questions as to whether Mexico has cast its lot more with North America than with Latin America, to be sure, and indeed questions at the broader level of whether integration is more a matter of hemispheric proximity, migration, and investment than a matter of language and culture.

Asia is increasingly knit together across the lines of such old subregional divisions as East, Southeast, South, and Central. Of course, China's neighbors are at once drawn into its political and economic orbit and resistant to domination by its regional hegemony. Many are making efforts to maintain more distant alliances—not least with the United States—as counterbalances. At the same time, old geopolitical fault lines have re-emerged and are attracting attention. In Northeast Asia, the North Korean remnant of the Cold War may attract the most attention, but eyes are also on the division between China and Taiwan, the question of oil and maritime rights involving contested claims to various islands, and the Amur River frontier between Russia and China. In Central Asia, a cluster of newly independent states sits amid the larger powers of Iran, Russia, and Turkey and straddles the boundaries of the Muslim and Christian worlds. And the volatile conflicts on the Indian subcontinent are not just matters of religious division but of geopolitics. What happens in Afghanistan shapes Pakistan's regional influence. Though India is by far the region's strongest power, it feels itself encircled by enemies or at least unreliable allies. And across the continent, the influence of political Islam is influential and often intertwined with national and regional struggles.

This is not just a matter of the developing world. Geopolitics and issues like uneven development and migration remain powerful in Europe. While the division of East and West within Europe has been redrawn, it has not disappeared. Even with the successes of the European Union, there are substantial internal divisions, as can be seen in German anxiety about being called on to support "profligate" Greeks. More generally, in the context of financial crisis, the distance between richer and poorer European countries seems large; so too the distance between those with deep macroeconomic imbalances—Britain included, not just the southern Europeans with their conventionally weaker economies—and those without. Europeans are rattled thus by some of the implications of European unity. But they seem to be rattled even more by immigration and by Islam.

Religion has become a significant factor in global political economy, surprising theorists who had thought it destined to fade with modernization.[42] The patterns are distinct in the cases of Christianity, the world's fastest growing religion, and Islam, the one attracting the most new attention in politics.

Christianity is changing from within, as for example, Latin American Catholics convert to Pentacostalism, sometimes in the very process of migrating to the United States. Pentacostalism is also a major factor in Africa, producing both converts to Christianity and revitalizations and reorientations for long-time Christians (and those who had drifted in and out of more loosely defined religious allegiances). And it is not a tiny movement in the former USSR. But Christianity is also attracting new converts in Asia, in uncertain but apparently large numbers. Pentacostalism offers among other things a mode of adaptation to new economic circumstances, a religious organization of personal self-discipline, entrepreneurial motivation, and connections to potentially helpful business associates.[43]

Islam is also growing by new conversions, though not to the same extent. The renewal of Islam is largely a matter of revitalization of already Muslim populations and the promulgation of new ideologies. But Islam's geographic distribution in the world is changing, largely by patterns of migration. This has generated the most publicized response in Europe, where panic over the prominence of Islam has been widespread. It has challenged both the secular and the democratic traditions of France, Germany, and perhaps most problematically, the Netherlands, but it has also become a factor in the politics of Britain, Spain, and other countries. Anxiety over Islam has impeded the seemingly logical incorporation of Turkey into the EU. This in turn has altered the geopolitics of central Asia and the Middle East. At the same time, Islam is itself a global ecumene, linking populations (and polities) from the Middle East to Indonesia and China's northwest, the Mediterranean to Central Asia, and the Indian Ocean.

Anxiety over extremism (a term often deployed in the West as though it applied only to Islam) has made Islam a much bigger issue in global political economy since the 1990s and especially 2001. There is of course a reality to the threat of terrorist attacks throughout the world as there is to the role of Islam in more geographically specific mobilizations in Afghanistan, Central Asia, or the Middle East. But just as clearly, "extremism" is as much an issue on the Israeli side of the most basic of the Middle Eastern conflicts. And extremism is hardly foreign to Christianity.

Religion is usually only one dimension in large-scale conflicts or even narrower phenomena like terrorist acts—and seldom the sole and decisive dimension. But religion is prominent in conflicts that are able to draw great powers into response. This is as true of China in Xinjiang, Russia in Chechnya, and India internally and in relation to Pakistan as it is in regard to the United States or Europe. It appears as a global dimension of conflicts that are also shaped by a variety of local circumstances, including national or ethnic inequalities and discriminations. It shapes lines of solidarity and connection that may be influential in a reorganizing post-crisis world.

Inequality and Social Welfare

Raising issues of geopolitics is already a reminder that globalization is poorly described as simply the spreading of market relations everywhere. The political and the economic are always entwined. If there are new technologies for transcending distance in some relationships, there are still conflicts at borders and frontiers, alliances along lines of ethnic or

into concrete next steps of improved incomes or family and community life. In such contexts, diseases like HIV/AIDS and natural disasters from floods to famines often appear as more deadly negative lotteries (even though patterns of social organization and failures of social policy may lie behind each).

Upheaval in global political economy is shifting the meaning of categories like rich countries, rapidly developing, and poor, though not overnight. While China and India are each home to rapidly growing middle classes and dozens of newly minted billionaires, both also have large populations of very poor citizens. In each, prosperity is very unevenly distributed. Nonetheless, rapid development is moving them increasingly into core positions in the modern world system. The scale and momentum of their economies suggest that they will be among global leaders. It is possible that during the coming decades they will experience something akin to the industrial growth and strengthening of service provision that Europe and North America experienced during the post–World War II boom. This may exacerbate global environmental challenges, but it holds prospects for continued dramatic material gains within some of the world's largest economies.

Conversely, Russia faces a future pattern of development limited by its dependence on the sale of natural resources—especially gas and oil. This has created wealth, though so far the benefits have been concentrated in a narrow elite and the nature of the wealth has been conducive to corruption. For Russia to enjoy more balanced growth would require a concerted effort to improve its productive industries—which have languished since the days of the USSR. This is particularly a challenge given the head start enjoyed by Brazil, China, India, South Korea, and other stronger productive centers. Russia previously enjoyed an advantage in human capital thanks to strong Soviet programs of education and training. This has been eroded by brain drain, however, and by a failure of investment only now being partially reversed. In varying degrees, Russia's situation is shared by eastern European countries that also face semi-peripheral futures. Many have the advantage of stronger industrial production thanks partly to more modernization in recent decades, and also to membership in the EU. They do not, however, have the wealth of natural resources that makes Russia potentially a world leader if it can manage greater economic balance.[50]

Natural-resource dependence is everywhere a mixed blessing. Several Latin American countries have made oil and mineral wealth the basis for substantial social programs. Whether this will become a successful strategy for long-term development, in Venezuela, for example, is unclear. Many are currently prosperous because of the sale of agricultural and mineral products to more industrial countries, notably China. But counting on agriculture and extraction alone is a limiting strategy. On such bases Argentina was one of the world's richest countries in the early twentieth century but did not translate this into productivity growth or national wealth. In recent years, Brazil has done a better job than most others of integrating natural-resource wealth with productive industry.

In Africa too a number of currently poor countries hope that rich endowments of natural resources will become bases for transformative economic development. In the past, however, those natural resources have too often turned into a curse leading to predatory states, warlords who turn ethnic differences into criminal conflicts, and long-term dependence on foreign powers intent on buying natural resources at the lowest possible prices.[51] Natural-resource trade, legal and illegal, is implicated even in humanitarian crises, like those of Congo, Liberia, and Sudan. Strong states operating relatively honest and competent bureaucracies seem to be the main vehicle for resisting this fate.

It is not only the rich countries but also the rapidly developing that demand the natural resources of others—energy resources first and foremost but also timber and minerals vital to new technologies. There seems no end to the demand, though clearly there are limits to the supply, which only makes conflicts more likely. While these may bring direct combat between major consuming powers, it is likely the conflicts will continue to be played out nearer the sites of production than the sites of consumption, claiming the lives of the poor, harnessing states that might aid in development to the tasks of extraction, reifying the fault lines of region, religion, and ethnicity into bases for mobilization, and encouraging the leaders of liberation fronts and resistance movements to degenerate into the bosses of armed criminal gangs.[52]

In short, for all the globalization of recent decades, the financial crisis affected the world's regions and countries very differently. They were differently situated with regard to level and kinds of industry, nature of involvement in finance, strength of government structures, natural-resource endowments, human capacities, and labor costs. The current crisis has struck especially hard at relatively rich countries. This creates opportunities for some others, but it also unsettles relations in and among regions, making for challenges and risks in the years ahead.

Some of today's rapidly developing countries will become new world powers; their citizens will enjoy growing material consumption, and their industries will benefit from the combination of imported natural resources and relatively cheap labor. Most of today's rich countries will remain rich, even if in relative decline. But few of today's poor countries will enjoy equitable economic development—at least not unless there are massive changes in the social organization of power, the cultural constructions of identity, belonging, and moral obligation, and the systemic relationships that govern the exploitation of nature and human labor-power, the distribution of wealth, and the accumulation of capital. So far, movements to change these basic patterns of inequality are weak.[53] And while attention to climate change and environmental degradation is growing, practical action is lagging behind.[54]

Conclusion

To grasp the full meaning and implications of the financial crisis, we have to go beyond its immediate precipitating factors to situate the crisis in a longer-term history and a more complex view of capitalism and global relations.

Today we face an abundance of crises. We use the word most for what has happened in financial markets, but there are also crises in domestic politics and global governance—crises of environmental degradation, refugees and forced migration, infectious disease, and war. Each creates both intellectual and practical puzzles. Each shapes what possible futures are open to us, but seizing more rather than less attractive futures depends on deepening our knowledge of what is going on and what is possible.

It is a Chinese proverb and a business adage that crises create opportunities. Perhaps it is just an opportunity to buy cheap. But sometimes it is more, the chance to shift direction. Of course it is not only crises that create opportunities. History is always open-ended. There are always ways to do things better: to invent new technologies, to transform work processes, to start or save relationships, to make money. Crises focus our attention, at least sometimes, though they can also distract and disorient us. Crises actually constrain our choices. But they also encourage us not to take the future for granted, to try to make choices, and to achieve the better among the possible futures.

Introduction

Craig Calhoun and Georgi Derluguian

No adequate account of the contemporary crisis can be limited to short-term problems inside the finance industry. Overleveraged investment banks, the spread of proprietary trading, ever more opaque and poorly understood derivatives, and hedge funds operating beyond regulation all played significant roles. So did a culture of gambling and greed. But it is just as important to explain why the finance industry became so central to capitalism in this period and why risks became so large, concentrated in private hands, yet globally linked. The short-term failings of business as usual are also connected to larger-scale transformations.

This is missed by surprisingly many. There is a temptation to think that the crisis was the work of errant individuals, not the product of systematic operations. Ideology and self-interest reinforce this view among many on Wall Street. *New York Times* business columnist Joe Nocera calls it denial, a refusal to see what is evident, as exemplified by the fund manager Anthony Scaramucci, who, speaking on behalf of "the Wall Street community," complained that President Obama had been "whacking Wall Street like a piñata." It was a strange attack on a president who had sponsored billions of dollars in bailouts to rescue Wall Street. But the point is not simply that Mr. Scaramucci represents the distorted view of those who benefited from economic arrangements that transferred massive amounts of money from those who work to those who make financial deals. Rather, the larger point is that he represents a widely held theory of what went wrong in 2008. "You have 500 to 1,000 rogues on Wall Street," he said. "They were the ones who did counterproductive things to the society."[1] In other words, the crisis represented the work of a few overly greedy traders, rogues, or "bad apples." In this view, there are no lessons to be learned about the importance of financial regulation, the pitfalls of trading in securities neither buyers nor sellers fully understand, or the disastrous consequences of financialization—let alone about capitalism itself.

The contributors to this book do not all agree with each other, but they all disagree with Anthony Scaramucci. They disagree with all those who hold that there is nothing problematic about the system that produced the crisis, that only the excesses of a few individuals are at fault. That there were excesses of individual greed is not in doubt; of course, the greed and the payments made to satisfy it are both outrageous. But greed is not a satisfying explanation. This crisis has been shaped in basic ways by capitalism, by financialization since the 1970s, by politically organized limits to regulation, and by organizational as well as individual irresponsibility. In other words, what we are witnessing is a crisis resulting from business as usual, not simply a disruption of business as usual.

By now there are enough journalistic narratives of the crisis and explorations of its dramatis personae to fill multiple bookshelves. With titles like *Fool's Gold, House of Cards*, and *A Colossal Failure of Common Sense*, they tell—some of them extremely well—the story of how the new business as usual was formed within the financial industry.[2] The best and brightest from Princeton and Harvard were drawn into working for investment banks; traders became the sexiest and most highly rewarded players on Wall Street; "quants" developed algorithms and strategies to trade with increasing speed on the basis of more factors than they, let alone their managers, could understand; banks became proprietary traders on their own accounts; and a huge range of derivatives and specialized financial instruments were developed—in some cases, initially in an effort to stabilize markets and manage risk, but they were increasingly used to expand leverage and simply make money, lots of money. This is a crucial dimension of the crisis. But it needs to be integrated with a longer-term view of why financialization happened, how neoliberalism made a difference, and what futures are open now.

This first volume in the Possible Futures series takes on the core task of deepening historical understanding of the crisis. This means both showing how it fits into the patterns of previous decades and even centuries and, crucially, asking how it shapes our choices, capacities, and challenges for the future.

First of all, contributors show how the crisis today reflects problematic responses to previous crises and also the underlying contradictions that make capitalism prone not just to crisis but to specific kinds of crises. As Beverly Silver and Giovanni Arrighi make clear in chapter 1, a crisis of industrial overproduction is very different from a financial crisis—and not every crisis is a systematic crisis. Following Arrighi's theory, they show how cycles of innovation intersect with recurrent crises and stabilization of capitalism under a series of hegemonic leading economies.[3] The rise of each new hegemon—like the United States in the early to mid-twentieth century or Britain in the eighteenth—is marked by the solving of problems inherited from the previous period. But of course new problems arise, and each cycle ends with the hard-pressed hegemonic power withdrawing into financial speculation. This produces a late phase of secondary prosperity—prosperity built more on finance than the production of things. And it is crises of these financial phases that gain the capacity to transform the larger system. The question today, then, is whether a new hegemon will emerge. Will China, or perhaps a group of countries, succeed in stabilizing the economic system?[4] This would mean making material production ascendant again and meeting environmental, natural-resource, energy, and other challenges. It would probably also mean finding a way to reduce rather than exacerbate inequality.

Immanuel Wallerstein's chapter 2 account complements Arrighi and Silver, showing in more detail how in the 1970s a major crisis marked the end of a phase of industrial capitalism. Wallerstein introduced world systems analysis precisely in the context of the 1970s crisis, emphasizing the extent to which the dynamics of capitalism had to be understood through analysis of an international division of labor, recurrent crises and waves of problem-solving, and the stabilization and leadership provided by successive hegemonic powers.[5] Here, Wallerstein details the different challenges to capital accumulation that coincided in the 1970s, making clear that these involved political demands for a greater share in wealth as well as long-term economic cycles. A turn to finance temporarily restored economic momentum and capital accumulation—though with sharp limits, including limits on how wide a population would share in prosperity. The current crisis, he argues, is a return of problems not addressed in the 1970s. Like Arrighi and Silver, Wallerstein maintains that it is not clear that capitalism can recover. Among the possible futures we must consider is an era of chaos and instability as the world system gropes toward a new form of organization. It may regain stability and capital accumulation may remain its driving force—or the chaos may give way to some other future.

In chapter 3, David Harvey situates the current crisis in relation both to capitalism, as such, and to the era of neoliberalism and finance capitalism. He stresses in particular how an era obsessed with managing risks failed to come to terms with "systemic risk." Figuring prominently in this is the question of what would happen to a highly leveraged financial system if liquidity dried up. We now know a good deal more about this in practical terms, thanks to the experience of recent years. But Harvey argues that to make deeper sense of it, we should address the internal contradictions of capital accumulation. Drawing on Marx, but challenging most conventional Marxism, Harvey shows that capitalism works in part by repeatedly challenging, transcending, or working around limits, barriers to growth. It suffers temporary crises and regains momentum as limits are overcome. As Wallerstein argues, the crisis of the 1970s reflected one set of barriers to growth. But the radical financialization by which leading capitalist economies "recovered" sowed the seeds of a deeper crisis. Harvey sees the potential for renewed capitalist momentum with China in the forefront, until the next crisis, but he also emphasizes the possibility of trying to create a new and different kind of economy more directly focused on meeting human needs.

Since the 1970s, many of the world's leading capitalist countries have turned significantly away from advancing underlying "real economies"—the parts that produce usable goods—toward seeking profits from financial transactions. In chapter 4, Daniel Chirot documents the culture of extreme risk-taking that became business as usual in this era of "financialization." His stress is on the internal world of capitalist elites, but less on the ethics of capitalism and the proverbial bad apples than on how relatively honest and upstanding bankers were transformed into highflying financiers who ignore risks. Chirot suggests that the crisis of 2008 was a more or less conventional capitalist crisis and that it can potentially be met by a more or less conventional, largely Keynesian government response. But it was also a panic, a product of social psychology, and Chirot closes by asking what happens when such a panic coincides with deeper capitalist crisis and long-term technological cycles. We face a choice of possible futures: serious reforms (which seem increasingly unlikely as anxiety about a deep depression subsides), muddling through and leaving in place the sources of future crises (most likely), and an even greater crisis produced not by economic failure but by political madness or war.

Financialization was not simply a trend but a response to previous crises in profit rates and the accumulation of capital, most notably in the 1970s. It was encouraged by politicians preaching the virtues of marketizing almost everything and thus turning public property into private assets, often leveraged by massive credit. This, in turn, reflected deeper ideological work seeking to discredit regulation and public enterprise; to reduce business corporations to commodities themselves, bought and sold; and to encourage the notion that all human needs could best be met on the basis of private-property transactions. Yet, of course, as the financial crisis has demonstrated, those private-property transactions had massive public consequences, and most of the world's richer states used tax funds on an enormous scale to bail out private investors.[6] Even those who argued that individualism should rule and wanted to minimize the importance of the collective found themselves relying on state action to avoid economic disaster.

Neoliberalism and financialization went hand in hand during the late twentieth century. They produced a form of capitalism based in many ways on the proposition that the social didn't matter. What mattered were individual property owners and economic transactions among individuals.[7] Welfare systems and social protection were hollowed out or eliminated. Educational systems, health care, and transportation and other infrastructures all suffered, not least in the twentieth century's rich countries. Inequality increased to a startling extent, reversing a long previous trend in which benefits from both private enterprise and government spending were distributed more and more equally.

This raises the second major theme of the chapters in this book, the question of how rich and middle-income countries may reorganize to bring the social back into central consideration. This is the question approached in the Marxist tradition as "social reproduction"—the reproduction of the collective conditions required for continued renewal of material production and the economy more generally. Nancy Fraser, in chapter 5, and Caglar Keyder, in chapter 6, both show why the current crisis is not just a financial crisis, narrowly conceived, but also a crisis shaped by the attempt to increase short-term capital accumulation by reducing social supports that capitalism in the long run requires.

Fraser introduces a "neo-Polanyian" conception of capitalist crisis. Polanyi described a "double movement" by which societies typically correct for the predations inflicted by unregulated markets (and thus secure their future). Government is crucial to providing social insurance, education, food or health support, and other benefits—and since Bismark, it should be obvious that this is as important for conservative as for leftist governments. Social movements are crucial to producing government action (and also, often concessions from businesses). But these are not simply class or labor struggles. Nor does the double movement imply overcoming capitalism; it can be a push for "repurposing" capitalist wealth as well as for simple redistribution.

Drawing on Polanyi, Fraser also demands that we go beyond him. Polanyi failed to see that state action "correcting" for failures of markets could also be a form of domination. There are conservative as well as progressive ways to provide social support. Fraser protests against approaches that protect some groups at the expense of others—and calls for public contestation to reshape the "norms infusing social protection." Polanyi calls our attention to the disembedding process by which markets are made ends to themselves rather than means of meeting social needs. Fraser suggests it is not enough to re-embed markets in social relations and purposes; it is crucial to do this in ways that expand rather than restrict opportunities.

Keyder stresses social reproduction at the level of not just the nation-state but also the world system. He emphasizes that as much as members of the middle class of rich countries have suffered, the burden of globalization's inequality, exploitation, and crises is borne most by the world's poorest. The dynamics of the current crisis come largely from underconsumption. Absent major government interventions, there is no guarantee that capitalists will invest in forms of production that serve the everyday needs of majority populations (let alone the very poor). And in the last several decades, governments have not counteracted capitalist tendencies to inequality but exacerbated them in the name of neoliberal freedom from regulation and constraint. Not surprisingly, the distributions of wealth and income have become much more unequal. Rich countries rolled back social welfare provisions and less well-off ones sacrificed hopes for better living conditions to the competition for external investment.

Keyder is pointed in emphasizing the extent to which a large part of the world's population is more or less irrelevant to the calculations of capitalism—central neither to production nor consumption. He argues that failure to expand consumption is one of the reasons for overreliance on financial sources of profit. The current crisis is an opportunity for social democracy to regain the initiative after neoliberalism has so strikingly faltered, though this is hardly guaranteed.

Closely related to social reproduction is the question of whether there may be a new economic culture to supersede that of the recent past. In chapter 7, Manuel Castells offers encouragement to think this may be so. He sees the global financial crisis as a direct outgrowth of the institutional arrangements and practices adopted as capitalism shifted into a global informational economy in the late twentieth century. Deregulation combined with technology to transform financial markets; nearly every economic asset was securitized, often in the form of exotic new assets. The crisis reverberated globally, but as a turbulent flow of information, not just the market transactions that conventional economic theory (and indeed financial engineering) anticipates will "clear"—reaching a new level of equilibrium even if the new level of stability is sometimes lower.

Financialization allowed global imbalances to grow more and more extreme—as, for example, China accumulated massive investments in US debt. Global creditors (like China) and global energy suppliers took on pivotal new roles. But even as this capitalist global structure was becoming fragile, seeds of a new economy were sprouting in its interstices. From experiments in barter and alternative currencies to cooperatives and projects like urban farming, these are generally of very small scale today. Nonetheless, they suggest that alternatives are possible if the institutional constraints of conventional capitalism are reduced. Technological innovation, networking, and higher levels of education underwrite this new economy. They were important to capitalism in its ascendant financial phase, though it blocked their transformative potential by concentrating capital and limiting wages. And they support alternative-lifestyle communities today. Castells anticipates partially successful remedial action within the old framework but increasing pressure to change it and growing spaces free from its direct domination.

In chapter 8, Gopal Balakrishnan explores the contrary possibility, that capitalism may not this time be able to generate innovation enough to renew its dynamism. Balakrishnan acknowledges that a new phase of more dynamic capitalism, marked for example by technological innovation, might yet follow the current crisis. But he examines what it would mean for capitalism neither to revitalize itself nor to end but instead to enter a long-term, near steady-state of stagnation. This idea challenges Marxists as well as neoclassical economists—ironically joined by faith in an inevitable new age of expansion. Balakrishnan notes the expansion of capitalism to a truly global scale in the era of financialization but argues that this masked a long downturn in the "real economy" of goods and services that meet human needs. Relying on finance also made speculation nearly unstoppable, which produced its own problematic effects. And the debt accumulated by many of the world's rich countries sharply constrains their capacity to act in support of capitalist markets. Balakrishnan considers the possibility that China might rise to be capitalism's savior but thinks it is still too poor and too dependent on production for export (precisely to the countries facing economic crisis). With massive productive capacities that it is already having difficulty matching to consumers, capitalism may enter a long era of deflation.

These are economic questions, but not merely questions about "the economy." They are also questions about how ordinary people think about the future—indeed, whether they feel they can think about the future. As Fernando Coronil suggests, writing about Latin America in chapter 9, the very future has come into question. Not only there but in much of the world, many people find it hard to connect concrete actions today to long-term plans for tomorrow. Saving for retirement, seeking education for upward mobility, and working hard to advance a career are all projects that made sense in the previous era and now seem like illusions to many. It is not just social institutions that need to be rebuilt, thus, but a cultural orientation that makes sense of economic life and connects it to personal life.

Latin America was the one world region in which a version of the Left regained the initiative during recent decades. Regimes variously described as "new populist" or "new nationalist" came to power in Bolivia, Brazil, Chile, Ecuador, Nicaragua, Peru, and Venezuela. These involved different leaders, some with backgrounds in the military, some with long roles as social movement leaders, some with much deeper commitments to electoral democracy than others. They shared a refusal to accept the free-trade ideology of the "Washington Consensus" (see further discussion in volume 3).[8] They shared also a capacity to speak to and for the poor in countries long governed by elites who maintained a nearly caste-like distinction, frequently marked by race. They reached out to indigenous populations, often drawing electoral support from regions that had previously been only weakly mobilized for national politics. Many were explicit in denouncing both the long history of colonialism and US domination and the more recent one of neoliberal policies and their depredations. They were also willing to use the state to control natural resources and exercise a strong economic role generally, and in many cases to commit national resources directly to programs for the poor. For a time, the new Latin American Left inspired considerable optimism in the hope that its leaders had developed a basic challenge to rapacious neoliberalism. As Coronil makes clear, the situation looks more complicated now.

Brazil's Luis Inácio Lula da Silva was perhaps the most successful of the new leaders, not only staying in power but also overseeing large-scale expansion of educational opportunities and other social welfare programs. Brazil's economy has grown rapidly and diversified industrially, placing it alongside Russia, India, and China as an emerging global leader. And in many ways, Lula's challenge to neoliberal consensus came in the form of successful state-led development, not unlike that in China, revealing orthodox prescriptions to be faulty as well as unjust. Brazil has not merely resisted neoliberalism and US domination, it has delivered incremental but noticeable improvements in social welfare.

The relevance of this here is twofold. On the one hand, part of the story of the current crisis is the extent to which countries like Brazil passed through it with minimal damage. This is true also of other "BRIC" countries, with the exception of Russia. And this raises the second point of relevance. Brazil's success was based significantly on economic diversification and industrial development. It is neither a petrostate nor a creature of finance capitalism. Achieving a similar success is vital for Russia if it is to grow alongside Brazil, India, and China. These themes are minimally addressed in this volume but are central to the third volume in the Possible Futures series, which takes up possibilities for growth after the crisis and locates these largely outside the previously rich countries.[9]

Few other Latin American countries have been able to diversify as effectively as Brazil or to weather the financial crisis with as little upheaval. And crucially, few others have been able to maintain as strong a connection between everyday life and incremental change, on the one hand, and high ideals, on the other. Coronil presents this as a dilemma for the Latin American Left. The critiques offered by Hugo Chavez and Evo Morales are resonant: the need for social transformation is evident; yet the socialist ideal seems always deferred and the quotidian present virtually disconnected from it. No "next steps" seem clearly to connect the future to the present. This is both an important challenge for the Latin American Left and an insight of much more widespread significance. The current crisis has engendered only very weak social movement response, particularly from the Left. But it is entangled in many places with populist politics, more often linked on this occasion to the Right, but expressing alarm and anxiety over a sense of disconnection from the future.

This volume opens by situating the current crisis in larger perspective, that of global capitalism. It poses the questions of (a) whether capitalism will regain its dynamism and incorporate this crisis as temporary damage and the occasion for new growth and (b) whether this will be marked by a shift in the location of hegemonic power and its capacity to stabilize and guide the system. The next set of chapters raises the question of who wins and loses in this system—and especially whether the system can survive without providing wider distribution of benefits (and whether this will come about without political movements demanding it). Implicitly, the final three chapters offer three scenarios: capitalism may muddle through the current crisis, it may enter a long era of low dynamism and perhaps deflation, or it may be transformed by a new economic culture that has grown partially in its interstices and partially on the basis of new technologies it has produced. These may not be all the possibilities, but they remind us that we are facing deeply divergent possible futures and that which we suffer or enjoy is partly a matter of collective choice.

CHAPTER 1

The End of the Long Twentieth Century

Beverly J. Silver and Giovanni Arrighi

Writing almost twenty years ago—shortly after the collapse of the Soviet Union—the British historian Eric Hobsbawm pointed to a widespread sense of confusion about where the world was headed: he wrote that it was as if we were "surrounded by a global fog." The citizens of the world at the end of the twentieth century "knew for certain that an era of history had ended. They knew very little else."[1] In the two decades since this was written, the shape of the "new era" has continued to take form, but the "global fog" has not dissipated.

Understandings about the direction of global change have shifted wildly. In the late 1990s—with the long economic boom in the United States and no serious challengers to US global military power—it became common to hear predictions of an impending "Second American Century." Such predictions reached a high point in the aftermath of the 1997 East Asian financial crisis. But then the tables turned, first, with the bursting of the New Economy stock-market bubble in the United States in 2000–2001, followed by the debacle in Iraq and the failure of the Bush administration's Project for a New American Century. With the 2008 US-centered financial meltdown and the continued rapid growth of China, talk of a Second American Century faded. Instead, speculation about an impending Chinese Century took off. At the same time, speculation about the demise of US global dominance reached levels not seen since the 1970s, when the US defeat in Vietnam, oil shocks, and economic stagflation produced a sense of deep crisis.

How can we make sense of these wildly shifting perceptions about what era of world history we have entered? In this chapter, we argue that a comparison with past periods that are broadly analogous with the present can help both in explaining the shifting perceptions and in dissipating the global fog that still surrounds us.[2] But to what period should we compare the present? It has become relatively common to point to similarities between the beginning and the end of the twentieth century. In both periods, finance capital rose to a dominant position in the global economy relative to capital invested in production. In both periods, moreover, the financialization of economic activities proved destabilizing, culminating in major crises, notably in 1929 and 2008.

These two periods of financialization are indeed analogous. But the rise of finance to a dominant role in world capitalism was not unique to the late nineteenth and the late twentieth centuries. As the French historian Fernand Braudel has pointed out, the financialization of capital has been a recurrent feature of historical capitalism from its earliest beginnings. Writing in the 1970s (that is, before the takeoff of the latest phase of financialization), Braudel identified three periods of systemwide financial expansion: in the mid-sixteenth century (centered in the Italian city-states), in the mid-eighteenth century (centered in Holland), and in the late nineteenth century (centered in the United Kingdom).[3] In this chapter, we take these three earlier instances of financial expansion as the appropriate historical comparisons for understanding the current (fourth) period of systemwide financial expansion.

Like today, each of these past periods of financialization was preceded by a long period of *material expansion* of the global economy— that is, a period in which capital flowed predominantly into trade and production rather than financial intermediation and speculation. Genoa, Holland, Britain, and the United States successively rose to global preeminence by taking the lead in a major *material expansion* of the global economy (as was the case, for example, during the US-led "golden age" of Fordism-Keynesianism in the 1950s and 1960s). At a certain point, these material expansions reached their limits (for reasons to be discussed later), and when this happened, the dominant power of the epoch led a systemwide shift away from investment in trade and production and toward financial speculation and intermediation.

A phase of material expansion followed by a phase of financial expansion constitutes what we have called a *long century*, or a systemic cycle of accumulation (SCA). We can identify four (partially overlapping) long centuries, or SCAs: (1) a Genoese-Iberian cycle, stretching from the fifteenth through the early seventeenth centuries; (2) a Dutch cycle, stretching from the late sixteenth through the late eighteenth centuries; (3) a British cycle, stretching from the mid-eighteenth through the early twentieth centuries; and (4) a US cycle, stretching from the late nineteenth century to the present. Each cycle is named after (and defined by) the particular complex of governmental and business agencies that led the world capitalist system toward the material and financial expansions that jointly constitute the long century.

In all three cases discussed by Braudel, financial expansions led to a dramatic resurgence of power and prosperity for the leading capitalist country of the time (e.g., a second golden age for the Dutch; the Victorian belle époque for Britain). Yet in each case, the resurgence of world power and prosperity was short-lived. For Braudel, the successive shifts by Genoese, Dutch, and British capitalists away from trade and industry and into finance were each a sign that the material expansion had reached "maturity"; it was "a sign of autumn." Financialization turned out to be a prelude to a terminal crisis of world hegemony and to the rise of a new geographical center of world economic and military power.

Is this pattern repeating itself today? Are we experiencing the "autumn" of US world hegemony? In this chapter, we argue that the 2008 financial meltdown is one of the latest indicators that this is indeed the case. Like the Genoese, Dutch, and British before it, US capital shifted increasingly into finance and away from trade and production as the major world-scale material expansion founded on Fordism-Keynesianism reached its limits in the 1980s. By shifting to a focus on finance, the United States succeeded in attracting capital from all over the world, financing both a major boom in the stock market and a dramatic expansion of the US military. The Soviet Union collapsed under the strain, while the United States experienced its own belle époque in the Reagan-Clinton years. By the late 1990s, the crisis of the 1970s seemed a distant memory, and forecasts of a Second American Century became common.

Seen from the perspective of this chapter, however, those who forecast an impending Second American Century were mistaking the "autumn" of US world hegemony for a "new spring." Put differently, we are witnessing the end of the *long twentieth century*—a long century that has stretched from the late nineteenth-century financial expansion through the current financial expansion, a long century that is coextensive with the initial rise, full flowering, and demise of the US-centered era of capitalist world history. The chapter also addresses the question as to whether the "autumn" of US world economic and military power is likely to be seen (in retrospect) as the "spring" of a new world economic and military power, as has been the case during the three previous financial expansions.

In the remainder of this chapter, we compare the present with previous periods of financialization, and we compare the long twentieth century with previous long centuries. We do this in three main steps. In the following section, we identify similarities among the three previous periods of financialization, pointing to patterns of *recurrence* across time. In the next section, we focus on patterns of *evolution*. For long centuries should not be understood as primarily recurrent (cyclical) phenomena; rather, the financial expansions that mark the beginning and end of each long century have been periods of fundamental reorganization of the world system. We show how these successive reorganizations have produced an evolutionary pattern in which the dominant governmental-business complex increased over time in size, power, and complexity—*including social complexity*.

The pattern of recurrence and evolution summarized in the following two sections helps us narrow down the possible alternative futures open to us at this time. But as we argue in the last section of the chapter, there are good reasons to think that we cannot simply project into the future from past patterns of recurrence and evolution. The last part of the chapter identifies significant *anomalies* that can be expected to make future outcomes deviate from past patterns and concludes with a discussion of "possible futures."

Recurrence

A repeated theme in the second and third volumes of Fernand Braudel's trilogy *Civilization and Capitalism*—which takes us on a sweeping tour from the fifteenth through the eighteenth centuries—is that the periodic resurgence of finance has been a characteristic of historical capitalism from its earliest beginnings. "Finance capital," Braudel wrote, "was no newborn child of the 1900s." Instead he points to at least two earlier waves of financial expansion—periods in which "finance capital was...in a position to take over and dominate, for a while at least, all the activities of the business world." The first wave of financialization began around 1560, when the leading groups of the Genoese business diaspora gradually withdrew from commerce to specialize in finance; the second began around 1740, when the Dutch began to withdraw from commerce to become "the bankers of Europe."[4]

Seen from this perspective, the financial expansions that began in the late nineteenth and the late twentieth centuries are the third and fourth waves of a recurrent world-systemic process. During and after the Great Depression of 1873–96, when it became clear that the "fantastic voyage of the industrial revolution" had created an overabundance of money capital that could not all be profitably reinvested in industrial activities, the British increasingly withdrew from industry to specialize in finance. At the time Braudel was writing his trilogy, the fourth (that is, the current) wave of financialization had not yet taken off; but we can recognize today a repeat of the same phenomenon: that is, when, in the final decades of the twentieth century, it became clear that the golden age of Fordism-Keynesianism had created an overabundance of money capital that could not all be profitably reinvested in industrial activities, US capital switched to specialize in finance rather than industrial production. By the mid-1990s, the share of total US corporate profits *on a world scale* accounted for by finance, insurance, and real estate (FIRE) had surpassed the share of profits accounted for by manufacturing.[5]

It is helpful to reformulate Braudel's insights about the periodic resurgence of finance capital in light of Marx's general formula of capital, which is often understood as depicting the logic of investment decisions by individual capitalists.[6] Capitalists put their money capital into commodities for use in production (e.g., machinery, labor) with the expectation of obtaining a greater mass of money capital at some future point in time. They do not participate in production *as an end in itself.* If capitalists do not expect that their money capital will increase by investing in production, or if this expectation systematically goes unfulfilled, then they will tend to move out of production and revert to more flexible (liquid) forms of investment.

But Marx's formulation can also be understood as depicting a systemic logic. There are phases in which the dominant tendency among capitalists is to invest the mass of their money capital in production and trade, thus leading to phases of overall material expansion. But the very success of any material expansion eventually leads to an overaccumulation of capital that drives down the rate of return in the activities that had previously fueled the material expansion. The attendant squeeze on profits results in a switch: the dominant tendency among capitalists becomes to hold an increasingly large portion of their capital in liquid form, creating the "supply conditions" for financial expansions for the system as a whole. Financial expansions are thus symptomatic of a situation in which investment in the expansion of trade and production no longer serves the purpose of increasing the cash flow to the capitalist stratum as effectively as pure financial deals can.

As already noted, past financial expansions temporarily restored the power and fortunes of the leading capitalist state of the epoch (most recently seen in the Reagan-Clinton belle époque). How has this happened? In very broad terms, the slowdown in the material expansion associated with the initial takeoff of the financial expansion puts a squeeze on the fiscal positions of states, which in turn begin to compete more intensely for the mobile capital piling up in financial markets, fueling the financial expansion on the "demand side" of the equation. The world hegemonic power at any given time (Dutch, British, US), thanks to its continuing centrality in networks of high finance, is best positioned to turn the intensifying competition for mobile capital to its advantage and to gain privileged access to the overabundant liquidity that accumulates in world financial markets. This was clear in the 1980s and 1990s, when the United States succeeded in attracting mobile capital from around the world, fueling a long boom in the United States and provoking severe debt crises elsewhere in the world. The first major debt crisis was centered in Latin America in the early 1980s, producing what the United Nations dubbed "the lost development decade." Debt crises in eastern Europe and East Asia followed.

In the past, a new systemwide material expansion took off only if and when there was a hegemonic power capable of creating the needed global institutional preconditions (financial, geopolitical, and social). When this was the case—as it was in the 1950s and 1960s, when the

US-sponsored global institutions provided a certain degree of security and predictability—capitalists routinely plowed profits back into the further expansion of trade and production. However, such global institutional conditions are not created quickly or easily. In the past, declining powers lost their ability to maintain the necessary global institutional conditions before rising powers had the capacity or inclination to take over the role of leader. Thus, periods of transition from one long century to the next historically have been periods of widespread warfare and economic crises. This was clearly the case in the first half of the twentieth century—with the transition from British to US hegemony. We can see signs of a similar dilemma facing the world today.

Interestingly enough, Marx, in his discussion of primitive accumulation, took note of a historical pattern whereby expansions of the financial system recurrently played a key role in the transfer of surplus capital from declining to rising geographical centers of capitalist trade and production. Marx observed a sequence that started with Venice, which "in her decadence" lent large sums of money to Holland; then Holland lent out "enormous amounts of capital, especially to its great rival England" when the former "ceased to be the nation preponderant in commerce and industry"; and finally, England was doing the same vis-à-vis the United States in Marx's own day.[7] Thus, expansions of the credit system played a crucial role in restarting capital accumulation in a new geographical center again and again over the lifetime of historical capitalism—or to put it in our terminology, financial expansions have played a crucial role in launching each new systemic cycle of accumulation.[8]

Put differently, financial expansions historically have been periods of *hegemonic transition,* in the course of which a new leadership emerged interstitially and over time reorganized the system, setting the stage for a new material expansion on a world scale. Financial expansions have not only been the "autumn" of the existing hegemon; they have also marked the "spring" of a new major phase of capitalist development under a new leadership—that is, the start of a new long century with a different geographical center. But because this process has been neither simple nor smooth, financial expansions have culminated in fairly long periods of widespread systemic chaos.

Evolution

In the previous section, we focused on the similarities among long centuries. If we were to draw conclusions based on patterns of recurrence alone, then we would conclude that we are now in the "late autumn" of US world hegemony and the "early spring" of a new long century with a different (perhaps East Asian) geographical center. We might well be worried that we are entering (or have entered) a more or less long period of systemic chaos, with attendant widespread human suffering. However, precisely because the global system has evolved over time, we are limited in what we can conclude about the present and near future by focusing solely on patterns of recurrence. In this section, we focus on the pattern of evolution.

Figure 1.1 sums up a historical pattern of evolution that can be seen by focusing on the changing characteristics of "the containers of power" that have housed the headquarters of the leading capitalist agencies (i.e., the dominant governmental-business complex) of the four successive long centuries: the Republic of Genoa, the Dutch Republic, the United Kingdom, and the United States.[9] One key aspect of the evolutionary pattern shown in figure 1.1 is a trend toward an increase in the size, power, and complexity of the dominant governmental-business complex from one long century to the next.

At the time of the Genoese-centered material expansion, the Republic of Genoa was a city-state. It was small in size, simple in organization, deeply divided socially, rather defenseless militarily, and by most criteria a weak state in comparison with all the great powers of the time. Genoa's wealth made it a tempting target for conquest, but because it lacked any significant military power, the Genoese had to depend for their protection on the Iberian monarchs from whom they "bought protection." The Dutch Republic, in contrast, was a larger and far more complex organization than the Republic of Genoa. At the time of the Dutch-centered material expansion, it was powerful enough to win independence from imperial Spain, to carve out a highly profitable empire of commercial outposts, and to keep at bay military challenges from England and France. Thus, unlike the Genoese, the Dutch did not have to "buy" protection from other states; they "produced" their own protection. The Dutch, in other words, "internalized" protection costs that the Genoese had externalized, as figure 1.1 shows.

Figure 1.1: Evolutionary patterns of world capitalism

Leading Governmental Organization	Regime Type/Cycle		Costs Internalized			
	Extensive	Intensive	Protection	Production	Transaction	Reproduction
World-state		US	Yes	Yes	Yes	No
	British		Yes	Yes	No	No
Nation-state		Dutch	Yes	No	No	No
	Geno-ese		No	No	No	No
City-state						

At the time of the British-centered material expansion, the United Kingdom was a fully developed national state with a world-encompassing commercial and territorial empire that gave its ruling groups and its capitalist class an unprecedented command over the world's human and natural resources. Like the Dutch, the British capitalist class did not need to rely on foreign powers for protection (i.e., both internalized protection costs). But as the "workshop of the world," Britain also did not need to rely on others for the manufactured goods on which the profitability of its commercial activities rested. The British went beyond the Dutch by internalizing production costs.

Finally, the United States was a continental military-industrial complex with the power to provide effective protection for itself and its allies and to make credible threats of economic strangulation or military annihilation toward its enemies. This power, combined with the size, insularity, and natural wealth of the United States, enabled its capitalist class to internalize protection and production costs, as the British capitalist class had already done. But in pioneering the formation of vertically integrated multinational corporations, the US capitalist class was also able to internalize "transaction costs"—that is to say, to internalize the markets on which the self-expansion of its capital depended.

If we were to draw conclusions based on patterns of evolution discussed so far in this section, then we would predict that the governmental-business organization leading any future systemic cycle of accumulation would necessarily be of greater size and complexity than the United States. It is not plausible that any single country could meet this requirement. For example, China is much larger but also much poorer than the United States—not withstanding decades of rapid economic growth. Thus, the future evolution depicted in figure 1.1 is a movement toward some type of "world state."

The clear linear trend toward greater size and complexity is, however, partially moderated by another aspect of the historical pattern, which is summed up in figure 1.1 as a pendulum-like swing back and forth between "extensive" and "intensive" regimes of accumulation. Dutch chartered companies, such as the Dutch East India Company (VOC), were *formally* more complex organizations than the family-based business networks of the Genoese capitalist diaspora. But the family business enterprises on which the British textile industry flourished were formally less complex than the Dutch chartered companies; moreover, the overall success of British capital on a world scale depended on reviving in new and more complex ways the combined strategies and structures of Genoese cosmopolitan capitalism and Iberian global territorialism. Likewise, the US multinational corporations were formally more complex than the British family firms, while the success of US capital on a world scale depended on reviving in new and more complex forms the strategies and structures of Dutch corporate capitalism.

What are the implications for the present of this pendulum swing back and forth between "extensive" (cosmopolitan-imperial) regimes and "intensive" (corporate-national) regimes superimposed on a linear trend of increasing complexity? If the pattern were to hold into the future, then we would expect the strategies and structure of the governmental-business complex leading the next long century to be "extensive" in comparison with the "intensive" US regime, although of greater formal complexity than in the nineteenth-century British-centered material expansion of the world system. For now, we will only note that the multilayered subcontracting systems and other forms of flexible production associated with post-Fordism (which were, not incidentally, largely pioneered in East Asia) can be seen as signs of a pendulum swing back in the "extensive" direction.[10] Notwithstanding the pendulum swing, however, a linear trend toward increasing complexity is still clear.

Problems with projecting this linear trend into the future arise more clearly when we take note of the current split in the control of global financial and military resources, with the former concentrated in East Asia and the latter concentrated in the United States. This split is an unprecedented phenomenon, whose implications we discuss in the next section.

Anomalies

A significant anomaly in the present transition is the unprecedented bifurcation in the geographical locus of military and financial power. US multinational corporations have been investing heavily in China, repeating the historical pattern observed by Marx in which declining centers transfer surplus capital to rising centers. However, in a major departure from past patterns, the *net* flow of surplus capital, *from the beginning of the US-led financial expansion,* has been *from the rising to the declining economic center*—most notably, in the form of massive East Asian purchases of US Treasury bonds, first by Japan, later by China. As in past hegemonic transitions, the declining hegemon (the United States) has been transformed from the world's leading creditor nation to a debtor nation. This transformation, in the case of the United States, has taken place on a scale and at a speed without precedence (see figure 1.2).

Yet military resources of any global significance are overwhelmingly concentrated in the hands of the United States. There is no credible sign that any of the rising economic states, including China, has any intention of directly challenging US military power. Even without a direct challenge, however, the United States no longer possesses the financial resources needed to support its worldwide military apparatus (and now does so only by going deeper and deeper into international debt). Moreover, as was made clear by the failure of the Bush administration's Project for a New American Century, the projection of military power has not been particularly effective in bending the world to the will

Figure 1.2: Current account balance

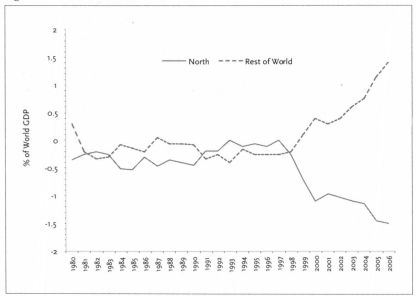

Source: Based on data from International Monetary Fund, World Economic Outlook Database, 2010, http://www.imf.org/external/pubs/ft/weo/2010/01/weodata/index.aspx.

of the United States or in countering escalating system-level social and political crises.

The future scenario suggested by the historical patterning summarized in figure 1.1—that is, the emergence of a world state—presupposes that the world state would somehow gain access to global surplus capital, now mostly located in the Global South, especially in East Asia. The recent expansion of the G7 meetings of wealthy countries to include large countries of the Global South (for example, the G20 meetings) is a more or less explicit recognition of this prerequisite and suggests at least a partial recognition of the fact that a world-state project that is Western- and Northern-dominated (e.g., primarily based on an alliance between the United States and western Europe) is no longer a feasible political project. The West now finds itself without one of the two most important ingredients of its fortunes over the preceding five hundred years: control over surplus capital. This is a major anomaly with respect to previous hegemonic transitions—all of which were transitions *within* the West and Global North.

If a Western-dominated world state seems unlikely, what then are the prospects for China itself becoming the center of a new material expansion of capitalism on a world scale in the twenty-first century? First, it is important to eliminate irrelevant considerations from the discussion. In the aftermath of the East Asian financial crisis of 1997–98, many observers dismissed the East Asian ascent as a mirage; and today, it is common to hear predictions of an impending financial crisis in China that, it is claimed, will reveal assessments of the Chinese ascent to have been overblown. Whether or not a major financial crisis will break out in China is an open question. But any such crisis would be of little relevance for understanding whether the center of world capital accumulation has been and continues to be shifting to China. As we pointed out in the conclusion of *Chaos and Governance in the Modern World System*, historically, the deepest financial crises were experienced in the newly emerging centers of capital accumulation on a world scale—London in 1772, New York in 1929—as their financial prowess outstripped their institutional capacity to manage the burgeoning flows of capital. It would make no sense to argue that the Wall Street crash of 1929–31 and subsequent Great Depression were signs that the epicenter of capital accumulation had *not* been shifting to the United States in the first half of the twentieth century. Likewise, it would make no sense to make the same argument about late twentieth- and early twenty-first-century financial crises centered in East Asia.

However, as we noted earlier, past systemwide material expansions only took off once the rising economic power was able to become hegemonic, in the Gramscian sense of the word—that is, to lead the world toward the creation of global institutional arrangements (financial, geopolitical, and social) capable of providing the necessary safety and security for a broad-based material expansion. Since the world system has evolved in fundamental ways from one long century to the next, the nature of these global institutions has also fundamentally changed from one long century to the next.

Today, as in the past, the barriers to a new material expansion are as much *social* as they are economic. As we argued in *Chaos and Governance*, successive hegemons have had to find ways to accommodate demands from a wider and deeper array of social movements. Thus, the evolutionary pattern of increasing size, scope, and complexity described earlier also entails increasing *social complexity*. The firm establishment of US hegemony after the Second World War (and the takeoff of the system-wide material expansion) did not just depend on the country's preponderance in military and economic power. Rather, it also depended on the implementation of policies designed to accommodate, at least in part, the mass labor, socialist, and national liberation movements of the first half of the twentieth century. The US-led solutions—the mass-consumption social contract for workers in the Global North and decolonization and the promise of development for the Global South—were only temporary solutions, as they were unsustainable within the context of historical capitalism. For one thing, to fully implement these solutions would bring about a squeeze on profits, given their substantial redistributive effects.

Indeed, the initial crisis of US hegemony in the late 1960s and 1970s was in important measure a social-political event, sparked by worldwide social unrest as a variety of movements in both the First and Third World mobilized to demand what in essence was a quicker fulfillment of the implicit and explicit social promises of US hegemony. This crisis, which marked the end of the US-led material expansion, was both an economic event and a social-political event; or more precisely, both elements of the crisis were intertwined. The financial expansion of the late twentieth century temporarily resolved these intertwined crises for US capitalists and the US state, leading to the belle époque of the 1990s. Financialization—the massive withdrawal of capital out of trade and production and into financial speculation and intermediation—had a debilitating effect on social movements worldwide, most notably via the mechanism of the debt crisis in the Global South and mass layoffs at the heart of the labor movement in the Global North.

If all previous long centuries presupposed a fundamental social-political reorganization of the global system—for example, the end of the Atlantic slave trade under British hegemony, the end of formal colonialism under US hegemony—what does the type of analysis carried out in this chapter suggest about the kind of fundamental reorganizations that would be required today? First, a new world hegemony (whether led by a single state, a coalition of states, or a world state) would have to accommodate and foster a greater equality between the Global North and

Global South, given the financial power of the latter. If the linear trend toward increasing social complexity were to continue into the future, then it would mean that such North-South equalization would take place, at least in part, through the incorporation of a wider and deeper array of social movements from below. (The widespread social unrest in China in both urban and rural areas since the late 1990s—and the efforts of the Chinese government to respond—may be a precursor to another move toward increased social complexity on a world scale.)

But what would this mean more concretely? This question brings us to a third point, which is highlighted in figure 1.1 but which we have not yet discussed. All previous world hegemonies have been based on the *externalization* of the costs of reproduction of labor and of nature. That is, profitability in all past material expansions has depended on treating the natural world as a no-cost input to production. Moreover, profitability has depended on paying only a small minority of the world's workers the full cost (or nearly the full cost) of the reproduction of their labor power. Instead, a large share of the costs of reproduction has been shifted onto households and communities involved in nonwaged activities (such as subsistence agriculture or unpaid household labor relied on for child care and care of the sick and elderly).

The externalization of the costs of reproduction of nature has been taken to an extreme in the long twentieth century with the highly resource-intensive and wasteful mass-consumption and production model associated with the "American way of life." Moreover, development for all—that everyone could achieve the American way of life—was an explicit promise of US hegemony (institutionalized through, among other things, the United Nations Development Program). That this promise was "false" first became clear with the crisis in the 1970s, the oil price shocks being a particularly relevant indicator.

Mohandas Gandhi already recognized the problem in 1928: "The economic imperialism of a single tiny island nation [England] is today keeping the world in chains. If an entire nation of 300 million [India's population at the time] took to similar economic exploitation, it would strip the world like locusts."[11] Gandhi's insight of more than eighty years ago remains fundamental today: the rise of the West has been based on an ecologically unsustainable model, which was possible only as long as the vast majority of the world's population was *excluded* from that same path. Given the shifting geographical distribution of economic power on a world scale discussed earlier, it is not clear how access to this style of consumption can be limited to only a small percentage of the world's total population. Yet any serious attempt to generalize the American way of life can only lead to social, political, and ecological conflicts that are more likely to form the basis for a long period of systemic chaos than the basis for a new material expansion.

The model of accumulation that drove the material expansion of the long twentieth century cannot provide the basis for a new material expansion in the twenty-first century. Any new world-scale material expansion presupposes a vastly different social, geopolitical, and ecological model— different not only from that of the long twentieth century but from those of previous long centuries as well. It presupposes an alternative path to the resource-intensive Western model of capitalist development—one that is more labor-absorbing, less resource-wasteful, and *not* premised on the *exclusion* of the vast majority of the world's population from its benefits.[12]

We have reached the end of the long twentieth century. It remains an open question whether we will find it meaningful to refer to whatever eventually emerges as another "long century" of historical capitalism or whether we will decide that we have (in retrospect) also reached the end of historical capitalism. In the meantime, a long and deep period of systemic chaos—analogous *but not identical* to the systemic chaos of the first half of the twentieth century—remains a serious historical possibility. While the end of the long twentieth century is inevitable, there is nothing inevitable about it coming to a catastrophic ending. Avoiding the latter is our urgent collective task.

CHAPTER 2

Dynamics of (Unresolved) Global Crisis

Immanuel Wallerstein

Since about 2007, politicians, pundits, and economists have all been talking about a global crisis, with considerable disagreement about the nature of this crisis and the measures that should be taken to resolve it. Memories are short, but actually, there was a quite similar discussion in the 1970s.

In 1982, I published a book, jointly with Samir Amin, Giovanni Arrighi, and Andre Gunder Frank, entitled *Dynamics of Global Crisis*. This was not its original title. We had proposed the title *Crisis, What Crisis?* The US publisher did not like that title, but we used it in the French translation. The book consisted of a joint introduction and conclusion and a separate essay by each of us on the topic.

We opened the book with our observation that "throughout the 1970s, 'crisis' had become an increasingly familiar theme: first in obscure discussions among intellectuals, then in the popular press, and finally in political debates in many countries."[1] We noted that there were many different definitions of the so-called crisis as well as different explanations of its origin. What seemed to be central in most analyses was that there had been two significant increases in the world price of oil—in 1973 and in 1979—each triggered by a decision of the Organization of the Petroleum Exporting Countries (OPEC). There were hysterical fears among some people in the United States that Libya could "buy" up the country's major property.

By the 1980s, the term *crisis* seemed to disappear from world discourse, to be replaced by another buzz word, one with a much more optimistic gloss—*globalization*. The origins of globalization were a matter of much debate, as was how recently it had begun. It was generally presented as something very new, transformatory, and inevitable. In the famous words of then prime minister Margaret Thatcher of Great Britain, people had no choice, or TINA—there is no alternative. Globalization was generally presented not only as inevitable but as something that promised wonderful benefits for everyone, at least in some middle run.

It was only beginning in 2008 that the tone turned dour again, and the word *crisis* resurfaced, this time more sharply than in the 1970s, but just as loosely. So the question "Crisis, what crisis?" seems again very relevant.

In my view, globalization (if it is defined as relatively open frontiers and relatively free flows of commodities and capital) is nothing new but rather is a cyclical phenomenon within a wider historical system that I think of as the modern world-system, one that is a capitalist world-economy. In my view, this world-system has existed since the sixteenth century, first in only part of the world but eventually expanding to encompass the entire globe. It is within this world-system that entrepreneurs operate and states juggle to strengthen their relative positions.

Something did indeed happen to this world-system in the late 1960s–early 1970s, but not what the proponents of the concept of globalization suggested. Rather, it was both the moment of normal cyclical shifts in the functioning of the world-system and also the moment of the beginning of its structural crisis as a system. These are two different things, and if we are to understand what has been occurring, we must spell out the details of each. I start by analyzing what I think of as normal cyclical shifts and then turn to what I think of as the structural crisis of the system.

The "Normal" Cyclical Downturns

There have been two extremely important cyclical phenomena during the whole history of the modern world system. One has to do with the long waves of global expansion and global stagnation of the world economy.

We sometimes call them Kondratieff waves, after the work of a Russian economist who wrote about them, although he was not the first. The other has to do with the rise and decline of what are called hegemonic powers of the world system—that is, those countries that are able, at least for a relatively short period, to lay down and enforce the basic operating rules of the interstate system.

The period 1967–73 was the moment when both the hegemonic cycle and the overall economic cycle each began its downturn. The period 1945 to circa 1970 had been the moment of the height of US hegemony in the world system and also the moment of the most expansive Kondratieff A upturn of global economic prosperity that the capitalist world economy had ever known in its history. The French refer to that period as "les trente glorieuses" (the thirty glorious years)—a most apt expression.

I call these downturns absolutely normal. To understand why, one must bear in mind two things. All systems have cyclical rhythms. It is the way they live, the way they deal with the inevitable fluctuations of their operations. The second thing to bear in mind has to do with how capitalism as a world system functions. There are two key issues: how producers make profit and how states guarantee the world order within which producers may make profit. Let us take each in turn.

The Long Economic Waves
Capitalism is a system in which the *endless* accumulation of capital is the raison d'être. To accumulate capital, producers must obtain profits from their operations. However, truly significant profits are possible only if the producer can sell the product for considerably more than the cost of production. Those who preach the virtues of a free market normally argue that competition is what permits the maximization both of profit and of general welfare. Actually the opposite is true. In a situation of perfect competition, it is absolutely impossible to make significant profit. If there is perfect competition (that is, in the classical definition, a multitude of sellers, a multitude of buyers, and universally available information about prices), any intelligent buyer will go from seller to seller until he or she finds one who will sell at a penny above the cost of production, if not indeed below the cost of production.

Obtaining significant profit requires not competition but a monopoly, or at least a quasi-monopoly of world economic power. If there is a monopoly, the seller can demand any price, as long as he or she does not go beyond what the elasticity of demand permits. That is, there are price limits from the point of view of the buyer. When a price becomes too high in terms of the buyer's capacity to pay or assessment of the worth of such an expenditure in relation to other possible ones, the buyer declines to buy. This is what economists call the elasticity of demand. It is crucial to note that it is limited.

Any time the world-economy is expanding significantly, one will find that there are some "leading" products, which are relatively monopolized. Once upon a time, steel production and automobile production were relatively monopolized. This is no longer true. At even earlier times, cotton textiles were relatively monopolized. This can seem incredible today, when there are countless producers of cotton textiles.

It is from these relatively monopolized products that great profits are made and large amounts of capital can be accumulated. The forward and backward linkages of these leading products are the basis of an overall expansion of the world-economy. We call this the A phase of a Kondratieff cycle.

The problem for capitalists is that all monopolies are self-liquidating. This is because there exists a world market into which new producers can enter, however well politically defended is a given monopoly. Of course, entry takes time. But sooner or later, others are able to enter the market, and the degree of competition increases. And when competition increases, prices go down, as the heralds of capitalism have always told us. At the same time, profits go down. When profits for the leading products go down sufficiently, the world-economy ceases to expand, and it enters into a period of stagnation. This is what we mean by the B phase of a Kondratieff cycle. Empirically, the A and B phases together have tended to be fifty to sixty years in length, but the exact lengths have varied. Of course, after a certain time in a B phase, monopolies can be created in new leading products, and a new A phase can begin. We often call this "innovation," as distinguished from "invention."

The Geopolitical Cycles

The second condition for capitalist profit is that there exists some kind of relative world order. Capitalists need to be relatively confident that wars will be at most relatively local affairs. They need to know that currencies do not fluctuate too much. They need to know that there is some relative political guarantee that their profits will not be confiscated. While world wars offer the possibilities for some entrepreneurs to do very well, they also occasion enormous destruction of fixed capital and considerable interference with world trade. The overall world economic balance sheet of world wars is not positive, a point the great economist Joseph Schumpeter repeatedly made in his writings. A relatively stable situation is necessary for a positive overall balance sheet. Ensuring this relatively stable situation is the task of a hegemonic power, that is, a power strong enough to impose such relative stability on the world system as a whole.

These so-called hegemonic or geopolitical cycles have been much longer than the Kondratieff cycles of world economic expansion and stagnation. It is not so easy, in a world of multiple so-called sovereign states, for one state to establish itself as the hegemonic power. It has in fact been done only three times in several hundred years: first by the United Provinces (more or less what is today the Netherlands) in the mid-seventeenth century, then by the United Kingdom in the mid-nineteenth century, and finally by the United States in the mid-twentieth century.

The rise of a hegemonic power is the result of a long struggle with other potential hegemonic powers. It has been won each time up to now by that state which, for various reasons and by various methods, has been able to put together the most efficient productive machinery and then to win a "thirty years' war" with its principal rival. The United Provinces became hegemonic after the original Thirty Years' War (1618–48). The United Kingdom became hegemonic after what historians call the Revolutionary and Napoleonic Wars (1792–1815). And the United States became hegemonic after what I think of as the "thirty years' war" between Germany and the United States that ran from 1914 to 1945. Thirty years' wars are not continuous, but they do involve eventually all the major military powers of the world-system, and they do lead to immense physical destruction.

The key point is that once a given state finally achieves hegemony, it is able to set the rules by which the interstate system operates, seeking simultaneously to ensure its smooth functioning and to maximize the flow of accumulated capital to its citizens and productive enterprises. One could think of this as a quasi-monopoly of geopolitical power.

The problem for the hegemonic power is the same as the problem for a leading industry. The monopoly is self-liquidating. This is so for two reasons. On the one hand, in order for the hegemonic power to maintain the order it imposes, it has to make use on occasion of its military power. But potential military strength is always more intimidating than actually used military strength. Using the military strength is costly in money and lives. It has a negative impact on the citizens of the hegemonic power, whose initial pride in victory tends to turn to distress as they pay the increasing costs of military action, and they begin to lose enthusiasm. Furthermore, big military operations tend almost always to be less efficacious than both supporters and opponents of the hegemonic power had feared, and this strengthens the future resistance of others who wish to defy the hegemonic power. The most recent example of this was the negative effect of the Vietnam War both on the economy of the United States and on the internal willingness of the American people to support further such wars, to which we often refer as the Vietnam syndrome.

There is a second reason. Even if the hegemonic power's economic efficiency does not immediately falter, that of other countries begins to rise. In the 1960s, the economic rise of western Europe and Japan in relation to the economic strength of the United States was quite striking. And as the others rise, they are less ready to accept the dictates of the hegemonic power. The hegemonic power enters into a process of slow decline relative to the rising powers. The decline may be slow, but it is nonetheless essentially irreversible.

The World-Revolution of 1968

The conjoining circa 1965–70 of the two kinds of decline—that marking the end of the historically most expansive Kondratieff A phase and that marking the beginning of decline of the historically most powerful hegemonic power—is what made that turning point so remarkable. It is no accident that the so-called world-revolution of 1968 (actually 1966–70) took place at that turning point, as an expression of the turning point.

The world-revolution of 1968 marked a third downturn, one however that has occurred only once in the history of the modern world-system—the decline of the traditional antisystemic movements of the world-system, the so-called Old Left. The Old Left—essentially the two varieties of world social movements, the Communists and the Social-Democrats, plus the national liberation movements—arose slowly and laboriously across the world-system, primarily throughout the last third of the nineteenth century and the first half of the twentieth century. The Old Left movements ascended from a position of political marginality and weakness as of, say, 1870 to one of political centrality and considerable strength as of, say, 1950.

These movements reached the summit of their mobilizing power in the period from 1945 to 1968—exactly the moment of both the extraordinary Kondratieff A-phase expansion and the height of US hegemony. I do not think this was fortuitous, although it might seem counterintuitive. The incredible world economic expansion led to a strong preference of entrepreneurs not to suffer interruptions of their production processes because of conflict with the workers. It followed that they tended to believe that concessions to the material demands of their workers cost them less than such interruptions. Of course, over twenty-five years or so, this meant rising costs of production, one of the factors that led to the end of the quasi-monopolies of leading industries. But most entrepreneurs make decisions that maximize short-term profits—let us say, profits over the succeeding three years—and leave the future to the gods.

Parallel considerations influenced the policies of the United States as the hegemonic power. Maintaining relative stability in the world-system was an essential objective. The United States had to weigh the cost of repressive activity on the world scene against the cost of concessions to the demands of national liberation movements. And reluctantly at first, but later more deliberately, the United States began to favor a controlled "decolonization," and this had the effect of bringing such movements to power.

Hence, by the middle of the 1960s, one could say that the Old Left movements had achieved their historical goal of state power almost everywhere—*at least on paper*. Communist parties ruled one-third of the world—the so-called socialist bloc. Social-democratic parties were in power, at least alternating power, in most of another third of the world—the pan-European world. (I include New Deal Democrats as a variant of a social-democratic party.) One has to bear in mind in addition that, at that time, the principal policy of the social-democratic parties— the welfare state—was accepted and practiced as well by their conservative alternating parties. The conservative parties simply wanted to make some minor adjustments to the welfare state. And of course, national liberation movements had come to power in most of the former colonial world (as well as various versions of populist movements in Latin America).

To be sure, I have said "at least on paper." Most analysts and militants tend today to be very critical of the performance of all these movements and doubt that their coming to power made much difference. But this is a retrospective view and is historically anachronistic. The critics forget the sense of worldwide triumphalism that pervaded the Old Left movements and their supporters in the 1960s, a triumphalism based precisely on their achievement of state power. The critics forget as well the sense of deep fear that pervaded the world's wealthier and more conservative strata about what looked to them like a juggernaut of destructive egalitarianism.

The world-revolution of 1968 changed all that. Three themes pervaded the analyses and the rhetoric of those who engaged in the multiple uprisings. All three themes bespoke a revised triumphalism. The first theme was that the US hegemonic power had overstretched and was vulnerable. The Vietnam War was the model example, albeit not the only one. The Tet offensive was taken to be the death knell of the US military operation. As part of the new atmosphere, the revolutionaries attacked the role of the Soviet Union, which they saw as a collusive participant in US hegemony, a feeling that had been growing everywhere, since at least 1956.

The second theme was that the Old Left movements—of all three varieties—had failed to deliver their historical promises. All three varieties had built their strategies on the so-called two-step strategy—first take state power, then change the world. The militants said, in effect, "You have taken state power but have not at all changed the world. If we, the revolutionaries of 1968, wish to change the world, we must replace you with new movements and new strategies. And we shall do this." The Chinese Cultural Revolution was taken by many observers as the model example of this possibility.

The third theme was that the Old Left movements had ignored the forgotten peoples—those downtrodden because of their race, their gender, their ethnicity, their sexuality. The militants insisted that the demands by all of these groups for equal treatment could no longer be deferred to some putative future time after the main Old Left parties had achieved their historical objectives. These demands, they said, constituted part of the urgent present, not the deferred future. In many ways, the Black Power movement in the United States was the model example.

The Post-1968 Ideological Struggles

The world-revolution of 1968 was an enormous political success. The world-revolution of 1968 was an enormous political failure. It burned very bright indeed across the globe and then by the mid-1970s seemed to be extinguished almost everywhere. What had been accomplished by this wild brushfire? Actually, quite a bit. For over a hundred years, the centrist ideology of liberalism had dominated the world's ideological landscape. Both conservatism on the right and radicalism on the left had been reduced to being minor variants of the centrist vision. The world-revolution of 1968 dethroned centrist liberalism as the governing ideology of the world-system. Both conservatism and radicalism regained their ideological independence and ideological strength. It is not that centrist liberalism disappeared. But it was reduced to being simply one alternative among others. And the Old Left movements, identified with the period when radicalism was not all that different from centrism, were destroyed as mobilizers of any kind of fundamental change. Still, the immediate triumphalism of the revolutionaries of 1968, liberated from any subordination to centrist liberalism, proved shallow and unsustainable.

The world Right, equally liberated from any attachment to centrist liberalism, took advantage of the world economic stagnation and the collapse of the Old Left movements (and their governments) to launch a counteroffensive, which we call neoliberal (actually quite conservative) globalization. The prime objectives were to reverse all the gains that the lower strata had achieved during the Kondratieff A period (1945–circa 1970). The world Right, now reveling in the label of "conservative," sought to reduce all the major costs of production, to destroy the welfare state in all its versions, and to slow down the decline of US power in the world-system. The onward march of the world Right seemed to culminate in 1989. The ending of Soviet control over its east-central European satellite states and the dismantling of the Soviet Union itself led to a sudden new triumphalism of the world Right. One more illusion!

The offensive of the world Right was a great success. The offensive of the world Right was a great failure. What was sustaining the accumulation of capital since the 1970s was the turning from seeking profits via productive efficiency to seeking profits via financial manipulations, more correctly called speculation. The key mechanism of speculation is encouraging consumption via indebtedness.

Seeking profits from finance (speculation) rather than from production was of course what had happened in every Kondratieff B period throughout the history of the modern world-system. The difference this time has been the scale of the speculation and the indebtedness. After the biggest A-period expansion in the history of the capitalist world-economy, there followed the biggest speculative mania. The bubbles moved through the whole world-system—from the national debts of the Third World countries and the socialist bloc in the 1970s, to the junk bonds of large corporations in the 1980s, to the consumer indebtedness of the 1990s, to the US-government indebtedness of the Bush era. The system has gone from bubble to bubble. The world is currently trying one last bubble—the bailouts of the banks and the printing of dollars. This is a bubble because it depends on borrowing money (notably the United States borrowing from China, but not only) and printing money, which devalues the dollar.

The depression into which the world has fallen will continue now for quite a while and go quite deep. It will destroy the last small pillar of relative economic stability, the role of the US dollar as a reserve currency for safeguarding wealth. As this happens, the main concern of every government in the world—from the United States to China, from France to Russia to Brazil, not to speak of all the weaker governments on the world scene—will be to avert the uprising of the unemployed workers and the middle strata whose savings and pensions disappear. The governments are turning to protectionism (even as they are denying it) and printing money as their first line of defense, as ways of dealing with popular anger.

Such measures may postpone for a year or two or three the dangers the governments fear and may assuage momentarily the pain of ordinary people. But they will eventually probably make the situation even worse. We are entering a gridlock of the system, from which the world will find it extremely difficult to extract itself. The gridlock will express itself in the form of a constant set of ever-wilder fluctuations, which will make short-term predictions—both economic and political—virtually guesswork. And this in turn will aggravate popular fears and alienation.

And China?

Some observers are claiming that the greatly improved relative economic position of the Asian nations—especially first Japan, then South Korea and Taiwan, then China and to a lesser extent India—is allowing, will allow, a resurgence of capitalist enterprise, with a simple geographical shift of location. One more illusion! The relative rise of Asia is a reality but precisely one that undermines further the capitalist system. It does so by overloading the numbers of persons to whom surplus value is distributed.

China is already beset by serious popular discontent, as it has managed to go in thirty short years from one of the least internally polarized countries to one in which the gap between the upper third of the population and the lower two-thirds is remarkably large and growing. China counters this in various ways. One is a very strong insistence on national unity, which leaves little or no place for cultural minorities, which are restive. A second is to try to curb some of the excesses of the new entrepreneurial elements, who have great strength at the local and regional level within the party structure. A third is to allow a certain rise in urban wage levels, which will make China's exports less competitive.

China's biggest economic problem is its entanglement with the dollar. On the one hand, buying US Treasuries is feeding money to the United States so that it can purchase China's exports. On the other hand, as the dollar declines (and it has been declining for some twenty years), China is losing real wealth. The trick is to withdraw gradually from the dollar, neither too slow nor too fast. As anyone who invests in a volatile world market knows, this is a very tricky and uncertain game.

In the end, however, the real problem is the size of Asia. The top end of the capitalist system can never be too large, for this reduces (not increases) the overall accumulation of capital. China's economic expansion actually accelerates the structural profit squeeze of the capitalist world-economy.

Where Do We the World Go from Here?

In order to analyze what is likely to happen in the near future, it is necessary to turn from the discussion of the normal cyclical ups and downs—the cyclical rhythms—of the capitalist world-economy to its secular trends. All kinds of systems function in the same formal fashion. The cyclical rhythms are how they operate on a continuing basis, how they breathe, if you will. There are innumerable ups and downs, some more fundamental than others. But the B phases never end at the same point as where the preceding A phases began. There is always a systemic price to pay for renewing the upward phase of the cycles. The system has always to move just a little further from equilibrium, even its moving equilibrium.

We may think of each upturn as a contribution to a slow-moving upward curve, each heading toward an asymptote. In the capitalist world-economy, it is not all that difficult to discern which curves matter most. Since capitalism is a system in which the endless accumulation of capital is paramount, and since one accumulates capital by making profits in the market, the key issue for all capitalists is how to produce products for prices that are lower, preferably far lower, than the prices for which they can be sold.

We therefore have to discern what goes into the costs of production and what determines the prices. Logically, there are three different kinds of costs of production: the costs of personnel (all personnel), the costs of inputs (all kinds of inputs), and the costs of taxation (all kinds of taxation). I think it is not too hard to demonstrate that all three costs have been going up over time as a percentage of the actual prices for which products are sold. And this is so despite the repeated efforts of capitalists to push them down and despite the repeated technological and organizational improvements which have increased the so-called efficiency of production. I discuss briefly why this is so and then discuss briefly why there are limits to the elasticity of demand, or the price for which commodities can be sold.

The costs of personnel may be divided into three categories—the relatively unskilled workforce, the intermediate cadres, and the top managers. The costs of the unskilled tend to go up in A periods as a result of some kind of syndical action. This is because when there is relative prosperity, entrepreneurs often feel they will lose more from a work stoppage than from acceding to workers' demands for slightly higher wages. But when these costs go too high for given entrepreneurs and particularly for those in the most profitable (leading) industries, relocation to historically lower-wage areas in the B period is the main remedy. In the past thirty or so years, many jobs have been moved, for example, from the United States or western Europe to various other parts of the world. Of course, when there is later on, perhaps twenty-five to fifty years later, similar syndical action in the new location, a new move occurs, as has been happening for centuries. For example, in recent years, jobs that had moved to, say, Korea or Taiwan then moved to mainland China and may be moving today to Vietnam.

The moves are costly but effective. But worldwide there is a ratchet effect. The reductions never eliminate totally the increases. Since the source of low-cost labor is often primarily rural workers moving to urban industrial zones, this repeated process over five hundred years has begun to exhaust the loci into which to move. This can be measured by the deruralization of the world-system.

The increase in the costs of cadres is the result of two different considerations. One, the increased scale of productive units requires more intermediate personnel, whose salaries augment the total personnel bill. And two, the political dangers that result from the repeated syndical organization of the relatively low-skilled personnel are countered by the creation of a larger intermediate stratum of workers who can be both political allies for the ruling stratum and models of a possible upward mobility for the unskilled majority, thereby blunting its political mobilization.

The increase in the costs of top managers is the direct result of the increased complexity of entrepreneurial structures—the famous separation of ownership and control. This makes it possible for these top managers to appropriate ever-larger portions of the firm's receipts, thereby reducing what goes to the "owners" as profit or to reinvestment by the firm. This last increase was spectacular in size during the past few decades. Pay for CEOs and other top personnel is drawn from the profit that might otherwise go to the shareholders or to further investments by the corporation. Pay for top personnel is essentially rent, which is being diverted from profit.

The costs of inputs have been going up for analogous reasons. The basic effort of capitalists is to externalize costs, that is, to get others to pay these costs and therefore not to pay themselves the full bill for the inputs they use. There are three main costs one may externalize—handling toxic waste, renewing raw materials, and building infrastructure. For a very long time, from the origins of the capitalist world-economy in the sixteenth century to the 1960s, such externalization of costs was taken as absolutely normal. It was basically unquestioned by political authorities.

In the twenty-first century, when climate change is widely debated, and "green" and "organic" have become universal buzz words, it is hard to remember that, for five centuries, toxic waste was normally and almost always simply dumped in the public domain. What happened is that the world has been running out of such vacant public domains—the equivalent of deruralization of the world's workforce. Suddenly, the health consequences and costs have become so high, so visible, and so close to home that a major political response has occurred, in the form of demands for environmental cleanup and control.

The second externalization, that of renewing resources, has also only recently become a major concern, the consequence of the sharp increase in world population. Suddenly, there is a wide and quite plausible concern about shortages—of energy sources, of water, of forestation, of products of the soil, of fish and meat. Suddenly, we are worried about who uses what, for what purposes, and who pays the bill.

The third externalization has been that of infrastructure. Products produced for sale on the world market need transport and communication, the costs of which have gone up as they have become more efficient and faster. Entrepreneurs have historically only paid a small part of the real bill for infrastructure.

The consequence of all of this has been a popular political thrust for governments to assume directly some of the necessary costs of detoxification, resource renewal, and further infrastructure expansion. To do this, governments must increase taxes. And unless they wish to go bankrupt, governments have to insist on more internalization of costs by entrepreneurs, which of course cuts sharply into margins of profit of enterprises.

Consequently, taxation has been going up. There are multiple political levels of taxation. There is also the private taxation of corruption and organized mafias. For the entrepreneur, it does not really matter to whom the taxes go. They are a cost. The size of private taxation has risen as the extensiveness of world economic activity has gone up, and state bureaucracies have expanded as well. One major reason for the expansion of the bureaucracies and taxation in general has been the impact of the world's antisystemic movements on political culture—what might be called the democratization of world politics.

Over the past two hundred years, popular movements have pushed for three basic state guarantees—education, health, and lifelong revenue flows. Each of these has expanded in two ways over this period: in the levels of services demanded (for example, once only elementary education, then secondary education, now university education) and in the geographical locales in which the demands have been made (once only western Europe and North America, today Asia, Africa, and Latin America). The "welfare state" is good shorthand for such demands. And there is no government today exempt from the pressure to maintain a welfare state, even if the levels vary, primarily according to the collective wealth of the country.

If one adds up what has happened to the three major costs of production, one sees that all of them have risen steadily as a percentage of the real sales prices of products, albeit in the form of an A-B ratchet, over five hundred years. What I mean by an A-B ratchet is that they may rise two units of some measure in an A period but only go down one unit in a B period. The most dramatic increases have been in the post-1945 period.

Cannot the prices for which products are sold simply be raised, in order to maintain the margins of real profit? That is precisely what has been tried in the post-1970 period. This has taken the form of price rises sustained by expanded consumption sustained by indebtedness. The economic collapse in the midst of which we find ourselves is nothing but the expression of the limits of elasticity of demand. When everyone lives far beyond his or her real income, there comes a point where someone has to stop, and fairly quickly everyone feels he or she has to stop. Demand retracts. And at an individual level, people react according to the old saying: once burned, twice shy. It is not so easy to restore the level of demand, particularly when it had been so high on the basis of borrowed money.

The coming together today of the three elements—the magnitude of the "normal" crash, the real rise in costs of production, and the extra pressure on the system of Chinese (and Asian) growth—means that Humpty Dumpty has fallen off the wall, and the pieces can no longer be put together again. The system is very, very far from equilibrium, and the fluctuations are enormous. As a consequence, short-term predictions have become impossible to make, and this tends to freeze consumption decisions. This is what one calls structural crisis.

Capitalism is no longer viable not simply because it involves much oppression for the majority of the world's population but because it no longer offers capitalists the opportunity to achieve their principal objective, the endless accumulation of capital. The game is no longer worth the candle—something that is becoming more evident to the capitalists themselves.

Structural Crisis

From here on in, we are living amid the bifurcation of the systemic process. The question is no longer, how will the capitalist system mend itself and renew its forward thrust? The question is, what will replace this system? What order will be chosen out of this chaos?

Of course, not everyone is aware of this as yet. Most people continue to operate as though somehow the system were continuing, using its old rules. They are not really wrong. The system does continue to operate, using its old rules. But now, using the old rules only exacerbates the structural crisis. However, some actors are quite aware that we are in a bifurcation. And they know, perhaps only tacitly, that at some point in a bifurcation, the collectivity of all actors leans definitively in one direction or another. One can say that a decision has been made, even if the use of the word "decision" sounds anthropomorphic.

One may think of this period of systemic crisis as the arena of a struggle for the successor system. The outcome may be inherently unpredictable, but the nature of the struggle is very clear. The world is before alternative choices. They cannot be spelled out in institutional detail, but they can be suggested in broad outline.

We can "choose" collectively a new stable system that essentially resembles the present system in some basic characteristics—a system that is hierarchical, exploitative, and polarizing. There are, no doubt, many forms this could take other than that of a market-centered economic system, and some of these forms could be harsher than the capitalist world-system in which we have been living. Alternatively, we can "choose" collectively a radically different form of system, one that has never previously existed—a system that is relatively democratic and relatively egalitarian.

I have been calling the two alternatives "the spirit of Davos" and "the spirit of Porto Alegre." But the names are unimportant. What is important is to see the possible organizational strategies on each side in this definitive struggle—a struggle that has been going on in some form since the world-revolution of 1968 and may not be resolved before circa 2050.

Before, however, one looks at strategies, one must note two crucial characteristics of a structural crisis. Because the fluctuations are so wild, there is little pressure to return to equilibrium. During the long, "normal" lifetime of the system, these pressures were the means by which extensive social mobilizations (so-called revolutions) had always been limited in their effects. But when the system is far from equilibrium, exactly the opposite happens. Small social mobilizations have very great effects.

This is what complexity science refers to as the "butterfly" effect. We might also, in ancient Western philosophic discourse, call it the moment when free will prevails over determinism. Ilya Prigogine calls this way of understanding complex systems the "narrow path between two conceptions that both lead to alienation: a world ruled by deterministic laws, which leaves no place for novelty, and a world ruled by a dice-playing God, where everything is absurd, acausal, and incomprehensible."[2]

The second crucial characteristic of a structural crisis is that neither of the two camps has, nor can it have, a vertical structure with a small group at the top calling all the shots. There is neither a functioning executive committee of the ruling class nor a politburo of the oppressed masses, nor can there be. Even among those who are aware of and committed to the struggle for a successor system, there are multiple players, pushing different emphases, co-coordinating poorly with each other. These two groups of aware militants on both sides are also finding it difficult to persuade the larger groups that form the potential base of their strength of the utility and possibility of organizing the transition. In short, the chaos of the structural crisis is reflected as well in the relatively chaotic structures of the two camps struggling over the successor system.

Emerging Strategies of the Two Camps in the Struggle

What we can do, while in the very middle of this structural crisis, is to try to analyze the emerging strategies that each camp is developing, the better to orient our own political choices in the light of our own moral preferences. We can start with the strategy of the camp of "the spirit of Davos." They are deeply divided. There are those who wish to institute a highly repressive system which openly propagates a worldview that glorifies the role of skilled, secretive, highly privileged rulers and submissive subjects. They not only propagate this worldview but propose to organize a network of armed enforcers to crush opposition.

There is a second group who believe that the road to control and privilege is via a highly meritocratic system that would co-opt the large number of cadres necessary to maintain the system with a minimum of force and a maximum of persuasion. This group speaks a language of fundamental change, utilizing all the slogans that have emerged from the antisystemic movements—including a green universe, a multicultural utopia, and meritocratic opportunities for all—all this while seeking to maintain a polarized and unequal system.

And on the side of the camp of "the spirit of Porto Alegre," there is a parallel split. There are those who envisage a highly decentralized world, one which privileges rational long-term allocations over short-term economic growth, one which makes possible innovation without creating cocoons of expertise unanswerable to the larger society. This group envisages a system in which a universal universalism will be built out of the never-ending piecing together of the multiple wisdoms that humans have created and will continue to create in their different cultural flowerings.

There is a second group who have been, and continue to be, more oriented to transformation from above, by cadres and specialists who believe they see the politics of struggle more clearly than the rest. Far from being decentralizing, they envisage an ever more coordinated and integrated world-system, a formal egalitarianism without real innovation and without the patience to construct a truly universal but multifaceted universalism.

So, far from a simple twofold battle for the successor system, I envisage a fourfold battle—one between the two great camps and a second one within each of the great camps. This is a confusing situation, confusing intellectually, morally, and politically—all the more reason to insist that the outcome is fundamentally unpredictable and uncertain.

Practical Steps to Take

What then can we say of the practical steps any of us, as individuals and as groups of diverse kinds and strengths, can and should do to further this process? There is no formulaic agenda of action. There are only lines of emphasis. I would put at the head of the list actions that we can take, in the short run, to minimize the pain—the pain that arises from the breakdown of the existing system, the pain that arises from the confusions of the transition. Personally, I would not sneer at winning an election, at obtaining some more benefits within the states for those who have least materially. I would not sneer at some protection of judicial and political rights. I would not sneer at combating some further erosion of our planetary wealth and conditions for collective survival. I would not sneer at any of these, even though I do not consider any of these achievements more than momentary palliatives for immediate pain. They are not in themselves in any ways steps toward creating the new successor system that we want.

The second thing that we can do is to engage in endless serious intellectual debate about the parameters of the kind of world-system we want and the strategy of transition. We not only need to do this ceaselessly, but we need to do it with a willingness to hear, as part of the debate, persons we deem of goodwill, if not of our immediate viewpoint. A constant open debate may bring more insight, will surely build greater camaraderie, and will keep us perhaps from falling into the sectarianism that has always defeated antisystemic movements. The very volume in which this chapter appears may be considered to be a contribution to the constant open debate.

The third thing we can do is to construct, here and there and everywhere, on a small or large scale, alternative decommodified modes of production. We can learn from doing this the limits of many particular methods. We can demonstrate by doing this that there are other modes of ensuring sensible and sustainable production than reliance on the profit motive as the basis of our reward system.

The fourth thing we can do is to engage in moral debate, to sharpen our sense of the moral negatives of any and all particular modes of action, to realize that balances must be made between the realizations of alternative good outcomes.

And through this all, we must put at the forefront of our consciousness and our action the struggle against the three fundamental inequalities of the world—gender, class, and the multiple forms of identity (race, ethnicity, religion). This is the hardest task of all, since there is none of us guiltless and none of us pure. And the entire world culture that we have all inherited militates against this.

Finally, we must run like the plague from any sense that history is on our side, that the good society is certain to come, if only x or y. History is on no one's side. A century from now, our descendants may regret all that we have done. We have at best a fifty-fifty chance of creating a better world-system than the one in which we now live. But fifty-fifty is a lot. We must try to seize Fortuna, even if it escapes us. What more useful thing can any of us do?

CHAPTER 3

The Enigma of Capital and the Crisis This Time

David Harvey

There are many explanations for the crisis of capital that began in 2007. But the one thing missing is an understanding of "systemic risks." I was alerted to this when Her Majesty the Queen visited the London School of Economics and asked the prestigious economists there why they had not seen the crisis coming. She being a feudal monarch rather than an ordinary mortal, the economists felt impelled to answer. After six months of reflection, the economic gurus of the British Academy submitted their conclusions. The gist was that many intelligent and dedicated economists had worked assiduously and hard on understanding the microprocesses. But everyone had somehow missed "systemic risk." A year later, a former chief economist of the International Monetary Fund said, "We sort of know vaguely what systemic risk is and what factors might relate to it. But to argue that it is a well-developed science at this point is overstating the fact." In a formal paper, the International Monetary Fund described the study of systemic risk as "in its infancy."[1] In Marxian theory (as opposed to myopic neoclassical or financial theory), systemic risk translates into the fundamental contradictions of capital accumulation. The IMF might save itself a lot of trouble by studying them. So how, then, can we put Marx's theorization of the internal contradictions of capitalism to work to understand the roots of our contemporary dilemmas?

This is the task I set myself in writing *The Enigma of Capital: And the Crises of Capitalism*.[2] In writing it, I found, however, that conventional versions of the Marxian theory of crisis formation were inadequate and that it was necessary to take a fresh look at the arguments on crisis formation laid out in *Capital* and, even more important, in *The Grundrisse*. In the latter work, Marx argues that the circulation, and accumulation, of capital cannot abide limits. When it encounters limits, it works assiduously to convert them into barriers that can be transcended or bypassed. This focuses our attention on those points in the circulation of capital where potential limits, blockages, and barriers might arise, since these can produce crises of one sort or another.

Capital, Marx insists, is a process of circulation and not a thing. It is fundamentally about putting money into circulation to make more money. There are various ways to do this. Financiers lend money in return for interest; merchants buy cheap in order to sell dear; and rentiers buy up land, resources, patents, and the like, which they release to others in return for rent. Even the capitalist state can invest in infrastructures in search of an improved tax base that yields greater revenues. But the primary form of capital circulation in Marx's view was that of production capital. This capital begins with money, which is used to buy labor power and means of production, which are then brought together in a labor process, under a given technological and organizational form, that results in a new commodity to be sold on the market for the initial money plus a profit.

A part of the profit, for reasons I take up later, has to be capitalized and launched into circulation to seek even more profit. Capital is thereby committed to a compounding rate of growth. The quantity of global goods and services traded through the market (which now stands at around US$55 trillion) has grown at an average rate of around 2.25 percent since 1750 or so.[3] In some places and times, it has been much higher, and elsewhere, much lower. This fits with the conventional wisdom that a growth rate of 3 percent is the minimum acceptable level at which a "healthy" capitalism can operate. The average global growth rate from 2000 to 2008 was exactly 3 percent (with plenty of local variation). Anything less than 3 percent is problematic, while zero or negative growth defines a crisis that, if prolonged, as in the 1930s, defines a depression. So the problem for capital is to find a path to a minimum compound 3-percent growth forever.

There are abundant signs, however, that capital accumulation is at a historical inflexion point where sustaining a compound rate of growth is becoming increasingly problematic. In 1970, this meant finding new profitable global investment opportunities for US$0.4 trillion. Resumption of 3 percent growth right now would mean finding profitable invest-ment opportunities for $1.5 trillion. If that rate of growth were to be sustained until 2030 or so, we would be looking at $3 trillion. Put in physical terms, when capitalism in 1750 was about everything going on around Manchester and Birmingham and a few other hot spots in the global economy, then 3-percent compound growth posed no problem. But we are now looking at compounding growth on everything going on in North America, Europe, much of East Asia, Latin America, and increasingly South Asia, the Middle East, and Africa. The implications socially, politically, and environmentally are nothing short of gargantuan.

Note that the operative term here is *profitable* investment opportu-nities, as opposed to socially necessary and socially valuable investment opportunities. So where, then, are the potential limits to this profitability? Since capital is a process, not a thing, then the continuity of the pro-cess (along with its speed and geographical adaptability and mobility) becomes a feature crucial to sustaining growth. Any slowdown or block-age in capital flow will produce a crisis. If our blood flow stops, then we die. If capital flow stops, then the body politic of capitalist society dies. This simple rule was most dramatically demonstrated in the wake of the events of 9/11. Normal processes of circulation were stopped dead in and around New York City, with huge ramifications for the global economy. Within five days, then mayor Rudy Giuliani was pleading with everyone to get out his or her credit card and go shopping, go to the restaurants and the Broadway shows (seats are now available!), and shortly thereaf-ter, the president of the United States did an unprecedented thing: he appeared in a collective commercial for the airlines pleading with people to start flying again. When the banks stopped lending and credit froze in the wake of the Lehman collapse on September 15, 2008, the survival of capitalism was threatened, and political power went to extraordinary lengths to loosen the constrictions. It was a matter of life or death for capital, as everyone in power recognized. Inspection of the circulation of capital reveals, however, a series of potential blockage points, any one of which could induce a crisis by constricting capital flow. Let us consider each of these.

1. Assemblage of the Initial Capital

Capital accumulation presumes that adequate amounts of money can be brought together in the right place, at the right time, and in the right quantities in order to launch that money into circulation as capital. Marx for the most part treated this problem of the initial capital in terms of primitive accumulation (the robbery of moneys from the rest of the world). This is inadequate because, as Saint-Simon had earlier pointed out, the association of many capitals (eventually achieved via the corporate form, stock markets, etc.) is required to undertake large-scale projects such as railways, canals, and even large-scale industrial undertakings. It is the job of the financial system—almost invariably incorporating state powers—to assemble small-scale savings and surpluses and to redistribute the moneys so assembled across a range of potentially profitable projects. The Péreire brothers, for example, schooled in the ways of thought of Saint-Simon, created new credit institutions to facilitate the rebuilding of Paris in order to mop up surpluses of both capital and labor left stagnant in the aftermath of the economic crisis of 1848. They soon found that they themselves need not engage with production, that leveraging (borrowing at 3 percent and lending out at 5 percent) could yield them hefty profits.[4] The creation of a modern mortgage-finance system in the United States dates back to the 1930s (when a third of the unemployment was attributable to depression in the construction trades), and this laid the basis for the postwar suburban boom that played such a crucial role in preventing the United States from sliding back into depression.

Continuous financial innovation has been crucial to the survival of capitalism. But finance and money capitalists also demand their cut of the surplus value produced. Excessive power within the financial system can itself then become a problem, generating a conflict between finance and production capital. Financial institutions, furthermore, have always integrated with the state apparatus to form what I call a state-finance nexus.[5] This usually stays in the background except in a crisis, as happened in the United States in the wake of the Lehman collapse: the secretary of the Treasury (Henry Paulson) and the chairman of the Federal Reserve (Ben Bernanke) were making all the key decisions (President Bush was rarely seen). To the degree that state power favored City of London finance over production capital in Britain after the First World War, so it contributed to the malaise of industrial production in the same way that Wall Street finance connived at the deindustrialization of the United States after the mid-1970s. Crises have frequently centered on the financial sector and associated state powers either because finance is overregulated or not innovative enough (producing what is called "financial repression"[6]—a term often used in the 1970s) or because it is too powerful and too uncontrollable for the good of the system (as is often argued now).

At various points, Marx contemplates, as we must too, the possibility of autonomous financial or monetary crises forming from within the financial system and spreading to the rest of the economy. Financial innovation is absolutely fundamental to achieving compound growth, and capital cannot do without it. But this innovation can all too easily get out of hand, go insanely speculative, or simply empower excessively the financiers, who often look to their own self-interest rather than to the stability of capitalism. Deregulation of the financial system, seen as a necessary step in the 1970s in order to overcome the barrier of financial repression, has played a critical role in the crisis this time. But why the necessity of that financial innovation and deregulation from the 1970s onward?

2. The Labor Market

When labor is scarce or too well organized, then this can check the free circulation of capital. Wages rise at the expense of profits. The long history of class struggle over wage rates and conditions of contract (length of the working day, the working week, and the working life), along with struggles over levels of social provision (the social wage), is testimony to the importance of this potential limit to capital accumulation. This constriction was very marked in the core regions of capitalism in the late 1960s and early 1970s. This was the primary blockage that had to be overcome.

Labor markets (always geographically fragmented) were largely organized on a national basis in the period 1945–80 and were insulated from international competition by constraints on international capital flow. Nation-states could design their own fiscal policies, and these could be influenced politically by organized labor and left political parties. The social wage tended to increase at the expense of capital. The answer to this problem partly lay in the successful political assault (led by Reagan, Thatcher, and military leaders in Latin America) on organized labor and its political institutions. But the other prong of attack was to mobilize global labor surpluses through offshoring. After the collapse of the Bretton Woods financial system in the early 1970s and the subsequent deregulation of finance, constraints to international capital flow were loosened, and capital began to exercise greater discipline over nation-state fiscal policies. Welfare states were undermined, real wages stagnated or declined, and the share of wages in total GDP in the OECD countries fell. Capital gained access to a vast disposable labor reserve living under marginal conditions. By the mid-1980s, the labor problem (in the market, on the shop floor, and politically in social democracies) had disappeared. Wage repression was experienced almost everywhere. Note well, however, that the labor problem could not have been overcome without the financial deregulation and innovations that dismantled barriers to cross-border capital flows. The labor problem was solved at the expense of opening up the possibility of crises within the financial system (of which there were many after 1975 or so). But what converted that possibility into a certainty?

3. The Availability of the Means of Production and Scarcities in Nature

Several technical issues arise around access to adequate means of production. Supply bottlenecks can easily occur, sometimes for systemic reasons that cannot be elaborated on here. But beneath this lies the possibility of so-called natural limits to raw-material supplies and to the capacity of the environment to absorb wastes. The history of capitalism is replete with many phases when "nature" is held to be an ultimate limit to growth. But the Malthusian scenario has never as yet really grabbed hold. This history is a very good example of how capital, when it encounters limits, exhibits considerable ingenuity in turning them into barriers that can be transcended or circumvented (by technological changes, opening up new resource regions, and the like). Because capital has successfully done this in the past does not necessarily mean, of course, that it is destined to do so in perpetuity. Nor does it imply that past episodes of supposed natural limits were negotiated smoothly and without crises. Whether or not this is a moment when what James O'Connor calls "the second contradiction of capitalism" (the relation to nature as opposed to the capital-labor relation that Marxists typically privilege) comes to the fore as the main barrier to sustained accumulation is a matter for debate.[7]

But in exactly the same way that financiers have sometimes gained too much power and produced a general crisis by pursuing their narrow interests, so landlords and rentiers can do the same thing, as happened when the oil cartel OPEC added fuel (actually subtracted it!) to the crisis of the 1970s or when speculators drove up the price of oil and other raw materials, such as food grains, in the summer of 2008. Excessive political and price manipulation in raw-materials markets, in rents on intellectual property rights, or in the built environment can threaten the continuous accumulation of capital. When the rentier is the state (as it often is in the case of oil), then geopolitical struggles can also produce barriers and limits to the release of so-called natural resources into the circulation of capital. I write "so-called" because resources are always technological, cultural, and economic appraisals and in the form of the built environment—sometimes referred to as "second nature"—are actively produced as a new landscape for accumulation. Scarcities that threaten compound growth are largely socially produced.

The importance and power of the rentier classes has always been underestimated. There is evidence that the British upper classes (the landed aristocracy in particular) accumulated far more wealth from rising rents from the mid-seventeenth century onward than they did from the exploitation of factory labor in Manchester. The power of rentiers has been growing in recent times, as we have seen in land markets, in pursuit of intellectual property rights and patents, and in speculation in commodity futures. It is significant also that during the current crisis the well-heeled as well as state powers (the Chinese in particular) are buying up land and resources galore in Latin America and Africa. Land and property values in combination with finance capital are at the epicenter of this crisis and continue to constitute a dangerous potential barrier to the recovery of compound growth in the long run.

4. Technological and Organizational Forms

How labor power and means of production are brought together depends on the technological and organizational forms available to capitalists in a given time and place. The history of capitalism has been deeply affected by the ways in which productivity gains are achieved. New organizational forms such as just-in-time systems, subcontracting, the use of optimal scheduling, and the like have been just as important as new machines, robotization, and automation in achieving increases in productivity and in disciplining labor on the shop floor. Two general points are important to note. Excessive innovation can generate crises by displacing labor too rapidly or rendering production systems obsolete well before investments have been amortized. Innovation can, on the other hand, lag when "the coercive laws of competition" slacken because of monopolization.[8] The balance between monopoly and competition here is crucial. Excessive monopolization and centralization of capital can produce stagnation (as happened in the period of "stagflation" in the 1970s), whereas competition can be "ruinous" for many capitalists when it becomes too fierce and cutthroat (as became apparent in the deindustrialization of the 1980s).[9]

A low-profit-margin regime arose in almost all lines of conventional production in the 1980s, even as real wages stagnated. With the dismantling of capital controls over international movement, uneven geographical development and interterritorial competition became key features in capitalist development, further undermining the fiscal autonomy of nation-states. This also marked the beginnings of a shift of power toward East Asia. But it also led capital to invest more and more in control over assets—capturing rents and capital gains—rather than in production. The speculative-asset bubbles that formed from the 1980s onward were the price that was paid for unleashing the coercive laws of competition worldwide as a disciplinary force over the powers of labor and over the previously autonomous powers of the nation-state with respect to fiscal and social policies.

Deregulating and empowering the most fluid and highly mobile form of capital—money capital—to reallocate capital resources globally (eventually through electronic markets and a "shadow" unregulated banking system) facilitated the deindustrialization in traditional core regions. Capital then accelerated its reliance on a series of "spatial fixes" to absorb overaccumulating capital. Cascading patterns of foreign direct investments coursed around the world, fundamentally changing the geography of capitalist production and facilitating new forms of (ultraoppressive) industrialization and natural-resource and agricultural raw-material extractions in emerging markets. The hegemonic shift of economic power toward East Asia, a shift that Giovanni Arrighi had long been presciently anticipating, began to be more and more evident.[10]

Two corollaries then followed. One was to enhance the profitability of financial corporations relative to industrial capital and to find new ways to globalize and supposedly absorb risks through the creation of fictitious capital markets (the leveraging ratio of banks in the United States rose from around three to thirty). Nonfinancial corporations (such as auto companies) often made more money from financial manipulations than from making things. The other impact was heightened reliance on "accumulation by dispossession" as a means to augment capitalist-class power. The new rounds of primitive accumulation against indigenous and peasant populations (particularly in Asia and Latin America) were augmented by asset losses of the lower classes in the core economies, as witnessed by losses of pension and welfare rights as well as, eventually, huge asset losses in the subprime housing market in the United States. Intensifying global competition translated into lower nonfinancial corporate profits.

5. The Labor Process

The labor process is where profit originates and capital is produced. What happens on the shop floor, in the fields, or on the construction sites is therefore crucial. The discipline and cooperation of the worker is here essential to accumulation. Indiscipline and lack of cooperation on the part of labor is a perpetual threat that needs to be overcome either by co-optation and persuasion (the creation of quality circles, the mobilization of company loyalties and pride in work) or by coercion (threats of job loss or in some instances physical violence). The shop-stewards movements, the factory councils, and all manner of other forms of shop-floor organization empower labor, while the capitalists have to negotiate or fight their way to achieve a modicum of labor discipline. Capital here uses differences of gender, ethnicity, race, and even religion to great effect to divide and rule in the workplace if it possibly can. While such differences have obviously played a crucial role in the labor market as well, it is here at the point of production where they become all-important. Toward the end of the 1960s and well into the 1970s, the problem of labor discipline loomed large in the core regions of capitalism. Offshoring to more docile labor pastures proved helpful to capital, as did the availability of immigrants and undocumented workers. As in labor markets, the power balance within the labor process shifted markedly toward capital, and much of the shop-floor resistance crumbled from 1980 onward. But as the autonomista Marxists insist, labor discipline can never be fully assured. It is always a potential point of revolutionary resistance.[11]

6. Demand and Effective Demand

The new commodity produced has to be sold for the original money plus a profit. Someone, somewhere, must need, want, or desire the product and have enough money to pay for it. Capitalism exhibits an astonishing history of the production of new needs, wants, and desires, in part through the production of new lifestyles (consider what is needed to maintain a suburban household) but also through an incessant barrage of advertisements and other subliminal means to manipulate the human psyche for commercial reasons. Not all such attempts are successful (history is littered with new products that never found a market), but in a world where the consumer accounts for more than two-thirds of the driving force for capital accumulation, at least in the core regions of capital accumulation, the human limits to wants, needs, and desires constitute a potential barrier to which capital must perpetually attend in the search for compound growth.

But the other issue here is finding consumers with sufficient money to pay. Compounding growth supposes that there is more money available at the end of the day than there was at the beginning, and the big question is, where does the extra money come from? There are three basic answers. First, the moneys held by noncapitalist factions can be drawn into the system. The "gold reserves" of the feudal classes played a very important role in the early years of capitalism. Sucked out by usury and other forms of indebtedness as well as through normal marketing practices, this source of effective demand has much diminished (though the Catholic Church may yet have to melt down a lot of its gold plate to pay for the sins of its priests). The second option, which Rosa Luxemburg emphasized, was the gold and silver reserves of countries largely outside the orbit of capitalist development. Imperialism and colonialism here played a usually violent role in opening up new markets (e.g., the nineteenth-century opium wars in China), thus draining wealth from the once-rich regions of China, India, Africa, and Latin America.[12] But with the integration of many of these regions into the full circulation of capital, these forms of effective demand are now insufficient to sustain the compound growth of capital accumulation. The third option is to produce effective demand from within the capitalist dynamic. The total wage bill is insufficient and has in any case been falling in relation to GDP over the past thirty years. Capitalist consumption, no matter how conspicuous, cannot do it either. The answer is that the money spent on the expansion of investment tomorrow forms the effective demand to mop up the expanded product created yesterday. Tomorrow's growth creates the effective demand for yesterday's expanded product. The effective demand problem today is thereby converted into a problem of finding profitable new investment opportunities tomorrow. This explains why compound growth is so essential to the perpetuation of capitalism.

Three issues then arise. First, the time gap between yesterday's product and tomorrow's reinvestment has to be bridged, and this entails the use of money as money of account. The finance capitalists come back in as crucial players who operate not only at the beginning of the circulation of capital sequence but also at the end. For example, financiers lend to property developers, who hire labor to build houses, which are then purchased by the workers with a mortgage loan often from the very same financiers. Such a system is inherently speculative and prone to produce housing bubbles of the sort already noted.

But it is not only the financiers who do this. Commercial and merchant capitalists buy from the producers and specialize in marketing to consumers. Merchant capitalists, like financiers and rentiers, extract a rate of return from their own efforts and can come to exert an independent class-factional power, which has often played a significant role in crisis formation. The pressures put on producers by merchant-capitalist organizations such as Walmart, Carrefour, and a whole host of supermarket chains along with merchant organizations such as Benetton, the Gap, Nike, and the like step into the forefront of what capital circulation is about, both smoothing out potential barriers and creating potentially dangerous concentrations of economic power. As with the landlords and rentiers, the merchant-capitalist class's self-interest is not necessarily concordant with that of the whole capitalist class. When we track what happens to the price of sugar, for example, as it moves from the cane fields of the Dominican Republic to the supermarkets of the United States, we see that the actual producers receive less than 5 percent of the final retail price. Most of the profit is taken by merchant intermediaries.

The third issue is less easy to identify, even as it seems to be assuming more and more importance in the way capital circulation works. When capital primarily produced long-lasting things, it was always in danger of satiating markets. I am still using the silver-plated forks made in Sheffield that graced my grandmother's table. The lifetime of consumer products has therefore to be shortened if capital is to survive. This happens to some degree by resort of fashion, by planned obsolescence and making things that break down easily, by continuous innovation (from iPods to iPads), and so on. This pressure has, in recent years, produced a shift from the production of things to the production of spectacle—a shift that Guy Debord presciently understood when he wrote *The Society of the Spectacle* back in 1967.[13] Just consider what goes into the production of the Olympic Games, not only the new physical infrastructures but the vast employment and resources entailed in opening ceremonies (remember the spectacle of Barcelona and then later the astonishing spectacle of Beijing). More and more capital therefore circulates in the production of spectacular and ephemeral events, with all sorts of consequences for consumerism as well as for urban life. But productions of this sort are invariably debt financed, and as the history of the Olympics clearly demonstrates, finding the money to pay off the debts afterward is often problematic. It is perhaps no accident that Greece, which staged the Olympics in 2004, is now in a leading crisis role because of its sovereign debt.

With real wages stagnant or falling after 1980, the deficit in effective demand was largely bridged by resort to the credit system. In the United States in particular, household debt tripled from 1980 to 2005, and much of that debt was accumulated around the housing market, particularly from 2001 onward. All sorts of innovations in finance, along with state policies that often had the effect of subsidizing or even paying people and corporations to go into debt, kept the compounding rate of growth going. This was the fictional bubble that eventually burst in 2008. But, again, notice the sequence. Wage repression produces a deficit of effective demand, which is covered by increasing indebtedness, which ultimately leads into a financial crisis, which is resolved by state interventions, which translates into a fiscal crisis of the state, which can best be resolved, according to conventional economic wisdom, by further reductions in the social wage.

7. Capital Circulation as a Whole

When viewed as a whole, we see a series of potential blockage points to the circulation of capital, any one of which has the potential to be the source of a crisis. There is, therefore, no single causal theory of crisis formation, as many Marxist economists like to assert. There is, for example, no point in trying to cram all of this fluidity and complexity into some unitary theory of, say, a falling rate of profit. In fact, profit rates can fall because of the inability to overcome any one of the blockages identified here. It is the task of historical materialist analysis to wrestle with the question as to where the primary blockages are this time around. But solutions at one point have implications for what happens elsewhere. The labor problem (both in the market and on the shop floor) that was central in the late 1960s in the core regions could not be overcome except by opening up the coercive laws of competition across a global space. This required a revolution in the architecture of the world's financial system, which increased the likelihood of "irrational exuberance" within the financial system. The consequent wage repression depressed effective demand, which could be overcome only by resort to the credit system. And so on.

The fundamental theoretical conclusion is, *capital never solves its crisis tendencies; it merely moves them around.* This is what Marx's analysis tells us, and this is what the history of the past forty years has been about. No one now claims that the excessive power of labor is the source of the current problem, as it was back in the 1970s. If anything, the problem is that capital in general and finance capital in particular are far too powerful and that the state cannot step in to rebalance affairs because it is captive—politically and economically—to capitalist-class financial, rentier, producer, and commercial interests. The dynamic shift from a crisis within the financial system centered on the banks to a fiscal crisis of states is now producing a renewed assault on labor, particularly in the public sector, as well as the social wage. But if purchasing power and consumer confidence then sag, then where is the market? The big intangible here is, however, whether mass resistance will arise to contest the austerity required to reduce state deficits.

The Uneven Geographical Development of the Crisis

We know that the crisis for capital (as opposed to the crisis for many homeowners and workers, who had long been distressed) began in the housing markets of Southern California, Arizona, Nevada, and Florida in 2007. This was the primary epicenter of the crisis.[14] But why there, and why then? The crisis then quickly spread through the mortgage-finance companies (such as Countrywide in the United States) to the major financial institutions (such as Bear Stearns) that still held a goodly amount of what became "toxic" securitized mortgage debt. It then spread to other institutions that either held the debt (such as Fannie Mae and Freddie Mac), invested in the debt (everyone that invested in collateralized debt obligations), or insured the debt or other financial transactions (such as AIG). The parallel crash of Northern Rock in Britain indicated that there were problems lurking in property markets elsewhere (as ultimately became apparent in Spain and Ireland in particular). The financial institutions located in New York and London then became the epicenter of the crisis. It largely fell to the US and British governments, along with the US Federal Reserve and the Bank of England, to stabilize the situation.

The crash of Lehman Brothers in September 2008 sent the contagion global. (Was this a deliberate move to transform the crisis from the local to global scale, a cave-in to populist pressure to punish the sinners on Wall Street, or just a huge mistake?) The crisis was probably bound to go global anyway, given the interdependency within global financial networks. Banks elsewhere (e.g., in Germany and France) had bought into the toxic debt, as had municipal and state governments and pension funds from Norway to Florida. All of them felt the distress. No matter where located, the holders of the toxic debt were in difficulty. Canadian and East Asian financial institutions, on the other hand, remained unaffected because they had little exposure.

But after Lehman, the whole global credit system (in which interbank lending is crucial) froze, and this formed the immediate primary blockage to the continuity of capital flows. Perfectly good enterprises suddenly found themselves in difficulty because they could not roll over their debt. Many firms rescued themselves by laying off workers by the droves and intensifying wage repression. Debt-fueled consumerism and effective demand were halted, consumer confidence fell off a cliff, and unemployment surged, though at radically different rates both within and between countries: compare, for example, Minnesota and Ohio in the United States or Spain (20 percent) and the Netherlands (4.4 percent) in Europe in 2009. The major export economies then took a hit as world trade contracted by some 20 percent, sparking huge difficulties for businesses and emphatic surges in unemployment in East Asia as well as in Germany, Brazil, and elsewhere. An earlier boom in raw-material prices (oil in particular) that turned out to be largely speculative likewise collapsed in the face of declining growth. Raw-material producers were in trouble. The global economy was clearly headed toward a huge depression, unless government acted.

What then followed depended crucially on the imperatives, ability, and willingness of different governments to use their powers (either individually or collectively) to confront the crisis. Given the threat of a depression on the scale of the 1930s, there was a growing initial clamor to resurrect Keynesian-style solutions. The immediate response after the Lehman debacle was to rescue, stabilize, and eventually reform the financial architecture (both locally and globally) and to construct a debt-financed stimulus to deal with the collapse of effective demand. The United States could not, however, act alone, and so the G8 was replaced by the G20, a coalition of leading states that accounted for most of the world's market-based economic activity. The search for a systemic exit from the crisis was hindered, however, by a number of overwhelming difficulties, not least of which were the very different political ideologies, needs, and configurations of class forces and special interests within the G20 states.

The United States, for example, was already deeply in debt to the rest of the world.[15] While the "safe haven" of dollar-denominated assets was likely to sustain dollar inflows into the foreseeable future, it was nevertheless dangerous for the United States to attempt a stimulus on a large-enough scale to work internally, let alone to entrain the rest of the world back onto a compound growth path (as it had done after 1945). In the United States, there were also strong political objections from a Republican Party that pandered to the hysterical populist right-wing fears of excessive government intervention and that saw opposing further deficit financing as a means to prevent any recovery that might redound to Obama's and the Democratic Party's electoral advantage. Whatever stimulus could be had was also pushed, for ideological reasons, toward tax cuts to a class that might not spend, as opposed to needy population groups that would. Finally, the best forms of stimulus lie in the provision of social and physical infrastructures that will raise productivity and improve efficiency within the national space. But the United States had no clear projects of either sort in mind. The refusal of the Republicans to support aid for state and local finances indicated a determination to cut social services rather than to expand them (a determination partly offset by short-term stimulus funds for education). And the physical infrastructures had to be "shovel ready," which meant they were for the most part a continuation of investments in urban and suburban development that had led into the crisis, rather than an innovative move toward a national urban-development policy that would help the United States exit the crisis in the long term (e.g., by saving on energy rather than expanding demand for it). The only innovation was weak support for alternative energy sources. Finally, many key aspects of a full Keynesian program were kept off the table. Chief of these was the greater empowerment of labor as a way to reverse chronic income inequalities. Mitigating the huge social inequalities that had arisen in the 1920s was viewed in the 1930s as a way to stimulate effective demand. The neoliberal politics of the 1980s and 1990s had produced inequalities in wealth and income not seen since the 1920s, which needed similar reversal. But the imbalance of power between capital and labor could not be addressed for fear of being dubbed and damned as "socialist" or "communist" by a powerful right-wing propaganda machine. Dominant class forces (the "Party of Wall Street") with strong influence within both political parties refused point-blank to accept a state-led recalibration of the relative powers of capital and labor. The power imbalance that lay at the root of the crisis was to remain untouched.

After an early phase of recovery in which "green shoots" were spied all over the economic landscape, the US economy lapsed back into slow growth and high unemployment in the spring of 2010, with little prospect of any dramatic revival. Corporate profits and the stock market began to revive, but under conditions of lower turnover and savage cost cutting, particularly with respect to wages. What revival there was came at the expense of increasing unemployment rather than alleviating wage repression, with negative effects on consumer confidence and internal effective demand (the wage concession taken from the autoworkers in the GM bailout is a prime example). This was not a path toward sustainable growth. If it pointed anywhere, it was toward deflation. Revival of a more robust sort would have to come from elsewhere.

Possessed of huge surpluses and an untroubled banking system easily manipulated by the central government, China had the means to act in a more full-blooded Keynesian way. The crash of export-oriented industries and the threat of mass unemployment and unrest in early 2009 forced the government's hand. The stimulus package devised had two forks. Close to US$600 billion was put largely into infrastructural projects—highway building on a scale that dwarfs that of the US interstate highway system of the 1960s, new airports, vast water projects, high-speed rail lines, and even whole new cities. Second, the central government forced the banks to loosen credit for local state and private projects.

The big question is whether these investments will increase national productivity. Given that the spatial integration of the Chinese economy is far from complete, there are reasons to believe it will do so. But whether the debts can be paid off when due or whether China will later be the epicenter of yet another global capitalist crisis is an open question. One negative effect has been a renewal of speculation in housing markets, with a doubling of property prices in Shanghai in 2009. There are other troubling signs of overcapacity in manufacturing and infrastructures, and many banks are rumored to be overextended. There is evidence of the emergence of an uncontrolled "shadow banking" system that is repeating some of the mistakes that occurred in the United States from the 1990s on. But the Chinese have dealt with nonperforming loans before, as high as 40 percent of assets in the late 1990s. They then used their foreign exchange reserves to erase nonperforming loans. Unlike the TARP program in the United States, which was passed by a reluctant Congress and which prompted much public resentment, the Chinese can take immediate action to recapitalize their banking system and crack down on shadow banking behaviors.

The Chinese eventually embraced other aspects of a Keynesian program: the stimulation of the internal market by increasing the empowerment of labor and addressing social inequality. The central government suddenly appeared willing to tolerate or unable to resist spontaneous strikes (not organized by the official unions controlled by the Communist Party) at major producers such as Toyota, Honda, and FoxConn in the summer of 2010. These strikes resulted in significant wage increases (in the range of 20 or 30 percent or so). The politics of wage repression was being reversed. The government increased investments in health care and social services, and it pushed hard on the development of environmental technologies to the point where China is now a global leader. The fear of being called a socialist or a communist that bedevils political action in the United States obviously sounds comical to the Chinese. But there are dangerous signs of inflation and serious pressures (both internal and external) to revalue the renminbi. The banking system may not be as sound as it appears. As wages rise, so capital is moving offshore to lower-wage locations in Bangladesh, Cambodia, and other parts of Southeast Asia.

China has emerged from the crisis faster and more successfully than anywhere else, with growth rates quickly reviving toward 8 or even 10 percent. The increase in internal effective demand has not only worked within China but entrained other economies, particularly raw-material producers. Australia has flourished, for example. And General Motors makes more cars and profits in China than anywhere else. China had stimulated a partial revival in international trade and in demand for its own export goods (trade with Latin America has increased tenfold since 2000, for example). The export-oriented economies in general, particularly throughout much of East and Southeast Asia along with Latin America, have revived faster than others. China's investments in US debt have helped sustain effective demand for its low-cost products there. The effect has been to alter the balance of economic power, to produce a hegemonic shift within the global economy.

The revival of the export-oriented economies has extended to Germany. But this brings us to the problem of the fractious responses to the crisis across the European Union. After an initial burst of stimulus politics, Germany took the lead, dragging a more reluctant France along with it, in turning the eurozone to a monetary policy of deficit reduction through draconian reductions in public expenditures. This policy is now echoed by the new Conservative-led coalition in Britain. This politics coincided with the sudden deterioration in public finances elsewhere. The so-called PIGS (Portugal, Ireland, Greece, and Spain) found themselves in dire financial straights, in part through their own mismanagement but even more significantly because their economies were particularly vulnerable to the credit collapse and the sudden decline in property markets and tourism. Lacking the industrial base of countries such as Germany, they could not respond adequately to the fiscal crisis that threatened them.

The big question then was, has the financial crisis been stabilized at the expense of creating a fiscal crisis of the capitalist states (with California looking more and more like one of the biggest failed states in the world)? Rumors flew as to the state of Britain's finances, and the fact that many other weaker states such as Latvia and Hungary were already on the ropes suggested serious underlying problems in state finances that could even, at some point, affect the sustainability of the US deficit. It was in this climate that much of the capitalist world shifted its focus to deficit reduction rather than deficit stimulus financing of the Keynesian sort. Once the crisis shifted from being a financial crisis in the banking sector to being a fiscal crisis of the state, then the political opportunity immediately arose to take another savage cut at what remained of the welfare state. The banks had been saved, and it was, in classic neoliberal fashion, evidently time to sock it to the people by draconian austerity rather than stimulus measures.

As a result, the political fault lines shifted in many places back toward the more classic forms of class struggle, as unions (particularly in the public sector) and affected populations (students, retirees, etc.) fought back against the austerity from California to Greece. Why should the people pay for the errors and corruptions of a capitalist class that continued to consolidate its wealth and power?

But there were and are abundant variations both in impacts and responses. Lebanon was so busy reconstructing from the Israeli bombardment of 2006 that it scarcely noticed the onset of the global financial crisis (though it had political crises of its own galore). Brazil quickly recovered, in part on the back of the China trade but also because of the surge of internal demand based on President Lula's redistributive policies toward the poor (the Bolsa Família). India was relatively insulated from the crisis since its main export of services was less affected and its financial system relatively sound. Certain states, such as Kerala, suffered from the loss of remittances from the Persian Gulf states, but elsewhere a gathering but questionable boom, particularly in construction, underpinned high rates of growth. The number of Indian billionaires doubled in 2009 alone. Haiti, on the other hand, suffered a serious loss of remittances from the United States and then collapsed entirely as a result of the 2010 earthquake and its appalling aftermath.

The shifting of the crisis around the world both in its form and in its intensity created a dynamic of cascading geographical effects to the point where nothing could easily be predicted. From an epicenter in the US Southwest and Florida, to the collapse of Dubai World, to the Greek sovereign-debt crisis, no one could easily anticipate where the next aftershock would hit and how severe the shock or what the political response would be. By the same token, the rapid recoveries of China, India, and Brazil have been surprising. The geography of it all can, with a lot of effort, be tracked but not easily predicted. Yet the vulnerabilities within the global system are clear. A collapse of the property market and surging inflation in China, a fall in oil prices that hits Russia very hard along with Venezuela and the Persian Gulf states, a surge of political protests from Greece to Spain, France, Britain, and California, or simply a sudden further collapse of consumer confidence in the United States or of foreign-investor confidence in the viability of US debt will likely send the whole system into either a downward tailspin or a lurch into a different configuration of global power that sees one half of the world (almost certainly Asia) grow rapidly at the expense of the other half.

The Left Alternative

Many people have long dreamed that an alternative to capitalist (ir)rationality can be rationally arrived at through the mobilization of human passions in the collective search for a better life for all. These alternatives—historically called socialism or communism—have, in various times and places, been tried. In former times, such as the 1930s, the vision of one or other of them provided a beacon of hope. The practices that flowed from this source arguably improved the lives of many people and saved capitalism from autodestruction after 1945. But in recent times, such alternatives have lost their luster, in part because of the failure of historical experiments with communism to make good on their promises. Political protest at the crisis conditions has been spotty but in some instances vociferous (from both the left and the right) in response to the crash of 2008.

It could be that 2009 marked the beginning of a prolonged shakeout in which the question of grand and far-reaching alternatives to capitalism will step by step bubble up to the surface in one part of the world or another. The longer the uncertainty and the misery are prolonged, the more the legitimacy of the existing way of doing business will be questioned and the more the demand to build something different will escalate.

The central problem to be addressed is clear enough: *compound growth forever is not possible; capital accumulation can no longer be the central force impelling social evolution.* The troubles that have beset the world these past thirty years signal that a limit is looming that cannot be transcended. Add to this the facts that so many people in the world live in conditions of abject poverty, that environmental degradations are spiraling out of control, that human dignities are everywhere being offended even as the rich are piling up more and more wealth at the expense of everyone. Meanwhile, in most places the levers of ideological, political, institutional, judicial, military, and media power are under tight political control. This serves to perpetuate the political status quo and to frustrate opposition even as the economy and living standards deteriorate. "Freedom" then becomes just another word to justify repression.

A revolutionary politics that can grasp the nettle of endless compound capital accumulation and eventually shut down the class power that propels it forward requires an appropriate theory of social change. Marx's account of how capitalism arose out of feudalism in fact embodies such a "co-revolutionary theory."[16] Social change arises, he argues, through the dialectical unfolding of relations between seven moments within the social body politic:

1. Technological and organizational forms of production, exchange, and consumption
2. Relations to nature
3. Social relations between people
4. Mental conceptions of the world, embracing knowledges and cultural understandings and beliefs
5. Labor processes and production of specific goods, geographies, services, or affects
6. Institutional, legal, and governmental arrangements
7. The conduct of daily life and the activities of social reproduction

Each one of these moments is internally dynamic, marked by tensions and contradictions (just think of our diverse and contested mental conceptions of the world), but all of them are codependent and coevolve in relation to each other within a totality, understood as a Gramscian or Lefebvrian "ensemble" or Deleuzian "assemblage" of moments. The transition to capitalism entailed a mutually supporting movement across all seven moments within the totality. New technologies could not be identified and applied without new mental conceptions of the world (including that of the relation to nature and of new labor processes and social relations).

Social theorists often take just one of these moments and view it as the "silver bullet" that causes all change. We have technological determinists (Thomas Friedman), environmental determinists (Jared Diamond), daily-life determinists (Paul Hawken), labor-process determinists (the autonomistas), class-struggle determinists (most Marxist political parties), institutionalists, and so on and so forth.[17] From Marx's perspective, they are all wrong. It is the dialectical motion across the moments that really counts, even as there is uneven development in that motion.

When capitalism itself undergoes one of its phases of renewal, it does so precisely by coevolving all moments, obviously not without tensions, struggles, fights, and contradictions. Consider how these seven moments were configured around 1970, before the neoliberal surge, and consider how they look now; all have changed in relation to each other and thereby changed the workings of capitalism as a whole.

This theory tells us that an anticapitalist political movement can start anywhere (in labor processes, around mental conceptions, in the relation to nature, in class or other social relations, in the design of revolutionary technologies and organizational forms, out of daily life, or through attempts to reform institutional and administrative structures, including the reconfiguration of state powers). The trick is to keep the political movement moving from one moment to another in mutually reinforcing ways.[18] This was how capitalism arose out of feudalism, and this is how a radically different alternative can arise out of capitalism. Previous attempts to create a communist or socialist alternative fatally failed to keep the dialectic between the different moments in motion and failed to embrace the unpredictable and uncertain paths in the dialectical movement between them.

The problem for the anticapitalist Left is to build organizational forms and to unleash a co-revolutionary dynamic that can replace the present system of compounding accumulation of capital with some other forms of social coordination, exchange, and control that can deliver an adequate style and standard of living for the 6.8 billion people living on planet Earth. This is no easy task, and I do not pretend to have any immediate answers (though I do have some ideas) as to how this might be done. But I do think it imperative that the organizational forms and political strategies match the diagnoses and descriptions of how contemporary capitalism is actually working. Unfortunately, the fierce attachment of many movements to what can best be termed a fetishism of organizational form gets in the way of any broad revolutionary movement that can address this problem. Anarchists, autonomists, environmentalists, solidarity economy groups, traditional left revolutionary parties, reformist NGOs and social democrats, trade unions, institutionalists, and social movements of many different stripes all have their favored and exclusionary rules of organization, often derived from abstract principles and sometimes exclusionary views as to who might be the principal agent sparking social revolution. There is some serious barrier to the creation of an overarching umbrella organization on the left that can internalize difference but take on the global problems that confront use. Some groups, for example, abjure any form of organization that smacks of hierarchy. But Elinor Ostrom's study of common property practices shows that the only form of democratic management that works when populations of more than a few hundred people are involved is a nested hierarchy of decision making. Groups that rule out all forms of hierarchy thereby give up on any prospect whatsoever for democratic response not only to the problem of the global commons but also to the problem of continuous capital accumulation.[19] The strong connection between diagnosis and political action cannot be ignored.[20] This is a good moment, therefore, for all movements to take a step back and examine how their preferred methods and organizational forms relate to the revolutionary tasks posed in the present conjuncture of capitalist development.

Chapter 4

A Turning Point or Business as Usual?

Daniel Chirot

We are all Keynesians now.
—Milton Friedman, quoted in *Time,* December 31, 1965

I. A Local Story with Global Implications

In the spring of 2009, as the crash of 2008–9 seemed to be dragging the US economy toward a new depression and the entire world was following, I talked to some knowledgeable bankers in the state of Washington about the fall of Washington Mutual (WaMu) in 2008, the largest bank failure in US history up to that time.[1] (Lehman's collapse was bigger and more consequential, but that was because it was much more than a bank. Other likely candidates for collapse among banks bigger than WaMu, Bank of America and Citi, were saved by government intervention.) I asked them to explain what had happened. Their stories were all much the same.

WaMu's chief executive, ousted in 2008 as his bank was about to fail, was primarily a financial expert whose chief accomplishment was to acquire a large number of small to medium-sized banks (mostly thrifts specializing in mortgages) throughout the United States, thus turning his own bank into a giant. He further increased WaMu's business by then acquiring mortgage companies, especially in the five years prior to his bank's collapse. This included mortgage companies in Southern California, where an enormous housing-price bubble was developing. Maintaining the momentum of growth and keeping up profits was critical to keeping the stock price high. Falling or even stagnant profits would cause the stock price to decline, thus making WaMu itself vulnerable to being taken over by another giant. Bonuses for top executives and maintaining their own self-esteem as successful executives were dependent on keeping up the stock price. In order to maintain and even increase profits, WaMu had to initiate an increasing number of mortgages, as this was its principal business. By acquiring banks and mortgage companies throughout the country, it could increase its depository base and leverage this to make yet more loans.

Aside from never efficiently integrating the operating procedures and systems of the many institutions that WaMu took over, a problem that made it ever harder to control what these branches were doing, WaMu began to run into an even deeper quandary that was spreading throughout the global financial system. Keeping up profits was becoming increasingly difficult as the real economy's stock of investment opportunities was not growing fast enough, except through various kinds of financial speculation and in the mortgage market. To keep on generating rising profits, WaMu had to find ways of continuing to grow a housing market that was increasingly saturated and overpriced. Too much money was going into new constructions of ever-larger houses, more office space, and bigger shopping malls. But if there were too few other places to invest, this is where business had to be increased. So the bank pressured its executives to find new ways of increasing loans, and this led to a catastrophic decline in lending standards. Loans with absurdly small short-term payments were peddled to buyers with weak credit, who were promised that when their rates were increased, as specified in the contracts they were given to sign, they would be able to refinance or sell at a profit. (How this was done in a way that made it seem legitimate is detailed in the next section.) Of course, lending more money to ever more insecure borrowers made that much more cash available to buy property, thus increasing demand and inflating real-estate prices. But this could not go on indefinitely. Rising prices stimulated more speculative building until the combination of too much supply and ever more unrealistic prices caused the bubble to break. Then, collapsing prices created problems for those who were suddenly faced with higher interest rates as their short-term low-rate periods expired. Large numbers of loans went bad, and WaMu began to collapse.

The question I asked bankers who knew about WaMu's dealings, and those of other banks in the years before 2008's crash, was whether top executives at WaMu knew what they were doing. And, if so, was this deliberate fraud? Was it like the case of Bernard Madoff's sixty-plus-billion-dollar fraudulent investment company that never invested but only paid off old investors with the funds invested by new ones? There are certainly allegations that crimes were committed.[2] These are being investigated by US government officials. The consensus among bank executives familiar with events is that the top WaMu executives, including its chief executive officer, Kerry Killinger, did not think they were committing fraud at all, unlike Madoff, who knew he was a crook and eventually admitted it.[3] Rather, these top banking officials were caught up in a typical, frenzied kind of speculative bubble. New financial instruments were being produced that generated huge profits, made the bank's leaders highly successful, and created what seemed like thousands of good, secure jobs in their banks. They became ever more influential and admired community leaders. The top people at WaMu were generous donors to charities and socially prominent role models, as were their counterparts in big financial institutions around the entire country and world. The game was too good to stop, it all seemed perfectly legal, and it was making the United States increasingly prosperous. More people got their own houses, even poor families who could not afford them, and this was a socially desirable objective. National political authorities went along and touted the beneficial effects as proof that unregulated free markets worked.

To be sure, the causes of the crash of 2008 are more complicated than that. On the other hand, the transformation of WaMu's chief executive from a cautious, sober banker into a high-flying financier needing to show that he could generate growing profits lies at the heart of what caused institutions such as his to get involved with hugely insecure, speculative actions. That this happened came as a great surprise to the financial world and to a great many economists as well.

What I propose to do in the following pages is to show that, first of all, even in the nineteenth century farsighted economic thinkers, notably Karl Marx, understood that such speculative crashes were likely in capitalist economies. Second, ever since the Great Depression of the 1930s, it has been understood that enormous swings in the business cycle that follow some (but hardly all) speculative crashes need to be mitigated by government action and that speculative behavior has to be regulated. A good many prominent economists, including some of the greatest of all, such as John Maynard Keynes, understood this perfectly well. At the same time, dominant late-twentieth-century economic models became increasingly disconnected from reality and failed to take into account the hard-won lessons of the 1930s. The crash of 2008 has brought more realistic economic thinkers back to the fore. Finally, a bit over one year after the height of the crisis, but long before it will end, I intend to speculate briefly about its long-term consequences.

II. The Causes of the Financial Crash of 2008

The banking and stock-market crises of 2008 should not have come as such a surprise. The exact timing of panics that inevitably follow large asset bubbles cannot be predicted, but they have occurred repeatedly since at least the early 1600s. Robert Shiller, a well-known Yale economist, ascribes their advent partly to the rise of newspapers, though this coincided so closely with the beginning of the modern capitalist era that it is difficult to separate the two.[4] Shiller predicted the stock-market crash of 2001, when the "dot-com" high-tech bubble burst, and he is one of the best analysts of the current housing and mortgage crisis that led to the 2008 stock-market crash.[5] Shiller explains that bubbles are created by the rapid spread of news about spectacular gains to be obtained by certain kinds of investments, from Dutch tulips in the 1630s to securities and derivatives backed by subprime mortgages 370 years later. The rise of the Internet, huge increases in televised news about stock markets, and electronic trading have exacerbated the tendency toward "irrational exuberance," but such bubbles existed long before.

Karl Marx noted that capitalism generates its own regular periods of overinvestments, wild speculation, and subsequent crashes. These are as much a part of capitalism as sustained periods of economic growth and technological progress. Charles Kindleberger's classic *Manias, Panics, and Crashes* agrees and charts the history of such busts from the seventeenth to the twenty-first century.[6] Needless to say, since 2008, a huge number of new books and articles have been written about the same topic, some excellent, others less so, and classics such as Kindleberger's have again been reprinted, with a sixth edition in 2009. Before 2008, this was a somewhat marginalized but still well-developed area of economic history. Today, it is in the forefront of the news, though much of the new material goes over the same theories and history that were available long before this particular crisis. Almost every new issue of the *Economist,* the leading general news magazine for serious English-language readers in the world, reviews some new books on the crisis.[7] Some of the best broader new works for the general public are books by Carmen Reinhart and Kenneth Rogoff and by Paul Krugman.[8] All of these remind us that none of what has happened should have come as such a surprise. But it did.

Karl Marx would not have been so astonished. A century and a half ago, he wrote that as capital piles into the most lucrative investments available, the marginal rate of return falls, and capital gets attracted to risky investment areas in order to keep up profits.[9] Even if Marx's general theories about how capitalism's crises would inevitably lead to mass pauperization and the rise of communism turned out to be far off the mark, there was a lot about capitalism he did understand. He wrote:

> Concentration increases simultaneously, because beyond certain limits a large capital with a small rate of profit accumulates faster than a small capital with a large rate of profit.…This in turn causes a new fall in the rate of profit. The mass of small dispersed capitals is thereby driven along the adventurous road of speculation, credit frauds, stock swindles, and crises.[10]

In an article in the *Atlantic,* Simon Johnson pointed out that the share of total profits of all US businesses generated by the financial industry rose from around 10 percent in the early 1980s to 40 percent by the early 2000s.[11] During that time, the pay per worker in the financial sector went from being about the same as the average compensation for the United States as a whole to being 80 percent higher. This was not a pattern restricted to the United States but one that was spread throughout the world. Financial stocks became a much larger portion of total market capitalization. In a *New York Times* editorial, Paul Krugman pointed out that in the 1960s finance and insurance together accounted for less than 4 percent of US gross domestic product (GDP) and the Dow Jones Industrial index that is meant to reflect America's major big industries did not contain a single financial company until 1982.[12] Before the bursting of the financial bubble in 2008, 8 percent of US GDP came from finance and insurance, and five of the thirty Dow Jones companies were financial institutions. The evolution of General Electric (the only company in the original Dow Jones index, created in 1896, that remains part of it) approximates what happened. It went from being a company that produced some of America's most important industrial machinery to being one that generated more than half its profits from its purely financial business. It still makes major machines, including jet engines, but in 2008, before the effects of the financial crisis were felt, 62 percent of its total profits were from its financial services division.[13]

By the first decade of the twenty-first century, after the collapse of the speculative binge in Internet and computer-related stocks, the stock market had revived, and increasing amounts of investment funds went into the financial industry because it seemed safe as well as highly profitable. But this was where WaMu and other giant financial institutions got caught in a trap, as they plunged into what seemed like the surest way to increase profits, namely, housing, construction, and the many new financial instruments being devised to back loans in these areas.

Mortgage-backed securities were the key to staying on this accelerating treadmill. WaMu and others would securitize their mortgages (turn them into marketable securities) and get them off their books as quickly as possible. The money they would be paid for these securitized loans could then be used as the asset base for yet more loans, which would then be securitized and sold. Each operation earned WaMu and its branches fees for generating new mortgages and earned yet more fees for financial institutions such as Merrill Lynch and other big operators in this market that bought, split up, and repackaged these loans to sell to other financial institutions around the world. The word went out to WaMu branches to initiate as many mortgage loans as possible and not to pay close attention to whether they were lending money for overpriced houses to individuals unable to afford them. Securitizing mortgage loans began well before the current crisis developed, and this did indeed free capital for more loans. But another financial instrument that was much newer was invented to accelerate business. This was the variable-interest loan, which started at very low interest rates that were scheduled to hugely increase later. This would lure poorer purchasers with the promise that they could afford more-expensive houses with low monthly payments. This would not be a problem because presumably house prices always rose, so refinancing the loan as soon as payments went up would be easy. And with rising prices, if the purchaser defaulted, the holder of the mortgage could easily foreclose and sell the house at a profit. Beyond these assumptions, WaMu (and other loan institutions) would bear little risk anyway, as the mortgages would have been sold to other financial institutions. This was the common wisdom.

Some of the biggest buyers of these securities were Fannie Mae (Federal National Mortgage Association) and Freddie Mac (Federal Home Loan Mortgage Corporation). The fees they charged for these operations and the revenue flows from mortgages were deemed well worth the supposedly small risk. Fannie Mae was created in 1938 to securitize mortgage loans in order to stimulate the housing market. It was privatized in 1968, though it retained implicit government backing for its debt; this enabled it to take on ever-larger amounts of mortgages, vastly increase its profits, and provide generous dividends as well as big bonuses for its executives. Freddie Mac was created as a competitor to Fannie Mae in 1970 along the same lines and is also private with implicit government backing. This implicit support, never legally defined, allowed these institutions to obtain financing from investors at below-market rates because there was—supposedly—no risk.[14] Indeed, when the crash of 2008 occurred, and it turned out that Fannie and Freddie were bankrupt because of the vast number of failed mortgage securities they were holding, the US government took over their trillions in debts to prevent a complete collapse of financial markets around the world.

Legally, this may not have been a Ponzi scheme, particularly because of relaxing regulatory rules pushed through under the Reagan, Bush 41, Clinton, and Bush 43 administrations. The reality, however, was that these were actually quite similar to Ponzi schemes because they relied increasingly on passing risk to others as quickly as possible while creating loans that could never be paid off.[15] Furthermore, ratings firms, chiefly Moody's and Standard and Poor's (S&P), were collecting huge fees by giving AAA—meaning safest possible—ratings to the mortgage-backed securities that were being sold.

A further step to disaster was taken when these loans started to be split up into different parts, repackaged in complex ways, and sold as a new kind of instrument called CDOs (collateralized debt obligations). These CDOs were actually bundled combinations of so many different loans in so many places that it became impossible for anyone to know what they were really worth or how sound they were. The reason these were created was that repackaging ordinary mortgage-backed securities generated yet more fees for the initiators, and the fact that Moody's and S&P were rating them as ultrasafe AAAs meant that they could be sold easily. A number of senior bankers I spoke with admitted that by 2006 some of the securities floating around were incomprehensible because they were composed of so many different obligations split up into little pieces and it was only because of the trust placed in ratings agencies that they were still being sold; but even those agencies were no longer able to judge what they were rating, so they collected their own fees and gave them high marks because they were being issued by respected investment banks. The height of folly was reached when it became acceptable to extend so-called NINJA loans to people with "no income, no jobs or assets." Repackaged into trusted, complex financial instruments, these were camouflaged in ways that made the lunacy of the whole operation invisible.

The crash of 2008 brought back the work of a formerly rather obscure economist named Hyman Minsky. He had postulated three stages in the way credit is extended that lead to crashes. First, there is what he called "hedge finance," when loans go to firms with enough operating cash to easily pay back both interest and principal. As lenders seek to expand activities beyond the most reliable firms to increase their own profits, Minsky said they engage in "speculative finance," with firms that borrow the money having enough money to pay interest on the loan but having to borrow more to pay back owed principal. Finally, as lending expands more, money is loaned to firms that need to borrow merely in order to pay both interest and principal, meaning that such firms quickly fall ever more deeply into unpayable debt. Then, only a sudden appreciation in the borrower's assets can save the firm and allow the lender to get its money back. Minsky called this "Ponzi finance" because it turns into an ever-riskier gamble that asset prices will keep on going up or, ultimately, that a miracle will occur.[16]

Financial institutions, however, were reassured because they worked out complex risk models that showed that that they were operating within safe limits. Unfortunately for them, these risk models were worked out by well-paid math wizards who tended to be young and to have little financial experience. The models were based on historical, and therefore obsolete, assumptions that used prior rates of mortgage failure as a base for calculating risk. So, even if the math in the models was impeccable, the models themselves were useless, as default rates were no longer likely to be nearly as low as they had traditionally been. Before these new financial instruments had been devised, and older ones abused, the standards for providing mortgages had been stricter, so of course, default rates had been much lower.

Another source of reassuring stability was Fannie Mae, the single largest player in the game. It had long been involved in what amounted to a giant lobbying campaign (that sometimes amounted to sheer bribery) with the US Congress to keep the system going. It claimed to be doing all of this to help the poor and minorities obtain their own houses, but it was in fact boosting profits for the sake of its stockholders and its executives, who were receiving large bonuses for their work.

Perhaps bank executives should have known that they were increasingly engaged in "Ponzi finance," and in some sense they probably did, but as the measure of success in such circles was narrowly based on rising stock prices, as long as these were going up, it all seemed fine. To not play the game risked a backlash from shareholders, demands for resignations, and possibly a hostile takeover, resulting in embarrassment and loss of prestige for the institution's leaders. For Karl Marx, whether this was "criminal" would have been irrelevant, as it was the system that forced capital and, therefore, capitalists to act that way. Indeed, that is exactly the excuse given by the executives of the many failed institutions, including the former leader of WaMu, though it is unlikely that any of these bankers are Marxists or that many have even read any Marx.

We know the end of the story. Housing prices fell, loans became due that could not be paid, and complex securities based on packaged bundles of loans lost their value. American International Group (AIG), a huge insurance company, went bankrupt (not technically, as the US government stepped in to save it) because it had made a lot of money insuring the loans and investments of big financial institutions around the world. The assumption had been that these were all "secure" investments, so AIG never bothered to obtain reserves to pay policyholders if these insured products actually collapsed. Big banks, some insurance companies, and hedge funds turned out to be overleveraged because they had invested in risky loans without having adequate capital reserves to cover them in case of failure. WaMu was only one of the institutions to fail. Lehman Brothers, Merrill Lynch, and banks everywhere from Iceland to Switzerland to Hong Kong had to admit to huge losses; stock markets around the world crashed.

Karl Marx would have recognized this. There was too much capital investment going into products that were yielding decreasing marginal returns. This time, the "products" were financial instruments, not physical products, but otherwise, this is exactly what happened. Chasing profits, financial institutions created all sorts of new products, from subprime loans to complex, virtually incomprehensible securities and derivatives, that became increasingly tenuous. Finally, there were far too many such products around to keep them profitable, underlying values on which they were based fell, and the least efficient institutions, such as WaMu, collapsed. As Marx predicted, in such a crisis the most efficient firms survived and absorbed many of the failed ones. J. P. Morgan Chase, the most successful giant bank in the United States, obtained WaMu at a fire-sale price that ruined what was left of its stockholders. Top WaMu executives emerged with smaller, but still substantial, fortunes, while many employees lower down in the bank lost their life savings and pensions. Thousands lost their jobs.

Where Marx was wrong, however, was to think that that such crises would soon spell the end of capitalism. Contrary to Karl Marx's expectations, capitalist economies have shown a remarkable ability to rebound; furthermore, while Marxists from the late nineteenth century until now have always seen each new crisis as the beginning of the end of capitalism, it has turned out that only some of these crises have had long-term repercussions. But a few have provoked major changes, and why that is so needs to be explained.

III. Conflicting Explanations of Why Some but Not Most Panics Change the World

Panics have happened many times before. Kindleberger and Aliber's book on this topic lists thirty-eight periods when major panics (the old word for what are now called recessions) in the capitalist world caused deep economic troubles between the start of the seventeenth century and the end of the twentieth.[17] If we were to count lesser panics, there would be many more. But most, including those of the 1980s and 1990s from the United States to Japan to Russia to Southeast Asia and Latin America, did not cause major worldwide disruptions, only some localized, mostly temporary pain.

That was the case with the stock-market crash of 1987 that actually saw a bigger one-day percentage drop in the New York stock market than the crash of 1929 that many think set off the Great Depression. Other panics, such as the one in the United States in 1907 or, even more recently, the dot-com stock-market crash of 2000–2001, extended by the panic generated by the 9/11 terrorist attack on New York, dissipated quickly. On the other hand, the crash of 1929 and the subsequent Great Depression of the 1930s permanently altered the world capitalist system. When do financial panics lead to fundamental changes? What will be the outcome of the crisis that began in 2008?

One reason for the seriousness of the 2008–9 financial panic is that the US economy is so big and US dollars are such an important reserve currency that when there is a panic in the United States, it is a world-shaking event. Japan's burst real-estate and stock-market bubble in the 1990s did not cause a major global economic setback, whereas the United States' problems in 2008 did.[18] Yet not every American burst bubble has such major consequences. The largest ever one-day stock-market crash, on October 19, 1987 (the S&P average fell 20 percent), was quickly handled as the US Federal Reserve (the Fed) pumped enough liquidity into markets to ease the panic. There were few long-term effects. Stock markets collapsed around the world, but there was no subsequent recession.[19] Similar Fed action in 1997 at the time of the Asian economic crisis, in 1998 when Russia's currency collapsed along with its new and highly speculative stock market, and at the time of the 2000–2001 US market crash also contributed greatly to limiting damage.[20]

More serious than these temporary panics was the mid- to late-1980s massive savings-and-loans (S&Ls) and thrift-banks debacle. This was the most costly financial failure in US history until that time (but dwarfed by the failures of 2008). More than seven hundred banks failed, and the US government laid out over $100 billion to pay off depositors and merge failed banks into viable ones. The reasons for this failure can be summarized by saying that Ronald Reagan's administration deregulated what had been a sedate kind of banking devoted to making home-mortgage loans at fixed rates and opened the door to wild speculation in home construction. The S&Ls had been run by small bankers who did not understand the new system and fell prey to takeovers by speculators, some of whom were, to say the least, engaged in fraudulent development schemes. They created a housing bubble, with a lot of buildings booked at inflated prices, but when these could no longer be sold or leased, loans defaulted, and S&Ls failed.[21] WaMu was one of the successful survivors at that time and used the occasion to launch its vast expansion by taking over less successful banks. This made it a leader in the banking disaster that initiated the current global crisis two decades later, but in the 1980s the US and world economies did not suffer greatly because the US government stepped in and limited the damage.

In other words, there can be fairly serious US financial panics that get contained. So why has 2008 caused the most serious global economic downturn since the 1930s? Will it result in changes as important as the ones provoked by the Great Depression? To answer that question, we must look at the nature of long-term technological economic cycles in the world capitalist economy. There is a huge literature in the field of economics about business cycles, but much of it seems rather inconclusive and more focused on short-term fluctuations than very long ones. This was not always true. A 1944 volume published by the American Economic Association (AEA) on business cycles reprinted leading articles on that subject from the 1920s and 1930s. Its first two substantive articles were by Joseph Schumpeter and Nikolai Kondratieff. There followed pieces authored by Wesley Mitchell, Jan Trinberger (later to share the first Nobel Prize in economics with Ragnar Frisch in 1969), Paul Samuelson (winner of the second such prize in 1970), Friedrich Hayek (co-winner of the 1974 prize), Alvin Hansen, and other luminaries. If most of the articles in that collection dealt with cycles measured in terms of a few years, many reflected on the causes of long-term cycles. Alvin Hansen's article, the 1938 speech he gave as president of the American Economic Association, said,

> The growth of modern industry has not come in terms of millions of small increments....Characteristically it has come by gigantic leaps and bounds,...discontinuous, lumpy, and jerky....And when a revolutionary new industry like the railroad or the automobile, after having initiated in its youth a powerful upward surge of investment activity, reaches maturity and ceases to grow, as all industries finally must, the whole economy must experience a profound stagnation, unless, indeed, new developments take its place. It is not enough that a mature industry continues its activity at a high level on a horizontal plane....It is the cessation of growth that is disastrous....And when giant new industries have spent their force, it may take a long time before something of equal magnitude emerges.[22]

Schumpeter himself also believed that long-term cycles were caused by the arrival of new technologies in "swarms." He looked at the work of Nikolai Kondratieff, a Soviet Marxist economist who had postulated that there were long "waves" of rise and decline in capitalist economies. A long "A" phase of growth of roughly twenty-five to thirty years would be followed by a declining "B" phase of roughly the same length.[23] Kondratieff had no explanation for why this happened, so it is Schumpeter's theory that these waves are caused by the uneven rise of new technologies that has become accepted by those who believe in Kondratieff waves. (Kondratieff himself was imprisoned in the 1930s by Stalin and executed for his deviationist views in 1938.)

Schumpeter was very conservative, even right-wing (he had an embarrassing tendency to say nice things about Hitler),[24] and he is rarely cited by contemporary economists except as a historical figure. Ironically, both he and Kondratieff appeal far more to the academic far left than to conservative economists,[25] though some others, for example, the economic historian Walt Rostow,[26] have had some faith in this approach. The problem is that repeated efforts to justify these long-wave theories with empirical facts have failed to do so. As early as 1940, Simon Kuznets (who developed his own theory of long-term cycles of growth) analyzed Schumpeter's *Business Cycles* and concluded that its use of statistical data to confirm Kondratieff waves was incompetent.[27] Similarly, a more recent test by Solomos Solomou also found that the evidence for Kondratieff waves simply does not hold up. There are business cycles and obvious periods of growth and decline, but they are not regular and cannot conceivably be explained by any simplistic mechanism.[28] Solomou, on the other hand, favors Kuznets's theories about swings or cycles. A more recent statistical test of cycles by Bert de Groot and Philip Hans Franses concludes that there are indeed cycles in the economy, but looking at US, British, and Dutch data, they find a large number of such cycles that are not systematically correlated with each other.[29] Therefore, they conclude, the cycles tend to negate each other and to produce smoother economic growth than if they were interconnected or than if any one of them were dominant.

Kuznets's cycles, worked out during a long and productive career that also led to his being awarded the third (in 1971) Nobel Prize in economics, essentially laid out a multicausal explanation of changes in rates of economic growth in the nineteenth and twentieth centuries. In the nineteenth century, agricultural swings were important: a good market for certain products led to overproduction, and that lowered prices, which in turn led to farm failures. Investment swings in all areas followed similar patterns. Climate, international trade, migration, demographic trends, and many other variables could account for cycles that lasted roughly some fifteen to twenty-five years each. As Kuznets spent more of his time on accumulating international comparative data on the history of economic growth, however, his earlier work on cycles took a secondary place. Interestingly, in his 1971 Nobel Prize speech in Sweden, he did not mention cycles or swings but talked about the causes of economic growth and backwardness. In this speech, he emphasized the role of technology and how it interacted with social and political institutions that were more permissive of growth or blocked it. He also discussed what he called major technological epochs:

> The major breakthroughs in the advance of human knowledge, those that constituted dominant sources of sustained growth over long periods and spread to a substantial part of the world, may be termed epochal innovations. And the changing course of economic history can perhaps be subdivided into economic epochs, each identified by the epochal innovation with the distinctive characteristics of growth that it generated.[30]

Contrary to this rich tradition in economic thought, for a while in the 1980s and 1990s, a leading economic line of business-cycle research came to rely instead on the rational-expectations theories of Robert E. Lucas. Finn E. Kydland and Edward C. Prescott won a Nobel Prize in economics in 2004 for their work in this area. What they claim is that because markets anticipate various kinds of future pressures such as those from policy changes by governments, the economy should always be in equilibrium. Firms anticipating changes will alter their behavior to adapt, and supply and demand should quickly match each other. Since, however, that is not always the case, an explanation must be found, and this amounts to unanticipated technological shocks.[31] Lawrence Summers in a 1986 paper demolished the Kydland and Prescott arguments by saying that essentially they were too abstract and based on models that do not correspond to reality. Obviously, Summers's argument had little effect on the reputation of this kind of theorizing (since its proponents won Nobel Prizes), but it remains persuasive. Summers concluded his short, powerful paper by saying that economists cannot explain economic fluctuations that are caused by too many variables.[32]

N. Gregory Mankiw said something similar about "real business cycle" theory in a 1989 article. While admiring the theory's elegance and parsimony, he pointed out that it lacked empirical evidence about the nature of technology shocks. Rather, he said that what he called a "New Keynesian perspective" would prove more persuasive, despite being messier, because it rejected "the axiom of rational, optimizing individuals."[33]

What are we to make of all this? In the arguments just cited, there does appear to be some (but by no means total) agreement that technological changes are important, even if there is not much consensus about how or about why in some cases uneven technological "shocks" produce catastrophic recessions or depressions and at other times only mild economic swings. Schumpeter, for all the defects in his theories, was on to something important in making technological change the centerpiece of his work on cycles. Other explanations—climate cycles, rates of population change, wars, policy errors by governments, among many—work poorly if used too mechanically or alone, even if they seem to explain some individual cases.[34]

How do these arguments work if applied to the Great Depression of the 1930s? One of the most famous arguments about the Great Depression was pioneered by the University of Chicago's Milton Friedman, who won the Nobel Prize in 1976. This argument pays no attention to technological waves or cycles at all and claims that the Depression was primarily caused by errors made by the Fed in tightening the money supply at the wrong time.[35] Because the US economy was so important, the whole world was affected.

As a result of the crisis of 2008, however, the whole monetarist and related rational-expectations approach of the Chicago School is being increasingly questioned.[36] From John Maynard Keynes to John Kenneth Galbraith to Charles Kindleberger and most recently Paul Krugman (winner of the 2008 Nobel Prize), the main assumptions about the causes of the Great Depression have been different. Demand was too weak (and therefore had to be stimulated by government action), and the financial system was in a precarious state to begin with because of excessive, unregulated speculation. Kindleberger concluded that the international financial system had to be backed by a single powerful actor able to sustain liquidity in times of panic, but in 1929 the British could no longer do this, and the United States, which could have, was unwilling.[37] Keynes believed this, and such thinking was behind the Bretton Woods reforms carried out after World War II to prevent another depression. Weak demand in the 1930s had various causes, among them too high a degree of income inequality.[38] So, in that respect, too, government action was required.

Underlying these explanations is the idea that is at the core of the recent book by George Akerlof and Robert Shiller.[39] Depressions and recessions are caused by a psychological breakdown in confidence and, therefore, a retrenchment by investors, bankers, and consumers. Akerlof and Shiller follow Keynes in calling the desire of investors to invest in risky new products and firms the "animal spirits" that are essential to keep capitalism working and progressing. Though Akerlof (who won the Nobel Prize in 2001) and Shiller's book is provocative and reflects sophisticated new work on the psychology of economic decision making going well beyond the static rational-expectations models, it does not quite explain why these psychological shifts occur. This is where technology shocks can play a useful role.

We can admit that the way in which financial institutions are regulated (or not) and the degree to which excessive speculation creates problems can increase or decrease the likelihood of financial panics and that government actions or inactions can mitigate or worsen panics. Policy errors by major central banks in the 1930s certainly contributed to prolonging the Great Depression of the 1930s.[40] But ultimately, no such explanations can adequately deal with the fact that some economic crises are world shaking, while most are not. Without trying to pretend that the kind of analysis that follows would satisfy a quantitative economist, I would like to suggest how major technological changes lie at the heart of any explanation of why some financial panics lead to far more serious outcomes than others do.

IV. When Panics Coincide with Changes in
Long-Term Technological Cycles

Basic innovations have initiated new industrial ages. Application of new technologies in cloth making created the first industrial period in England in the late eighteenth century, and this spread to western Europe and the United States until markets were saturated and weaker firms began to fail, producing a running series of depressions in the industrial West from the 1820s to the 1840s. This lengthy crisis became the basis of Karl Marx's theories about capitalism's inevitable ultimate demise. But then new products, led by railroad construction and the demand for iron, produced a new and spreading period of growth until the 1870s, when a new series of crises opened up a troubled couple of decades into the 1890s. By then, however, new products, chiefly in the chemical and electric-machinery industries, and the rapid growth of steel production had created another long period of growth that was only stopped by World War I.[41]

After the recovery from World War I, automobiles and household consumer electric machines should have led the way to another boom, and in some ways they did. On the other hand, after the recovery from the war, commodity prices, particularly in agriculture, fell as supply recovered, and there resulted a long-term agricultural depression in the United States and elsewhere. The new technologies, particularly in the United States, led to a speculative boom in the stock market that went well beyond what demand could bear. On top of this, conservative British policies trying to sustain the pound sterling destroyed London's capacity in the 1920s to sustain the international financial system (which it had done before 1914) and depressed the British economy, a major world importer. Then overly conservative economic policies in reaction to the stock-market panic of 1929–30 in all the leading economies failed to overcome these problems and were compounded by growing trade protectionism from 1930 on, led by the adoption of the completely irresponsible US Smoot-Hawley tariff in June 1930. This created enormous trade barriers and provoked similar protectionist measures among other industrial powers, thus contributing greatly to making the depression more serious. Herbert Hoover signed the tariff bill, giving in to Republican xenophobia and hysteria about falling agricultural prices, despite the unanimous recommendation by America's one thousand leading economists not to sign.[42] This combination of factors, behind which lay a failure to adapt to and to fully understand the consequences of the dramatic changes brought about by the vastly increased capacity to produce new kinds of consumer goods, especially in the United States, was the main reason for the Great Depression. Financial institutions capable of dealing with the new situation by ensuring the flow of credit and backing international trade at adequate levels did not exist. The nature of the new kind of consumer-oriented economy was not well understood. All this made the transition to this new age particularly traumatic.

The political consequences of the Great Depression, however, were even more serious than the economic ones, as it was in reaction to perceived economic problems that Germany became Nazi and Japan turned to aggressive militarism.[43] After World War II, the new economic age of mass personal consumption of the new machines, from automobiles to refrigerators to televisions, did take off in a spectacular way.[44] But by the 1970s, another series of crises occurred as new technologies made the old centers of automobile and steel production obsolete. The US stock market stagnated for a decade, the United States had to renege on allowing dollars to be converted into gold, and there emerged what has come to be called a "rust belt" in some of the major industrial areas of the American Midwest as well as in parts of industrial western Europe. Combined with the social changes of the 1960s and 1970s, some people saw this as the dawn of a new revolutionary age that would replace obsolete capitalism with something better.[45]

Once more, however, a new product revolution occurred, and instead of producing either major wars or depressions, the crises of the 1970s gave way to the rising boom stimulated by the electronics and computer revolutions of the 1980s and 1990s. For all the talk in the 1970s about the demise of the world capitalist system, nothing of the sort happened, and a calamity such as the Great Depression was avoided. To be sure, as usual, Neo-Marxists saw the disturbances, wars, and various panics of the 1980s, 1990s, and early 2000s as signs that a new cataclysm was about to occur,[46] but instead, international trade expanded, China and India as well as much of the rest of East and Southeast Asia began a rapid march toward greater economic prosperity, and despite wars and periodic financial panics, the United States and other Western economies remained prosperous.[47] Once again, technological innovation and the adaptability of entrepreneurial capitalists, if they are more than mere speculators, revived the world economy.

The panic of 2008 coincides with the rise of a new age led by revolutionary changes in communications, biotechnology, and health care and probably the start of the development of new sources of electrical power. Those are areas where enormous technological and scientific progress has been made and where many more advances are possible. The question, therefore, is whether, as in the late 1940s and 1950s and again in the 1970s and 1980s, the institutions exist to make this a relatively smooth transition. Or could it be that, as in the 1920s and 1930s, outdated institutions and ways of thinking will hinder and possibly block emerging new patterns of production and consumption from creating the right environment for progress.

It is the conjunction of the panic of 2008 with the failure of political institutions, social habits, and economic structures to keep up with the new age that has produced serious disruptions, particularly in the United States and Europe. As many critics have pointed out, neither regulatory rules for international finance nor distributive mechanisms to take into account the new technologies have kept up with changes that have occurred. Health care is a particularly important new area because of the enormous progress being made in biological and medical research, and in the long run, the demand for better health is practically unlimited, as long as ways are found to pay for it.

Paul Krugman has put it this way: "What does it mean to say that depression economics has returned? Essentially it means that for the first time in two generations, failures on the demand side of the economy—insufficient private spending to make use of productive capacity—have become the clear and present limitation to prosperity for a large part of the world."[48] Krugman does not think it very likely that the world will slip into another Great Depression (though he wishes he were absolutely sure), but he believes that for the first time since the 1930s, the US and world economies are not structured in ways that take advantage of high productivity.

Very few if any top bankers or financial managers of the sort who produced the panic of 2008 understood how big a change technology and new kinds of goods were producing or how badly many institutions had fallen behind the changes of the past generation. It does not take too many conversations with some of them to see that these are essentially socially and politically conservative, cautious people who find it difficult to think beyond conventional wisdom. That has always been the case and does not necessarily block progress that comes from more rash innovators and risk takers, but it does mean that institutional reforms that need to be made tend to be blocked by some of the very banking and Wall Street people who are supposed to understand the economy but really fail to understand the need for change until a massive crisis occurs or, perhaps, not even then.

In 2008, the social and political reforms necessary to produce enough demand for the dawning new age's innovations were not present, at least in the United States. Instead, the prosperity of the electronic and computer innovations in the 1980s and 1990s was leading to growing income inequality, as a fairly small proportion of the populations in rich and emerging countries was benefiting. And the investable surplus being accumulated was going into "safe" real-estate and financial products designed to promote a boom in traditional asset values. There is little question that the conservative atmosphere of the 1980s and 1990s (sometimes called the triumph of "neoliberalism" of the Ronald Reagan/ Margaret Thatcher kind, though most Americans do not think of this as being any kind of "liberalism" at all) contributed greatly to this lack of reform. In a way, the transition that had occurred in the 1970s to a new technological era was handled too well by the major capitalist powers and lulled them into believing that fundamental reforms to adapt to future changes were unnecessary. The panic of 2008 has exposed the flaw in this kind of conservative thinking.

V. The Benevolent and Postponing Scenarios: To Reform or Not

These observations lead me to speculate about the future consequences of the panic of 2008 by looking at three possible scenarios. First, there could be some serious reforms. For a while in 2009, it seemed that steps were being taken by most major economies, including those of the United States, China, and several of the major western European countries, to stimulate demand. These steps and the bailout of major financial institutions clearly demonstrated that the main errors of the 1930s were not going to be repeated. The Keynesian conclusions about that era have been learned. Most major central banks—including of course the most important one, in the United States—have poured liquidity into their economies, thus avoiding any possible repetition of the wrong policies criticized by Friedman and Schwartz. A major Great Depression was avoided. This is not enough, however, because confidence in future growth has to be fully restored to stimulate investment flows, and this in turn depends on creating both better economic institutions and a more equitable income distribution within and between economies.

Efforts are under way to significantly improve regulatory oversight of financial institutions to avoid the kind of speculation that was the immediate cause of the 2008 panic. China most of all but also India, Brazil, Russia, and a few other major players have been brought into the international economic system to join Europe, the United States, and Japan in reforming global policies.

In order to improve demand for the leading products of the new industrial age, governments have to take the lead, particularly in the United States. The required investments and product prices are too expensive and too risky to attract enough private capital or to be afford-able for ordinary consumers. Just as new products such as automobiles once created a huge new economic sector, so will health care, but invest-ment in usable products is hampered by uncertainty and the question of who will pay for expensive drugs and treatments.

This is even truer when it comes to producing and paying for new energy sources and improved infrastructure to accommodate an increas-ingly mobile world. This hardly means that making these changes is impossible or that private capital will not play a role, but it does mean that the ways of steering the economy toward less regulation and less government involvement championed by the United States in the 1980s, 1990s, and early 2000s cannot continue.

All this is entirely curable and can be remedied without bringing about the catastrophic events of the 1930s that led to World War II, as long as there is some recognition of what needs to be done by the politically powerful elites of the world.

On June 11, 2008, Kerry Killinger, then still head of WaMu, spoke to the Seattle Downtown Rotary Club and explained that his bank had strict lending standards and was not to blame for anything that had gone wrong and that the looming crisis was the fault of the Fed's low interest rates, the government's push to extend home ownership too widely, and various unscrupulous brokers. He did not mention any need for reform. A little over a year later, on July 15, 2009, Jamie Dimon, the head of J. P. Morgan Chase, by then America's largest bank and the one that had taken over WaMu, gave a speech to the same Seattle Downtown Rotary Club, with many of the area's most influential business people present. He stressed that the time had come to recognize that changes had to be made in how health care was delivered, that new sources of energy had to be developed, and that better ways had to be found to preserve the environment. He recognized that regulatory rules and institutions had to be updated and reformed. (I heard these speeches.) More than boilerplate public relations, he was expressing what had at the time become increasingly obvious to the thoughtful parts of the American establishment as well as to much of the electorate.

Of course, this perception was widespread throughout the world in 2009. The "emerging" powers of China, India, and Brazil as well as the Europeans all agreed that much reform was necessary and that they all need to cooperate with each other to accomplish this.[49] They also all were committed to preserving and expanding the world capitalist system that has served them well in recent decades.

Unfortunately, all that was when another Great Depression seemed very possible. Since then, many of these promises for major reform have fallen through. Mr. Dimon of Chase and the large financial firms saved by government actions have become less enamored of reforms that might curb their profits and bonuses.[50] Generally, there is less of a sense of urgency throughout the world and more of a tendency for various interests to block needed changes.

The second scenario, and probably the most likely one, is that the world will slowly get over the crisis caused by the financial panic of 2008, but without making enough reforms to prevent a possible calamity when the next bubble bursts. As Robert Aliber pointed out in a brief article during the summer of 2009, the large new emerging economies—Brazil, China, and India, in particular—have emerged quite well from the crisis and are accumulating surpluses that could well produce new, giant asset bubbles and another, even more serious crash in the future.[51] Meanwhile, in Europe and the United States, the sense of urgency about the need for major social, economic, and regulatory reform is lessening. In this scenario, the panic of 2008 will have turned out to be very serious but not quite catastrophic enough to reorient the world capitalist system in the right way. So the system will neither collapse nor fundamentally change. But because technological and social changes continue without slowing down in the least, when the next panic occurs, the consequences could be even direr. That seems to be what Joseph Stiglitz fears in his probably overheated denunciation of the Obama administration's efforts at reform as grossly insufficient.[52] By late 2010 it had become evident that the many forces hindering reform were winning, and all the current crisis has done is to provoke some fairly mild and temporary fixes. That could bring up a third possible, longer-term, and very dark scenario.

VI. The Catastrophic Third Scenario: Political Madness, Depression, and War

The world recovered from the Great Depression of the 1930s but at tremendous cost. What happened was that most political elites in Europe and Japan, supported by widespread popular discontent, turned to ultra-nationalism and autarkic measures to protect themselves. For Germany, Italy, and Japan, this led to fascism and disastrous wars that were supposed to guarantee their future security. The United States, France, and Britain failed to coordinate reform efforts that could have eased the effects of the Great Depression, so these institutional changes had to wait until after World War II. In the late 1930s, the major democracies were run by cautious, frightened conservative elites who resisted change until it was too late. Could all this happen again?

A sense of panic in a time when political elites and their people feel vulnerable can easily lead to protectionism, nationalist defensiveness, and ultimately wars. Though World War I was not caused by any obvious economic panic, it was the product of increasingly fearful nationalist hysteria among the largely conservative elites of the major powers.[53] In the 1930s, along with many of the same sentiments, there was the added shock of the Depression. That led to an even worse war that came close to destroying Europe and East Asia.

There is no shortage of political leaders in all countries, including the United States, China, Russia, and some of the most important and largest Latin American and Muslim countries, ready to follow this kind of path once more: moves toward economic protectionism and autarky, heightened xenophobic nationalism, rejection of international cooperation, and militarization. The economic disruptions that have followed the panic of 2008 feed popular resentment, fear, and anger against the seemingly hidden, hard-to-understand, distant financial dealings that led to all this.

Economic analysis is not well suited to predicting the future of the current crisis. Economists may propose possible solutions, and despite considerable disagreement about the causes of economic swings, there is an emerging consensus about the need for certain kinds of reforms. But as in the 1930s, academic economists are not the main decision makers. Crisis brings out on one side deep reactionary forces that want to prevent necessary change, and it calls forth revolutionaries on the other side who want to overthrow entire systems. It produces masses who do not know which way to turn. Political and ideological entrepreneurs spring up to lead various factions. Which of these political forces prevail in the major countries of the world will decide whether the outcome of the current crisis is delay and failure to reform or the more benign path toward necessary change. Inadequate institutional reform now seems likely, and this will open the way for another, possibly even more acute crisis in the future, and that could well result in something similar to what happened in the 1930s.

If we want to know what will happen, it is probably more useful to study what kinds of political elites emerge from this crisis in the world's most important countries than to untangle the arguments of their leading economic theorists. It is how these political forces react to the economic crisis and to future ones that will determine our fate. So far, prevailing political currents are not reassuring.

CHAPTER 5

Marketization, Social Protection, Emancipation: Toward a Neo-Polanyian Conception of Capitalist Crisis

Nancy Fraser

1. Introduction: Why Polanyi Today

By all rights, the current crisis of neoliberal capitalism should alter the landscape of critical theorizing. During the past two decades, most theorists kept their distance from the sort of large-scale social theorizing associated with Marxism. Apparently accepting the necessity of academic specialization, they settled on one or another branch of disciplinary inquiry, conceived as a freestanding enterprise. Whether the focus was jurisprudence or moral philosophy, democratic theory or cultural criticism, the work proceeded in relative disconnection from fundamental questions of social theory. The critique of capitalist society, pivotal for earlier generations, all but vanished from the agenda of critical theory. Critique centered on capitalist crisis, especially, was pronounced reductive, deterministic, and dépassé.

Today, however, such verities lie in tatters. With the global financial system teetering, worldwide production and employment in free fall, and the looming prospect of a prolonged recession, the economic aspect of capitalist crisis is impossible to ignore. But the same is true of the ecological aspect, given global warming, worsening pollution, resource exhaustion, and new forms of biocommodification that penetrate nature's very core. Then, too, the social dimension of crisis is increasingly salient—witness the devastated neighborhoods, displaced families, and war- and disease-ravaged communities that crisscross our planet of slums. Nor can one overlook the political dimension: the crisis, first, of the modern territorial state; second, of the latter's would-be regional successors, above all the European Union; third, of US hegemony; and fourth, of the institutions of global governance—all of which lack the imagination to envision solutions and the will and capacity to implement them. Finally, there is the crisis of critique itself and the crisis of emancipation, as neither critical theorists nor emancipatory social movements have so far risen to the occasion.

A crisis of this sort, multidimensional and overdetermined, supplies the inescapable backdrop for every serious attempt at critical theorizing. Henceforth, such theorizing can no longer avoid the question of capitalist society. Large-scale social theorizing, aimed at clarifying the nature and roots of crisis, as well as the prospects for an emancipatory resolution, should regain its central place in critical theory.

Yet how exactly should critical theorists approach these matters? How to overcome the deficits of discredited economistic approaches, which focus exclusively on the "system logic" of the capitalist economy? How to develop an expanded, noneconomistic understanding of capitalist society that incorporates the insights of feminism, postcolonialism, ecological thinking, and the cultural turn? How to conceptualize crisis as a *social* process in which economics is mediated by history, culture, geography, politics, ecology, and law? How to comprehend the full range of social struggles in the current conjuncture, and how to assess the potential for emancipatory social transformation?

The thought of Karl Polanyi affords a promising starting point for such theorizing. His 1944 classic *The Great Transformation* elaborates an account of capitalist crisis as a multifaceted historical process that began with the industrial revolution in Britain and proceeded, over the course of a century and a half, to envelop the entire world, entraining imperial subjection, periodic depressions, and cataclysmic wars.[1] For Polanyi, moreover, capitalist crisis was less about economic breakdown in the narrow sense than about disintegrated communities, ruptured solidarities, and despoiled nature. Its roots lay less in intraeconomic contradictions, such as the tendency of the rate of profit to fall, than in a momentous shift in the place of economy vis-à-vis society. Overturning the heretofore universal relation, in which markets were embedded in social institutions and subject to moral and ethical norms, proponents of the "self-regulating market" sought to build a world in which society, morals, and ethics were subordinated to, indeed modeled on, markets. That aspiration, inherently self-undermining and unrealizable, drove developments so deeply destructive of human society as to spark an ongoing countermovement for the latter's "protection." It was this "double movement"—the drive to expand and autonomize markets, followed by demands for social protection—that led, in Polanyi's view, to fascism and world war.

Here, then, is an account of capitalist crisis that transcends the cramped confines of economistic thinking. Masterful, capacious, and encompassing action at multiple scales, *The Great Transformation* weaves together local protest, national politics, international affairs, and global financial regimes in a powerful historical synthesis. Like Marx, Polanyi emphasized social struggle; but in place of the conflict between labor and capital, he foregrounded that between forces favoring marketization and cross-class movements for social protection. Like Marx, too, Polanyi sought to influence history, but his attitude to markets was more complex. Written with the aim of shaping the postwar order, *The Great Transformation* constitutes a brief for a new democratic regulatory regime that would defang markets, removing their sting without suppressing them altogether.

These points alone would qualify Polanyi as a promising resource for those who seek to understand the travails of twenty-first-century capitalist society. But there are other, more specific reasons for turning to him today. The story told in *The Great Transformation* has strong echoes in current developments. There is at least a prima facie case for the view that the present crisis has its roots in recent efforts to disencumber markets from the regulatory regimes (both national and international) established in the aftermath of World War II. What we today call "*neo*liberalism" is nothing but the second coming of the very same nineteenth-century faith in the "self-regulating market" that unleashed the capitalist crisis Polanyi chronicled. Now, as then, attempts to implement that creed are rending social bonds, destroying livelihoods, and despoiling nature. Now, as then, counterforces are mobilizing against the assault. On its face, then, today's crisis is plausibly viewed as a second great transformation, a great transformation redux.

For many reasons, then, Polanyi's perspective holds considerable promise for theorizing today. Yet critical theorists should not rush to embrace it uncritically. Even as it overcomes economism, *The Great Transformation* turns out, on closer inspection, to be deeply flawed. Focused single-mindedly on harms emanating from disembedded markets, the book overlooks harms originating elsewhere, in the surrounding "society." Occulting non-market-based forms of injustice, it also tends to whitewash forms of social protection that are at the same time vehicles of domination. Focused overwhelmingly on struggles against market-based depredations, the book neglects struggles against injustices rooted in "society" and encoded in social protections.

Thus, critical theorists should not embrace Polanyi's framework in the form in which appears in *The Great Transformation*. What is needed, rather, is a revision of that framework. The goal should be a new, quasi-Polanyian conception of capitalist crisis that not only avoids reductive economism but also avoids romanticizing society.

That is my aim in the present chapter. Seeking to develop a critique that comprehends society as well as economy, I propose to broaden Polanyi's problematic to encompass a third project that crosscuts his central conflict between marketization and social protection. This third project, which I call *emancipation*, aims to overcome forms of domination rooted in both economy and society. Central to both iterations of the great transformation, the one analyzed by Polanyi and the one we are living through now, struggles for emancipation constitute the missing third that mediates every conflict between marketization and social protection. The effect of introducing this missing third will be to transform the double movement into a *triple movement*. Embracing marketization, social protection, and emancipation, the triple movement is designed to map the collision of those three political projects, each of which remains salient today. Thus, this figure will form the core of a new, quasi-Polanyian perspective that can clarify capitalist crisis in the twenty-first century.

2. Disembedded Markets, Social Protection, and the Double Movement

I begin by recalling Polanyi's distinction between embedded and disembedded markets. Although seldom referenced explicitly in *The Great*

Transformation, this distinction is integral to all of that book's central concepts, including society, protection, crisis, and the double movement. Especially important for my purposes here, it carries strong evaluative connotations, which need to be subjected to critical scrutiny.

Famously, Polanyi distinguished two different relations in which markets can stand to society. On the one hand, markets can be "embedded," enmeshed in noneconomic institutions and subject to noneconomic norms, such as "the just price" and "the fair wage." On the other hand, markets can be "disembedded," freed from extraeconomic controls and governed immanently, by supply and demand. The first possibility, claims Polanyi, represents the historical norm; throughout most of history, in otherwise disparate civilizations and in widely separated locales, markets have been subject to noneconomic controls, which limit what can be bought and sold, by whom, and on what terms. The second possibility is historically anomalous; a nineteenth-century British invention, the "self-regulating market" was an utterly novel idea whose deployment, Polanyi contends, threatens the very fabric of human society.

For Polanyi, markets can never in fact be fully disembedded from the larger society. The attempt to make them so must inexorably fail, even when seemingly successful in the near term. For one thing, markets can function properly only against a noneconomic background of cultural understandings and solidary relations; attempts to disembed them destroy that background—for example, by eroding trust. For another, the attempt to establish self-regulating markets proves so destructive of the fabric of society that it provokes widespread demands for their social regulation; thus, far from enhancing social cooperation, the project of disembedding markets inevitably triggers social crisis. In the end, accordingly, Polanyi's distinction is better grasped as a difference in degree than as a difference in kind. While markets can never be fully disembedded, they can be more or less embedded. Equally important, as we shall see, they can be embedded in different ways.

The Great Transformation recounts the process by which British commercial interests sought to engineer that impossible creature, the "self-regulating market." In the process, they had to disable the noneconomic trappings in which markets had been embedded. Especially crucial was removal of restrictions on the buying and selling of land, labor, and money, previously limited by customary rights and community mores, moral and religious norms, structures of family and kin, local authorities, and the mercantilist policies of national states. When the new, commercially dominated government of the 1830s and '40s dismantled the system of outdoor relief and the tariffs and subsidies on corn, it effectively denuded land, labor, and money of their protective covering and transformed them into "fictitious commodities." Abandoned to the laws of "the dismal science," these fundamental bases of human society could now be bought and sold without regard for the consequences—human, social, natural.

According to Polanyi, however, "society" did not endure the assault with equanimity. From the beginning, rural landowners, urban workers, and other strata mobilized to protect endangered livelihoods, communities, and habitats. Despite their differences, Tories, socialists, cooperative movements, trade-unionists, religious activists, environmentalists, and opponents of international free trade effectively constituted a broad cross-class party of social protection. Aiming to protect labor, they sought to limit its commodification through legislation regulating wages and hours. Aiming to protect the agricultural lifeblood of rural communities, they sought tariffs on imported foodstuffs. In parts progressive, in parts reactionary, the forces of social protection opposed those of marketization. Defending society against economy, they turned to politics in order to reembed markets. Like their antagonists, they too mobilized in civil society and sought to capture state power. Thus, it was the sharpening struggle between these two camps, the marketizers and the protectionists, that leant the distinctive shape of a "double movement" to a century and a half of capitalist crisis.

To be sure, Polanyi's account depends chiefly on English developments. But he understood the double movement as a general schema with broad application. That assumption is plausible, I think, given British hegemony, which proved so consequential for developments elsewhere— for the colonies, for the rival European powers, and for the international regimes that structured their interactions. In country after country, commercial interests sought to loosen mercantilist restraints; in country after country, too, they encountered resistance. By the twentieth century, moreover, the free-marketeers had established an international regime of free trade, based on the gold standard, that effectively universalized capitalist crisis. In the context of global economic depression, iterations of the double movement appeared throughout the world, as counterforces of varied ideological stripes (from New Dealers to Communists to fascists) sought social protection in various forms (democratic, totalitarian, racist), eventually engulfing the planet in war. Thus, the resolution, in Polanyi's view, had to be international. Anticipating a new global financial regime, he advocated a framework that would foster market regulation and social provision by democratic welfare states. The goal should be to return the economy to its proper place in society.

. In general, then, the distinction between embedded and disembedded markets is integral to all of Polanyi's central concepts, including society, protection, crisis, and the double movement. Equally important, the distinction is strongly evaluative. Embedded markets are associated with social protection, figured as shelter from the harsh elements. Disembedded markets are associated with exposure, with being left to swim naked in "the icy water of egotistical calculation."[2] These inflections—embedded markets are good, disembedded markets bad—carry over to the double movement. The exposing pole signifies danger; the protective pole connotes safe haven.

What should we make of these ideas? On its face, the distinction between embedded and disembedded markets has much to offer to critical theorizing. For one thing, it points beyond economism, to an expansive understanding of capitalist crisis as a multifaceted historical process, as much social, political, and ecological as economic. Thematizing the commodification of nature, Polanyi integrated the ecological dimension, while also recognizing social disruption and political stalemate as constitutive aspects of capitalist crisis. In addition, his approach points beyond functionalism. Centering his account on the double movement, he gave pride of place to the projects of social actors—and to the collisions among them. In this way, Polanyi effectively jettisoned the orthodox view of crisis as an objective "system breakdown" and conceived it instead as an *intersubjective* process. Then, too, the distinction between embedded and disembedded markets makes possible a crisis critique that does not reject markets as such but only the dangerous, disembedded, variety. Consequently, the concept of an embedded market affords the prospect of a progressive alternative both to the wanton disembedding promoted by neoliberals and to the wholesale suppression of markets traditionally favored by socialists.

Nevertheless, the evaluative subtext of Polanyi's categories is problematic. On the one hand, his account of embedded markets and social protections is far too rosy. Romanticizing society, it occults the fact that the communities in which markets have historically been embedded have also been the locus of domination. Conversely, Polanyi's account of disembedding is a bit too dark. Having idealized society, it occludes the fact that processes that disembed markets from oppressive protections, whatever their other effects, contain an emancipatory moment.

Let me be clear. Polanyi never intended to idealize traditional society, let alone to endorse domination. An independent socialist, he advocated the defanging of markets by egalitarian, democratic means precisely in order to forestall the return of authoritarian, fascist alternatives. Thus, he recognized that not all regimes of protection were morally equivalent. But Polanyi never translated his moral intuitions into theoretical terms. Absent categorical distinctions between better and worse forms of embedding, his framework remained implicitly tied to an inadequate evaluative contrast between good embedded markets and bad disembedded markets.

Present-day critical theorists must revise this framework. Avoiding both wholesale condemnation of disembedding and wholesale approbation of reembedding, we must open both marketization and social protection to critical scrutiny. Exposing the normative deficits of society, as well as those of economy, we must validate struggles against domination *wherever* it roots.

To this end, I propose to draw on a resource not utilized by Polanyi, namely, the insights of emancipatory movements. Unmasking power asymmetries occluded by him, these movements exposed the predatory underside of the embedded markets he tended to idealize. Protesting protections that were also oppressions, they raised claims for emancipation. Exploiting their insights, and drawing on the benefits of hindsight, I propose to rethink the double movement in relation to *struggles for emancipation.*

3. Emancipation: The Missing "Third"

To speak of emancipation is to introduce a category that does not appear in *The Great Transformation*. But the idea, and indeed the word, figured importantly throughout the period Polanyi chronicled. One need only mention epochal struggles to abolish slavery, to liberate women, and to free non-European peoples from colonial subjection—all waged in the name of "emancipation." It is surely odd that these struggles should be absent from a work purporting to chart the rise and fall of what it calls "nineteenth-century civilization." But my point is not simply to flag an omission. It is rather to note that struggles for emancipation directly challenged oppressive forms of social protection, while neither wholly condemning nor simply celebrating marketization. Had they been included, these movements would have destabilized the dualistic narrative schema of *The Great Transformation*.

To see why, consider that emancipation differs importantly from Polanyi's chief positive category, social protection. Whereas protection is opposed to exposure, emancipation is opposed to domination. Whereas protection aims to shield society from the disintegrative effects of unregulated markets, emancipation aims to expose oppressive relations wherever they root, in society as well as in economy. Whereas the thrust of protection is to subject market exchange to noneconomic norms, that of emancipation is to subject both market exchange and nonmarket norms to critical scrutiny. Finally, whereas protection's highest values are social security, social stability, and solidarity, emancipation's priority is to overcome domination.

It would be wrong, however, to conclude that emancipation is always allied with marketization. If emancipation opposes domination, marketization opposes the extraeconomic regulation of production and exchange, whether such regulation is meant to protect or to liberate. Whereas marketization defends the supposed autonomy of the economy against encroachment from other social spheres, emancipation ranges across the boundaries that demarcate spheres, seeking to root out domination from *every* "sphere." Whereas the thrust of marketization is to liberate buying and selling from moral and ethical norms, that of emancipation is to scrutinize *all* types of norms from the standpoint of nondomination. Finally, whereas marketization claims as its values efficiency, individual choice, and the liberal norm of noninterference or negative liberty, emancipation's priority, as I just said, is to overcome domination.

It follows that struggles for emancipation do not map neatly onto either prong of Polanyi's double movement. Granted, such struggles appear on occasion to converge with marketization—as, for example, when they condemn as oppressive the very social protections that free-marketeers are seeking to eradicate. On other occasions, however, they converge with protectionist projects—as, for example, when they denounce the oppressive effects of deregulation. On still other occasions, finally, struggles for emancipation diverge from both prongs of the double movement—as, for example, when they aim neither to dismantle nor to defend existing protections but rather to transform the mode of protection. Thus, convergences, where they exist, are conjunctural and contingent. Aligned consistently neither with protection nor deregulation, struggles for emancipation represent a third force that disrupts Polanyi's dualistic schema. To give such struggles their due requires us to revise his framework—by transforming its double movement into a triple movement.

4. Rethinking "Society"

Conceptualizing the triple movement requires revising the social-institutional basis of Polanyi's framework. Critical theorists must replace his dualism of economy and society with a more complex societal schema that can accommodate sources of historical dynamism other than marketization.

In effect, Polanyi himself introduced a third social-institutional term. In his account, as we already saw, the conflict between marketizers and protectionists turned largely on control of the state. It turned out that, despite the marketizers' insistence that the "self-regulating market" was natural, they could advance their project only by deploying coercive state power. They needed the state both to disable the noneconomic regulations that had previously embedded markets and to impose the rule of supply and demand on populations that were often resistant. Likewise, protectionists could only hope to reembed markets by capturing and deploying state power. Only by recourse to the state's capacities could they devise and enforce regulations that would subject production and exchange to ethical norms. For both sides, then, the state was essential. Thus, the logic of Polanyi's argument supposed a triad of social institutions: society, economy, state.

On further reflection, however, even this triad proves inadequate to his problematic. In fact, the embedding of markets can only be a joint product of state and society. Before laisser faire, mercantilist states worked in tandem with nonstate institutions, such as the church and the family, which supplied the cultural meanings and ethical norms that informed their regulatory policies. The same was true of the democratic welfare states of the post–World War II era. The protections they instituted, too, were fashioned in part from meanings and norms that were already widely diffused throughout society. In fact, cultural meanings and norms constitute the indispensable *Sittlichkeit,* the ethical substance or normative "stuff," that lies at the heart of all embedding. States cannot create this ethical substance out of whole cloth. They rely, rather, on preexisting meanings and norms to meet them halfway.[3]

Therein lies the rub. Historically, the meanings and norms that have served to embed markets have often been hierarchical and exclusionary. When institutionalized, they have stamped the arrangements that Polanyi thought protected society as oppressive. What these arrangements protected was not society *simpliciter* but hierarchical exclusionary society—that is to say, they protected some people at the expense of others. Premised on oppressive norms, they entrenched disparities in social status, political voice, and access to resources. The effect has been to consolidate domination—and to inspire struggles for emancipation.

As we shall see, emancipatory movements often direct their struggles against the ethical substance that informs social protection. Protesting protections that are also predations, they criticize the normative understandings protections rely on—understandings not only of danger and safety but also of family, community, and belonging; of personhood, dignity, and desert; of dependency, contribution, and work; hence, of gender, nationality, and race. Making explicit this ethical substance, and subjecting it to critique, they transform taken-for-granted doxa into an object of political contestation. In effect, emancipatory movements bring matters previously immersed in what Polanyi called "society" into another societal realm: the public sphere of civil society.

To introduce emancipation, therefore, is perforce to introduce a new term, the public sphere of civil society. A communicative arena of contestation and public dispute, the public sphere of civil society is at once the space in which emancipatory movements critique the ethical substance of oppressive protections and the space in which those who defend the latter are forced to respond. It is the space, therefore, in which the tacitly diffused common sense of "society" is transformed into explicitly avowed propositional positions, subject to critique, on the one hand, and to explicit defense, on the other.[4] It is through the give-and-take among such opposing perspectives that emancipation can, under propitious conditions, become a historical force—a force no less dynamic than marketization.

By including emancipation, then, the triple movement transforms the triad of society, economy, state into a quartet, which also includes the public sphere of civil society. The effect is to alter the valence of "society," now contrasted with civil publicity. Whereas the latter operates in the modality of contestation, the former operates in the modality of doxa. Thus, the public sphere of civil society is a testing ground through which the norms infusing social protection may be forced to pass. Although it is itself replete with power asymmetries that compromise subordinates' voice, the public sphere nevertheless affords the chance to subject protection's *Sittlichkeit* to critical scrutiny.[5]

But the introduction of civil publicity also complicates the view of the state. State regulation can now be characterized in terms of its relation to civil society. In one scenario, social protections are administered in a top-down étatist fashion, treated as the province of experts, and severed from the communicative processes of civil society. In another, they are administered in a participatory-democratic fashion, as permeable to, and in ongoing dialogue with, civil society. Then, too, the public sphere of civil society affords the possibility of querying the manner in which social protection is framed. In one scenario, social protection is "misframed," designed to exclude some people whom markets expose to risk and/or some on whose labor society relies. In another scenario, protection is "well framed," including within its circle of refuge all who contribute their labor and are at risk.

In general, then, the triple movement transforms the social-institutional structure of Polanyi's thought. The effect is to open four lines of questioning he foreclosed. The first concerns the modality of the ethical substance that informs protection: have the operative norms been publicly vetted, or do they still exist in the mode of doxa? The second concerns the normative quality of that ethical substance: are the norms and meanings informing protection oppressive—in the sense that they violate the ideal of nondomination? Or are they emancipatory—in the sense that they accord with and advance that ideal? A third line of questioning concerns the modality of state regulation: is protection organized in a bureaucratic-étatist manner, which disempowers its beneficiaries, whom it treats less as active citizens than as passive consumers? Or is it organized in a participatory-democratic matter, as a mode of active citizenship? A fourth line of questioning concerns the framing of social protection: is protection misframed—in the sense that it excludes some who contribute their labor and are put at risk? Or is protection well framed—in that the set of those shielded from market vagaries coincides with the set of those exposed?

Such questions were forcefully posed by emancipatory movements throughout the period Polanyi chronicled. No less pertinent and pressing today, they deserve a central place in the critical theory of capitalist crisis in the twenty-first century. Although foreclosed in *The Great Transformation*, they can be accorded the importance they deserve in a neo-Polanyian framework that incorporates emancipation, along with marketization and social protection, in the figure of the triple movement.

5. Emancipation, Domination, Participatory Parity

But what precisely does emancipation mean in the present framework? To approach this question, let us briefly consider four of the many social movements that have mobilized under that banner: feminism, anti-imperialism, multiculturalism, and the New Left. Clearly, these movements did not share an explicit understanding of emancipation, and the forms of domination they protested were highly diverse. I believe, however, that a single normative aspiration subtends most (if not all) of their claims: to remove obstacles that prevent some people from participating fully, on a par with others, in social life. Thus, a major target of feminist protest is an androcentric status order, institutionalized throughout society, that subordinates women to men and precludes their full participation on terms of parity. For anti-imperialists, the central issue is a political-economic space divided between core and periphery, which denies non-Europeans the capacity to establish parity of participation in their own societies and prevents them from participating on a par with Europeans in transnational society. For multiculturalists, the chief target is a design of public space that institutionalizes majority-ethnic or majority-religious self-understandings, thereby denying parity of participation to members of minorities. For New Leftists, the burning issue was (and is) a bureaucratic organization of social protection that disempowers ordinary citizens and precludes their active participation in democratic life.

Clearly, these obstacles to participatory parity take different forms. In some cases, the principal locus of domination is society, while in others, it is the economy. In still other cases, the chief culprit is civil society and/or the state. Thus, the substantive content of emancipation varies accordingly. In some cases, emancipation means transforming the status order, replacing an ethical substance that supports hierarchy with one that fosters equal standing and participatory parity. In other cases, it means transforming political-economic space so as to overcome the division between core and periphery, while assuring access for all to the resources needed for full participation on equitable terms. Then again, emancipation sometimes means transforming the design of public space, deinstitutionalizing norms that advantage majorities, so as to enable members of minorities to participate as peers. In other cases, finally, it means transforming the mode of exercise of public power so as to foster equal participation and preclude domination. In practice, moreover, emancipation often means some combination of, or even all of, the above. In each case, however, its implicit thrust is to vindicate a single idea: the principle of participatory parity.

Elsewhere, I have sought to provide a fuller explication and philosophical defense of the principle of participatory parity.[6] Here, I want simply to note that this idea provides an account of emancipation that befits the figure of a triple movement. Equally sensitive to status hierarchies, class differentials, and political asymmetries (which is to say, to misrecognition, maldistribution, and misrepresentation), the principle of participatory parity targets harms associated with four major institutional centers: society, economy, state, and public sphere. Thus, it extends the reach of critique beyond modes of domination that derive from markets, to include as well those encoded in social protections.

6. Emancipation from Hierarchical Protections

To show how emancipation extends critique, I propose to look more closely at two of the movements mentioned in the preceding section: namely, feminism and anti-imperialism. Each of these movements' claims explodes Polanyi's double movement by disclosing a different way in which social protections can be oppressive. First, feminist claims unmask the oppressive character of social protections that are premised on status hierarchies; and second, anti-imperialist claims expose the oppressive character of social protections that have been gerrymandered to exclude some relevant actors. By discussing these claims, I aim to provide a concrete historical brief for the triple movement.

Consider, first, that the social and political arrangements that embed markets can be oppressive in virtue of being hierarchical. In such cases, they entrench status differentials that deny some who are included in principle as members of society the social preconditions for full participation. The classic example is gender hierarchy, which assigns women a lesser status, often akin to that of a male child, and thereby prevents them from participating fully, on a par with men, in social interaction. But one could also cite caste hierarchies, including those premised on racialist ideologies. In all such cases, social protections work to the advantage of those at the top of the status hierarchy, affording lesser (if any) benefit to those at the bottom. What they protect, accordingly, is less society per se than social hierarchy. No wonder, then, that feminist, antiracist, and anticaste movements have mobilized against such hierarchies, rejecting the protections they purport to offer. Insisting on full participation in society, they have sought to dismantle arrangements that entrench their subordination.

The feminist critique of hierarchical protection runs through every stage of Polanyi's history, although it is never mentioned by him. During the mercantilist era, feminists such as Mary Wollstonecraft criticized the traditional social arrangements that embedded markets. Condemning the gender hierarchies entrenched in family, religion, law, and social custom, they demanded such fundamental prerequisites of nondomination as an independent legal personality, religious freedom, education, the right to refuse sex, rights of custody in their children, and the rights to speak in public and to vote. During the period of laisser faire, feminists demanded equal access to the market. Exposing the market's instrumentalization of sexist norms, they opposed protections that denied them the right to own property, to sign contracts, to control wages, to practice professions, and to work the same hours and receive the same pay as men—all prerequisites of nondomination. During the post–World War II era, "second-wave" feminists targeted the "public patriarchy" instituted by welfare states. Condemning social protections premised on "the family wage," they demanded equal pay for work of comparable worth, parity for caregiving and wage earning in social entitlements, and an end to the gender division of labor, both paid and unpaid. In each of these epochs, feminists raised claims for emancipation, aimed at dismantling hierarchical protections. At some moments, they targeted traditional community structures that *embedded* markets; at others, they aimed their fire at the forces that were *dis*embedding markets; at still others, their principal foes were those who were *re*embedding markets.

Thus, feminist claims did not align consistently with either pole of Polanyi's double movement. On the contrary, feminist struggles for emancipation constituted a third prong of social movement, which cut across the other two. What Polanyi called a double movement was actually a triple movement.

7. Emancipation from Misframed Protections

The social and political arrangements that embed markets can also be oppressive in a second way: in virtue of being misframed. *Misframing* is a neologism I have coined for mismatches of scale—in this case, between the scale at which markets are embedded, which is usually national, and that at which they expose people to danger, which is often transnational.[7] The oppression of misframing arises when protective arrangements externalize the negative effects of markets onto "outsiders," wrongly excluding some of those exposed, while saddling them with the costs of protecting others.

The clearest examples are colonialism and its neoimperial successor regimes. Historically, the arrangements that protected nascent European industries had as their flip side the colonial subjugation of non-Europeans. Even today, moreover, social welfare provision in Europe and

North America is largely financed by economic domination of the Global South by means of debt and unequal exchange. In both cases, the arrangements that embed markets serve the citizens of the metropolitan powers at the expense of peripheral subjects. The latter's exploitation subsidizes the former's protection.

Misframing differs from hierarchy as a mode of domination. Whereas the latter denies parity to internal subordinates, the former constitutes as external "others" some whose labor is essential to society—for example, colonial subjects, undocumented workers, and other noncitizens. Thus, while hierarchical protections deny full membership to some who are recognized as belonging to society, misframed protections deny the status of membership to some on whose activities society relies.

Polanyi himself laid the basis for the critique of misframed protections, although he did not articulate it explicitly. In *The Great Transformation,* he observed, first, that political states are necessary prerequisites for successful social protection and, second, that they are unevenly available in the modern world. He writes,

> If the organized states of Europe could protect themselves against the backwash of international free trade, the politically unorganized colonial peoples could not.…The protection which the white man could easily secure for himself through the sovereign status of his communities was out of reach of the colored man as long as he lacked the prerequisite, political government.[8]

What exactly had caused the "colored man's" "lack"? European powers, at the height of what they called "laisser faire," used their colonies both as dedicated sources of raw materials and cheap foodstuffs and also as protected outlets for their manufactured goods. Thus, colonialism served to protect European industry and to cushion European peoples from the harshest effects of unregulated capitalism, while depriving colonized peoples of the means of protection.

It seemed to follow that colonized peoples would gain protection by achieving independence and acquiring states of their own. But even after decolonization, that goal proved elusive. The reason has to do with another Polanyian insight: the regulatory capacities of states depend importantly on international arrangements. Observing that the gold-standard/free-trade regime of the early twentieth century had prevented

European states from adopting protective policies, such as full employment or deficit spending, that depend on control of the money supply, Polanyi concluded that the post–World War II international regime should be designed in such a way as to permit, indeed to facilitate, protective policies at the national level. What he did not anticipate, however, was that the "Embedded Liberalism" established after the war would serve some states better than others.[9] In that period, when imperialism assumed the "nonpolitical" form of unequal exchange between newly independent ex-colonies and their erstwhile masters, the latter continued to finance their domestic welfare systems on the backs of the former. The disparity was exacerbated in the neoliberal era, moreover, by the policy of "structural adjustment," as international agencies such as the IMF used the weapon of debt to further undercut the protective capacities of postcolonial states, compelling them to divest their assets, open their markets, and slash social spending. Historically, therefore, international arrangements have entrenched disparities in the capacities of states to protect their populations from the vagaries of international markets. They have permitted the domestic reembedding of markets by the states of the core but not by those of the periphery.

No wonder, then, that anticolonial and anti-imperialist movements mobilized against misframed protections. In each historical era, they raised claims for emancipation, which cannot be fitted into Polanyi's schema. Prior to independence, they sought national liberation, whether by negotiated transition or by armed insurrection. After independence, they challenged the governance structures of the global economy, such as the World Trade Organization and the IMF. At some moments, anti-imperialists protested the forcible disembedding of their own local markets from their own precolonial societies. At others, they opposed the reembedding of European markets at their expense. Like the claims of feminists, then, the claims of anti-imperialists did not align consistently with either prong of Polanyi's double movement. In their case, too, struggles for emancipation constituted a distinct third force. Here, too, accordingly, what Polanyi called a double movement is better grasped as a triple movement, encompassing marketization, social protection, and emancipation.

8. Twenty-first-Century Capitalist Crisis in the Light of the Triple Movement

The previous discussion has established two points. We have seen, first, thanks to feminists and anti-imperialists, that the social arrangements that reembed markets can be seriously flawed. Even in democratic welfare states, social protections can be oppressive insofar as they are hierarchical and/or misframed. From this, it follows—and this is my second point— that neither the great transformation described by Polanyi nor the one we are living through now can be adequately understood by the figure of the double movement. In reducing the logic of crisis to a two-sided conflict between marketization and social protection, that figure not only occults projects of emancipation but also distorts our understanding of the two projects it purports to clarify. In fact, neither marketization nor social protection can be adequately understood without factoring in struggles for emancipation. I want to conclude by spelling out what is to be gained by transforming Polanyi's double movement into a triple movement.

The triple movement conceptualizes capitalist crisis as a three-sided conflict among marketization, social protection, and emancipation. In our time, each of these three orientations has committed adherents. Marketization is championed by neoliberals. Social protection commands support in various forms, some savory, some unsavory—from nationally oriented social-democrats and trade-unionists to anti-immigrant populist movements, from neotraditional religious movements to antiglobalization activists, from environmentalists to indigenous peoples. Emancipation fires the passions of various successors to the new social movements, including multiculturalists, international feminists, gay-and-lesbian liberationists, cosmopolitan democrats, human-rights activists, and proponents of global justice. It is the complex relations among these three types of projects that impress the shape of a triple movement on the present crisis of capitalist society.

To clarify this constellation, critical theorists should treat each term of the triple movement as ambivalent. We have already seen, contra Polanyi, that social protection is often ambivalent, affording relief from the disintegrative effects of deregulation while simultaneously entrenching domination. But the same is true of the other two terms. Deregulation of markets does indeed have the negative effects Polanyi stressed, but it can also beget positive effects to the extent that the protections it disin-tegrates are oppressive—as, for example, when markets are introduced into bureaucratically administered command economies or when labor markets are opened to former slaves. Nor is emancipation immune to ambivalence, as it produces not only liberation but also strains in the fab-ric of existing solidarities. Thus, even as it overcomes domination, eman-cipation may help dissolve the solidary ethical basis of social protection, thereby fostering marketization.

Seen this way, each term has both a telos of its own and a potential for ambivalence that unfolds through its interaction with the other two terms. None of the three can be adequately grasped in isolation from the others. Nor can the social field be adequately grasped by focusing on only two terms. It is only when all three are considered together that we begin to get an adequate view of capitalist crisis.

Here, then, is the core premise of the triple movement: the relation between any two sides of the three-sided conflict must be mediated by the third. Thus, as I have argued here, the conflict between marketization and social protection must be mediated by emancipation. Equally, how-ever, conflicts between protection and emancipation must be mediated by marketization. Thus, the critique I have made of Polanyi can also be turned against the adherents of emancipation. If he neglected the impact of struggles for emancipation on conflicts between marketization and social protection, they have neglected the impact of marketizing projects on conflicts between social protection and emancipation.[10]

As we saw, feminists, anti-imperialists, multiculturalists, and New Leftists have forcefully challenged oppressive protections in the postwar era. In each case, the movement disclosed a type of oppression and raised a corresponding claim for emancipation. In each case, too, however, the movement's claims for emancipation were ambivalent—they could line up in principle either with marketization or with social protection. In the first case, where emancipation aligned with marketization, it would serve to erode not just the oppressive dimension but the solidary basis of social protection *simpliciter*. In the second case, where emancipation aligned with social protection, it would serve not to erode but rather to transform the ethical substance undergirding protection.

As a matter of fact, all four movements encompassed both ori-entations. In each case, liberal currents gravitated in the direction of marketization, while socialist and social-democratic currents were more likely to align with forces for social protection. Arguably, however, emancipation's ambivalence has been resolved in recent years in favor of marketization. Insufficiently attuned to the rise of neoliberalism, the hegemonic currents of emancipatory struggle have formed a "dangerous liaison" with marketization.[11] In the view of some observers, they have supplied the "new spirit," or charismatic rationale, for a new mode of capital accumulation, "flexible," postfordist, transnational.[12] At the very least, the emancipatory critique of oppressive protection has converged with the neoliberal critique of protection per se. In the conflict zone of triple movement, emancipation has joined forces with marketization to double-team social protection.

The point suggests a rewriting of Polanyi's project. By theorizing the double movement, he portrayed the conflicts of his time as an epochal battle for the soul of the market: Will nature, labor, and money be stripped of all ethical meaning, sliced, diced, and traded like widgets, and to hell with the consequences? Or will markets in those fundamental bases of human society be subject to ethically and morally informed political regulation? That battle remains as pressing as ever in the twenty-first century. But the triple movement casts it in a sharper light, as crosscut by two other major battles of epochal significance. One is a battle for the soul of social protection. Will the arrangements that reembed markets in the postneoliberal era be hierarchical or egalitarian, misframed or well framed, difference hostile or difference friendly, bureaucratic or participatory? The other crosscutting epochal battle is for the soul of emancipation. Will the emancipatory struggles of the twenty-first century serve to advance the disembedding and deregulation of markets? Or will they serve to democratize social protections and to make them more just?

These questions suggest a "possible future" for those of us who remain committed to emancipation. We might resolve to break off our dangerous liaison with marketization and forge a principled new alliance with social protection. In thereby realigning the poles of the triple movement, we could integrate our longstanding interest in nondomination with legitimate interests in solidarity and social security, without neglecting the importance of negative liberty. Embracing a broader understanding of social justice, such a project would serve at once to honor Polanyi's insights and remedy his blind spots.

Chapter 6

Crisis, Underconsumption, and Social Policy

Caglar Keyder

I

This chapter seeks to analyze the reasons for the chronic problems experienced by the crisis-prone world economy and points to a possible future. As the greatest burden of globalization is borne by the poor, whose fortunes have worsened since the 1980s, any ethically desirable scenario for the future should seek to enhance their chances of securing a livelihood. In both the North and the South, there is a new poverty suffered by those segments of the population who are either not employed or employed at low wages, in precarious positions, and without security. Their incomes have stagnated, and premarket sources of household reproduction, such as recourse to peasant production or occupying public land for the construction of informal housing, are no longer permitted in an environment of full market dominance. Agricultural subsidies in the countryside and urban subsidies toward the city poor, which were integral components of Fordist and developmentalist regimes, have fallen by the wayside as governments have redirected their economic policies toward global competition. While these populist measures are being abandoned, more formal mechanisms of "welfare" provision, designed to protect the vulnerable against risks and exclusion, to secure minimum-income guarantees, and to alleviate poverty to some extent, are still in place. Contrary to popular belief, the programs of the welfare state have not been dismantled in advanced capitalist countries. In fact, more formal welfare policies have been adopted in some middle-income states to increase the overall impact of social expenditures. The scenario proposed in this chapter is the coming together of various strands of reaction against the ravages of neoliberalism to form a "double movement," in the sense described by Polanyi;[1] the primary object of this double movement would be to institute global and national social policies in order to redistribute global income toward the poor. The argument is that such a redistribution would also remedy the imbalances in the global economy and establish a more sustainable balance between an ever-expanding global production capacity and the effective demand for consumption that a more equitable distribution of global income would generate.

The present crisis has been described as the first crisis of globalization, due to its scope and the rapidity of its transmission to all geographies of the world. There is, however, a more fundamental sense in which the crisis is global: it can be understood properly only if the explanation takes the global economy as the unit of analysis. Furthermore, remedies also, at least to some degree, have to be global in order to counteract the tendencies leading to crisis. We are in the midst of an underconsumption crisis, which means that, given the prevailing income distribution, the capacity for consumption is inadequate to make investment attractive.[2] In other words, capitalists are reluctant to invest because they feel that there will not be sufficient demand for the eventual products. This is not a situation that characterizes one country only or a few. If that were the case, the country in which there are excess investable funds (say, the United States) could become a net creditor and invest in another part of the global economy (say, Asia) where there is demand for consumables, thus contributing to the overall deepening of capitalism. But if there is an underconsumption tendency generally in the world economy, meaning that the income distribution is bad everywhere and not conducive to bringing about widespread consumption, then such exports of capital cannot address the problem. This is why a global analysis (and a global cure) is called for.

What I argue in this chapter is that the bloating and the crisis of the financial sector are symptoms of underlying problems and that a superficial diagnosis that focuses attention on the financial sector cannot address these problems. Success in unclogging the financial pathways does not magically revive investment and employment. The policies intending to combat the crisis, as long as they remain at the level of "making credit flow again," will at best postpone a reckoning with the deeper imbalances and conflicts inherent in the global political economy. Such imbalances grow out of the lopsidedness in class balances and, by extension, in global income distribution. Because the period starting in the 1980s witnessed the defeat of the workers in the First World and the entry of several hundred million new workers of the South into the world capitalist economy, the world labor force has remained weak ever since. Additionally, First World states made no effort to advance the social-democratic policies of the postwar period. The welfare state was not dismantled, but it did not evolve or keep up with the increasing demands due to changing conditions either.[3] In the countries that became integral components of the world economy through the new globalization momentum, social policies made very little headway: in China and India, huge populations were still in the countryside, and therefore workers in the urban areas enjoyed no bargaining power. Governments had decided on industrialization strategies based on exports; hence, there was not much willingness to initiate social policy measures that would indirectly make labor more expensive. During the initial years of neoliberal ascendancy, there was an attempt to privatize all public services, which resulted in the dismantling of the provision mechanisms of collective goods. In the countries of the South especially, such denial of collective goods and subsidies increased the burden on the livelihood of the poor. The emerging inequality in class balances was manifested in a declining share of labor in all countries, including China,[4] and the worsening income inequality became the main factor leading to financialization and the crisis.

II

How can we argue that the conventional arsenal of social-democratic measures, which proved their worth during the post–World War II period in the nation-state environment, might in fact provide a solution to the problems faced by the emerging global political economy? Of course, the world is a different place now, and no government will attempt to replicate the policies of the glorious Fordist era. We have lived through three decades of neoliberal globalization, and that will leave its marks on any new policy. A simple rescaling from the national to the global level would seem attractive, except that this would require some degree of global governance that would be deployed for purposes of international redistribution of effective demand. At the moment, such global institutions are not there; nor is there any sign that they might be built in the near future. In the absence of this prospect, a concerted attempt to improve the income distribution in all countries is the second-best alternative. I suggest that increasing social expenditures may well be the most feasible policy toward this goal.

We might start the analysis with data concerning the symptomatic manifestation of the crisis. The most recent debacle was the explosive result of financial expansion in the American housing market. This was the third financial bubble within a decade, and the biggest. The East Asian credit expansion of the late 1990s and the dot-com exuberance around the turn of the millennium were the first two, and both culminated in crises, albeit without the global scope of the present one. In the years leading to 2008 too, it was the unchecked growth in credit, attempting to compensate for the underconsumption trend, that brought about the crisis. An unregulated Wall Street was more than willing to oblige in mediating the flow of easy money to borrowers. The new financial instruments invented by "quants" on Wall Street were built on the rickety foundation of consumer and housing loans, leveraged manyfold, and sold to high-income earners. These savings that flowed to Wall Street would have been borrowed by businesses and invested in the real sector, had the capitalists been able to garner the courage to expand production. But potential investors knew that the income distribution was such that consumption demand might not be forthcoming. Hence, savings were channeled into the new financial assets and served to inflate the bubble instead.

The bigger the bubble, the larger the financial sector. With the top graduates from top schools clamoring to work for investment banks, the financial sector increased its scope to insinuate finance into all economic transactions. This financialization implied that finance was now claiming a larger share of the total profits in the economy.[5] There is one statistic that highlights the enormous expansion of the financial sector in the United States during the past quarter of a century and that summarizes the concerns regarding imbalances in the economy: between the 1980s and 2006, financial-sector profits grew from around 15 percent to 40 percent of all corporate profits. This is a sign of an economy working with a disproportionately expanded credit volume relative to the *real* level of production, so that financial corporations are able to claim a much larger proportion of total profits than they would in a "healthy" economy.

Credit, of course, is an integral component of the capitalist cycle. The capitalist, before he or she embarks on the production process, has to buy the tools of production and raw materials and has to advance wages to the workers. After the goods to be sold are produced, the capitalist has to wait for the sale to take place before starting the production process again. Every time the capitalist wants to expand production and increase capacity, he or she has to resort to borrowing. Similar stories can be told of the merchant and of the workers, who often have to have credit advanced to them before they are paid for their work; otherwise they will not be able to survive until the date of payment. Consumer credit on an organized and formal basis, as opposed to merchants putting purchases "on tab," is a relatively recent addition to this rostrum, allowing buyers to owe part of the value they will access, thus temporarily creating additional consumption demand. Credit is a temporary expansion of claims to output; it is a way in which more can be spent than the purchasing power available through wage or profit income. Credit is not only a facilitator of exchange, however: it can also be a temporary solution to the problem of underconsumption, provided that there are willing borrowers. When credit is advanced to consumers, it increases their purchasing capacity; when it is repaid, the opposite occurs. This is why, if credit is going to be a provisional solution to the lack of purchasing capacity in the economy as a whole, the volume of credit has to expand in proportion to the incomes generated by the real economy.

In ordinary times, when wages are good and the income distribution is within the bounds of long-term trends, credit volume is more likely to maintain a "normal" proportion to the volume of real production. What we mean by an overextension of credit is when this proportion exceeds the normal range in an attempt to create unwarranted purchasing power, giving rise to a demand incommensurate with the actual capacity to purchase. Credit is advanced to consumers to artificially expand the market. Of course, this cannot happen in just any sector: there is a certain cycle to mundane purchases, and these items tend to lose value as soon as they are purchased. What might induce potential borrowers with greater certainty would be the possibility of purchasing an asset they believe to have a potential for appreciating in value. In the 1920s, people on the street borrowed to buy stocks; in the 1970s, developing countries borrowed to extend their industrialization based on imported inputs; in the years leading to 2008, lower-income Americans borrowed (with a lot of prodding by the lenders) to buy real estate. Naturally, all the artificially boosted demand for real estate also led the builders and developers to build to anticipate demand and thus created an oversupply of houses and office buildings and shopping malls, which remained unsold when the excessive ballooning of credit gave in to an inability of the debtors to service their debts. Although an item with a perceived potential to appreciate in value works best in creating the conditions for a ballooning of credit, consumer debt, funded through credit cards, might also have led to a collapse and created a similar situation if it had been given more time.[6] Lending to consumers with ever-lower chances of repayment would eventually result in overextension of the credit market and would end with bankruptcies of the borrowers unable to service their growing debt. Of course, mortgages are a faster route to the same result because they bring into play much greater sums of money.

The actual capacity to purchase, or "effective demand," depends on total income (as in national income) but also on its distribution. The answer to the question of why there is excessive credit in certain conjunctures is not only that there is irrational optimism of lenders who give up caution and instead seek to lend to any warm body; it is also that the incomes of the potential consumers have not kept up with the growing capacity to produce. In fact, the situation in the United States since the 1980s provides a good example: although workers' productivity (hence the output) increased by 70 percent over the 1980–2005 period, the average hourly wage increased by 4.4 percent only.[7] In other words, the income that was generated during the production of output did not translate to sufficient demand (because it was concentrated at the top). Hence, there was a need to flout the usual caution and to try to create additional purchasing capacity, and this was achieved through the supply of easy money and deregulated credit markets. In other words, the eventual risk of underconsumption, or production that could not be sold, could be avoided if the credit mechanism were deployed as a weapon to combat the imbalance between capacity to produce and capacity to consume.

The reason that what is produced cannot be sold should be sought in the inability to generate demand. This deficiency, that is, the shortfall in demand, has to be understood in the context of income distribution and class relations and the overall regulation of the economy. It follows that the recurrent crises of overextended credit resulted from an attempt to counteract deficient effective demand. In other words, credit was supposed to create consumption and investment, but its expansion got out of hand, resulting in repayment difficulties and defaults and eventually in the bursting of the bubble. As long as the structural problem is not addressed, credit inflation will lead to financial crises and will hurt the real economy with unemployment and loss of output. The bubble may take a longer time to develop with better regulation over the financial sector, but without the underconsumption problem addressed, it will surely inflate and will lead again to crisis.

III

If we leave out conceptual exercises based on the labor theory of value, classical political economy focuses on two complementary class-relations models of crisis, which together also describe the conditions for stability. One is the profit-squeeze model, stipulating a situation of weak capitalists, and the second is the underconsumption model of insufficient effective demand, the result of a weak working class. In the first model, capitalists find the profits they make insufficient. This may be because there is excessive competition and the cost of inputs is high, exercising pressure on profits. The biggest "input," of course, is labor. Because of low unemployment and the institutional strength of the workers, wages will be too high. Since profits and wages add up to the entire income created, or the value added in production, there is a zero-sum situation in this distributional model: if workers are strong, profits decline. This is a starkly political picture of class conflict in which distributional shares depend on relative strength and organizational ability.

In the real world, the state intervenes in a multitude of ways to influence the outcome of the struggle between the workers and the owners of capital. An empirical analysis would have to bring the state into the picture, primarily via its regulatory and fiscal roles (taxes and government expenditures). The Marxian framework suggests that taxes are extracted from surplus value; hence, the higher the taxes, the lower the profits. In other words, profits might be low with a given level of wages because the state, as another party in the distributional contest, may raise its share. On the whole, the experience of the decades since the end of World War II suggests that higher taxes improve income distribution: taxes are generally progressive, and higher state expenditures tend to redistribute income toward the lower-income groups. As was suggested in the capitalist-state debate of the 1970s, legitimation of modern states depends in large part on how much they provide for social consumption (public education, health and other welfare state expenditures, social assistance). The end of the Cold War and the winding down of the competition with the socialist bloc has perhaps, to some extent, liberated capitalist states from this constraint. Their capitalist nature has gained a more prominent role, as evidenced in the relative impunity with which they introduced policies described as neoliberalism. On the other hand, the entitlements that were put in place in postwar years have been popular and are now regarded by their clients as entrenched social rights. In most advanced capitalist countries, beneficiaries have proved to be able defenders of the "social wage" provided by the state. All social expenditures and subsidies—health, education, housing, child benefits, and social assistance—fall into this category of the social wage: they improve the income distribution and therefore counteract the tendency toward underconsumption.

It will be recalled that at the beginning of the neoliberal era, arguments were made against all the elements contributing to the strength of the working class: wages were too high, taxes took too much out of profit, there was too much regulation increasing nonwage costs to the capitalists, and social expenditures were rising. The complaint was that profits were squeezed. The sought-for ascendancy of the capitalist class would solve the problem of low profits by lowering wages and social expenditures and by deregulating. These measures would give the capitalists sufficient confidence that their profits would be satisfactory, and they would then invest. This was the recipe for the supply-side solution to the crisis of the 1970s: as political balances changed in capitalists' favor with a defeated working class, lower taxes, decreasing social expenditures, and deregulation, profits would rise and generate employment through increased investment. Neoliberalism was the outcome of the class struggle won by the capitalists.[8]

The second model of class balances thwarting the smooth working of the system, that of insufficient effective demand, often labeled as the underconsumption or oversaving hypothesis, has as its premise that workers who create value are not granted recompense sufficient to generate a purchasing power equal to the value created. Workers channel all their wages to consumption. Capitalists end up with profits; they spend a part of this sum as consumption and save the rest. For the economy to function at capacity, the same capitalists or others should use these savings to purchase investment goods. If, however, consumption demand is weak (this is the case because wages—private and social—are a smaller proportion of total income than they should be), then capitalists will not want to invest to increase the productive capacity. This outcome, the result of underconsumption, is what is termed oversaving. Surplus value will not be continuously ploughed back into capital accumulation to create higher production capacity if there is no anticipation of higher consumption.

Consumption is the ultimate validation of the capitalist process; it is the raison d'être of production. When capitalists save a high proportion of their profits, demand will not be sufficient to clear the market. Hence, eventually there will be surplus capacity, leading to layoffs: the usual picture of a crisis, with rising unemployment and unsold commodities. This was the situation ushering in the Great Depression. Keynesian policies of demand creation through government expenditure were meant to boost aggregate demand in response to the crisis. Keynesian management of the economy, however, appears to be a relatively superficial and necessarily temporary fix to the effective-demand problem since it only addresses the phenomenon of underconsumption without worrying about the cause (distribution of the total income) underlying it. The symptomatic prescription of a "stimulus package" against the insufficiency of effective demand may provide incentives for capitalists to invest and generate employment, but it will not necessarily alter the distributional calculus, unless lower unemployment shifts political balances in favor of wage earners.

The globalization of the past two decades provides a good example of shifting political balances leading to declining wages. Wages in high-wage countries have declined because of the competition of imports from low-wage countries; and capitalists discovered that they could employ low-wage workers to do the same work that was previously undertaken in high-wage locations. The distinguishing dimension of globalization of the recent period is precisely the geographical extension of the production circuit. As transnational corporations outsource more and more stages of the production process to workers in low-wage countries (increasingly in services as well as in manufacturing), the division of the produced value between wages and profits becomes more skewed. Hence, globalization has introduced an extreme instance of a shift in political balances against workers. There has emerged a large segment of the labor force in the North who are less formally employed and are essentially competing with low-wage labor in the South. They have to live with declining wages, while capitalists can increase their profits. The consequence is worsening income distribution.

The implication of this model is that the tendency to under-consumption may only be contained if the income distribution between capitalists and workers is at a sustainable level; crises arise when this distribution worsens against workers, that is, when workers' wages fall further short of being able to generate effective demand to purchase all the value created. This is therefore a theory of crisis in which the main causal factor is the functional distribution of income, the balance between classes. Taken together, the profit-squeeze and the underconsumption models suggest that capitalism must tread a narrow path, avoiding pitfalls on either side.[9] As "regulation theory" emphasized, maintaining this kind of sensitive balance is not something that capitalists may hope to achieve on their own; the necessary institutional capacity can only be deployed at the level of the state.[10] Regulation theory, which abstracts from the experience of the Fordist period, is based on the recognition that the balance between classes, implying the mutual relation between income shares, may only be maintained with the active construction of social structures employing the capacities of the state. This is not to argue that state activity pursues a fully thought-out project in the name of securing capitalist reproduction but that mutually reinforcing policies and institutions might, in time, come to constitute a constellation of relatively coherent regulatory practices.[11] It should be pointed out that such coherence does not guarantee success in freezing class balances and containing conflict.

There are economic, political, and social developments that will remain beyond management, outside the purview of any particular regulation, and will change the conditions within which the balances were initially struck, thus requiring a new mode of regulation.

Fordism maintained a balance between production and consumption until the 1970s; neoliberal globalization followed and led to global income inequality. Hence, globalization is *the* development of our time that requires a new mode of regulation. Whether it was technologically driven or pursued as policy by transnational corporations or by politicians, its distributional dynamics have so far remained beyond the regulatory capacity of states. There is, however, no global governance, let alone a global level for the coordination of social policies and institutions (such as labor unions) that are a factor in the distribution of income. Individual states, even in the case of the hegemonically powerful United States, find it impossible to manage the complexity of the impact of the global economy, while the absence of any regulatory body at the global level makes any attempt at maintaining balances impossible. There are, of course, agencies that have emerged or have transformed their mandates to take on global roles. The US government also provides some of the required services.[12] These attempts at global governance have so far been heavily skewed in favor of allowing capital to be mobile, of establishing markets in commodities and money, but have not ventured into the more complex field of shaping social structures. "Regulation" in the sense just described, however, is expected to produce a balance between production and consumption and not only to manage the collective affairs of capital. It, therefore, would have to entail both economic and social policy institutions with the requisite powers to tax and to redistribute, to grant rights and privileges to workers, and to conduct social policy toward the excluded.

IV

Growing inequality since the 1980s is very well documented. There has, however, been an argument as to which distribution statistics we must look at. Apologists who want to show that neoliberal globalization has had a positive impact look at the distribution of income among nations, with national averages taken to represent the income levels of entire populations of states. This distribution may in fact have shown an improvement, but this is mostly due to China's outstanding growth performance. If China is taken out of the picture, the distribution of income between the North and the South seems to have worsened.[13]

There is, however, no disputing the worsening of income distribution *within* most of the countries in the world. The United States is probably an extreme case, with the income accruing to the top 1 percent of the population increasing from 8 percent in the late 1970s to 23.5 percent in 2007.[14] With the exception of some countries in Europe, distribution of income has worsened in high- and middle-income countries. This is due in greatest part to the lowering of wages of less-skilled laborers who have to compete with the new working class of China. It is also the case that globalization has meant the higher remuneration of the managerial class at the top who could readily be inserted into global networks. In fact, the spectrum of wages in every country has widened because in every country there are highly paid educated personnel of transnational corporations and globally competitive sectors. Salaries and wages in these sectors and companies have soared, while at the low end there are low-skilled workers whose wages drift down toward Chinese levels. It is no longer the case that labor incomes can be predicted on the basis of where a worker lives. In every country, there are managers and high-end workers whose compensation packages are at the top of income scales and are becoming more similar internationally. Within China, as well, there is a new class of entrepreneurs and knowledge workers whose incomes have taken off. There are now billionaires everywhere.

When inequalities within countries increase while between-country inequality remains the same or increases, global inequality (income distribution for the entire world's population) also increases. There is a need, however, for a more direct measurement of the world income distribution. In a global economy where transnational corporations conduct one-third of the world trade within their own transnational organizations ranging over many countries, where production of each finished good takes place over dozens of national units, and where the division of labor in the most widely used commodities is fully supranational and the ownership of capital is multinational, income distribution measures would only be meaningful if they take the globe as a single unit. The annual celebration of wealth and the wealthy in magazines such as *Forbes* suggests that a few billionaires, domiciled all over the world, weigh as much in their command over resources as millions of poor. Such stories imply that world public opinion has started thinking in terms of a global distribution of income, although there is as yet no index measuring it.[15]

There is a question of which population to include in such an index of the global distribution of income. If the objective is to understand the capitalist production process and the distribution of value generated in its course, perhaps up to one-third of the world's population will be irrelevant to the analysis. We would like to know how the value added during production is distributed between workers and capitalists: this is the crucial relationship that determines the crisis tendency arising from underconsumption or oversaving. The incomes deriving from survival-oriented self-employment or household production, especially of the sporadically commodified peasantry, which have minimal impact on the market for commodities produced during the capitalist production process, have no bearing on capitalist crises. Those householders are not part of the distribution of incomes generated during the capitalist process. This, however, is a shrinking population. The ratio of the world's population participating in the production of global value in the sense of being part of the capitalist economy of production and consumption has increased rapidly since the early 1990s. Whereas a quarter of a century ago a much larger proportion of world households had to be satisfied with peasant incomes derived from noncommodified production, now a larger proportion of households and individuals are part of the global economy of commodity production *and* commodity consumption. There is an appreciably more unequal distribution when this new population is considered as part of the unit of analysis, along with the middle- and upper-income earners of the First World. In other words, there has been an addition of new populations to the global capitalist economy—mostly as low-wage workers in China and India or elsewhere in Southeast Asia and as producers of agricultural commodities in Africa, Asia, or Latin America—whose incomes are nowhere near the incomes of the majority of the workers in capitalist production a quarter of a century ago. Their wages fall far short of the values they create. Although their incomes in real terms are higher than in their earlier lives, their new consumption capacity does not and cannot approach the production capacity that they add to the global supply of commodities.

V

Income inequality and deficient effective demand, that is, insufficient capacity for consumption, are the ultimate causes of credit expansion.[16] The incomes of the middle classes in the world have not kept up with increases at the top. While incomes of the top earners have multiplied, the consumption potential of the middle categories has remained stagnant or increased modestly.[17] These are the social strata whose material improvement is the most system maintaining, which is why the *Economist* and similar journals were constantly celebrating the growing population that may be considered "middle class" in countries such as India. It is indeed their consumption potential that would counteract the tendency toward an underconsumption crisis. If, however, their incomes do not grow in tandem with the global increase in production, credit must be brought in.

The debt economy designed to boost consumption demand is everywhere, ranging from personal debt incurred through credit-card use to housing mortgages. The ratio of total credit-market debt to GDP in the United States was 350 percent in 2008, up from 150 percent in the late 1970s. In many middle-income countries, the number of credit cards in use has increased from none in the 1970s to millions now, and outstanding debt on them has increased especially rapidly in the past five years. Personal and commercial credit have always been necessary tools of the capitalist market, but on a temporary basis. What we have seen since the mid-1980s is that credit has increased steadily to become an integral component of effective demand. What the *New York Times* dubbed "the global lure of plastic" has contributed to the debt trap everywhere.[18] Wherever there is production of value that cannot be purchased because of inequality in incomes, wherever there is underconsumption, credit comes to the rescue in order to boost effective demand. More than a temporary fix to the structural problem, credit in this form addresses the social problem as well by actually allowing the middle class to "keep up" in the new consumption economy. The living standards of the middle classes are maintained by means of rising debt.

The other side of the inequality coin is what leads top earners to invest their savings in unproductive markets that we commonly associate with finance. There are limits to the conspicuous consumption of the rich, and if the incomes of the masses remain stagnant, there is no incentive to invest their savings to increase the production capacity of consumables. The money, instead, is placed in financial circuits, chasing higher returns in the form of appreciating prices, whether in real estate, art, shares, or sophisticated financial assets. As more money comes in, the price of the assets in which the rich put their money will increase; the markets will become attractive because of the gains; more money will be invested, this time by the less rich; and so on. This is, of course, the dynamic of bubbles. Bubbles are difficult to avoid when a lot of money is chasing gains in markets that deal not in value-producing investment but in a representation, at several degrees remove, of some real activity. Shares were the principal bubble-generating asset before the Great Depression; the recent period has introduced many new categories of such assets, including derivatives, various kinds of options, credit-default swaps, and the like. This again is not unexpected: the finance-industry operators, with so much money thrown at them, obliged. To absorb the supply of funds, they employed PhDs in technical wizardry, used all the available communications technology, and created new financial markets that straddle the global economy.

The flow of money into such asset markets constituted a pyramid (Ponzi) scheme because new money was continuously entering these new markets that nobody understood very well, and as long as new money could be attracted, returns on "investment" in the financial sector remained high. As in all pyramid schemes, the question of how so much money in the financial sector, increasing at a rate much faster than world income and amounting at its peak to many multiples of the global GDP, could possibly claim even a normal rate of return remained unasked. As long as the returns on paper were plowed back into the financial sector, the game could continue. When it became apparent that the foundations were less than strong and alert players started to leave the market, new money stopped coming and the pyramid collapsed.

Both because it leads to such financial bubbles caused by high incomes that cannot be invested in productive sectors and because of the necessary appeal to the credit economy in order to increase effective demand, underconsumption can be seen as the root cause of the expansion of finance. In other words, the growing inequality of incomes that is the reason for underconsumption is also the cause of the financial crisis that triggered the "Great Recession." The credit mechanism that temporarily solved the underconsumption problem was an obvious short-term measure that intensified the adverse effects of excessive financialization and left the economy vulnerable to speculation and busts.

As argued earlier, inequality engenders a consumption deficit, for the reason that the rich do not and cannot consume as much of their income as do the poor and the middle-income populations. Since consumption capacity is limited due to the prevailing income distribution, there is not much incentive on the part of capitalists to invest their savings in order to expand production capacity. But, as Marx and Engels argued in the *Manifesto,* the capitalist world economy has been expanding to new geographies and new populations ever since its inception. This is why oversaving in one part of the capitalist world can potentially become investment (and lead to the purchase of capital goods) in another part, where commodity relations are beginning to deepen. This is what Rosa Luxemburg had envisaged as the answer to the problems of "expanded reproduction" in the already capitalist countries: they could solve their oversaving dilemma by exporting capital, as long as there were new populations to incorporate into the capitalist economy to make into wage workers.[19] The index of such an escape, of successfully avoiding the underconsumption problem at home, would be the channeling of the excess savings into investment abroad. This means that there would ideally be a net outflow of value from the mature capitalist countries, where there is the risk of underconsumption, to the periphery, where populations newly introduced to capitalist markets would consume a much higher proportion of their incomes and might import the surplus production of the capital-exporting countries. In other words, economies running the risk of underconsumption crises should run trade surpluses (more exports than imports), to be purchased by the countries that are the destination of their capital exports.

As we know, however, during the years leading to the 2008 crisis, there was a net flow of capital *into* the United States, overshadowing the entire outflow of investment to the South. The United States was receiving close to 5 percent of its GDP annually as investment from abroad, allowing it to run a trade deficit—exactly the opposite of Rosa Luxemburg's solution to the underconsumption problem. At the same time, there was an outflow of capital from the one country that could potentially absorb the excess capital originating in mature capitalist countries. Until 2008, Chinese authorities did not opt to increase consumption by, for example, raising wages or social expenditures. This would have increased their capacity to import; instead they opted for higher savings and ran a trade surplus. With a more rapid increase in disposable incomes in China, the flow of surplus capital would not have been so perverse. As it was, Chinese savings contributed to further inflate the credit balloon in the United States. Since there was demand by China for US securities, the Federal Reserve could maintain low interest rates.

There is another way than direct or portfolio investment in which flows to developing capitalist countries may be assured—through what has been called international Keynesianism. Although it mostly remains wishful thinking, international aid has been on the agenda since the end of World War II, and the Cold War years witnessed a pragmatic application of aid policy, especially by the United States. The Brandt commission in 1983 proposed a more consistent and deliberate effort to transfer funds from the North to the South, with the intention of developing the South in a manner consistent with human dignity. The funds would serve to generate basic levels of health and education and sustainability and thus to combat poverty. There have, of course, been many such reports with the intention of creating a one-world consciousness, hoping for good acts on the part of the North. International Keynesianism is the broad label for such flows, mediated through states, designed to promote "development."[20] International Keynesianism redistributes world income downward and decreases global inequality and would contribute toward a solution to the problem of underconsumption.

As growth and crisis fluctuations become more obviously global, the issue of world-system-wide demand has come on the agenda. The calls for greater stimulation of demand in Asia are arguments in this line of thinking. The export-oriented growth, neglect of the domestic market, and high savings rates that had made the Asian miracle possible are now adding to the burden of global underconsumption. The crisis response in China in 2009 seemed to recognize the need for change, as economic managers shifted their emphasis from maximizing trade surpluses to spending stimulus money in domestic development projects and to promoting the purchase of consumer durables in the countryside.

Although world politics and global ideology do not seem inclined to produce a consensus around this project, the international transfer of excess capital to countries where it will be used for purchasing the excess production capacity of the world economy is an effective measure for increasing global aggregate demand. The problem cannot be addressed through national policy alone. Some form of international Keynesianism will have to be practiced as a measure of global regulation if recurrent underconsumption crises and the credit speculation they give rise to are to be avoided. There is, however, neither adequate institutional capacity at the global level nor sufficient political and moral awareness to implement global policies—even if they can be shown to serve the material interests of the rich countries.

VI

The argument based on underconsumption suggests that the only real solution with any chance to repair structural imbalances is a redistribution of incomes that would align consumption with productive capacity. Short-term fixes such as Keynesian stimulus packages where the government picks up the slack are temporary, unless they amount to greater equality through, for example, social expenditures that become permanent rights. Social expenditures are one form of improving income distribution since they liberate personal income to be spent on goods other than health, education, or child care.

In fact, J. A. Hobson based his theory of social democracy and imperialism on the choice between exporting the underconsumption problem and social democracy.[21] In Hobson's formulation, the imperialist exporting of capital becomes necessary because the capitalist system accumulates capital that cannot be put to profitable use domestically. The domestic market cannot absorb the potential output since the workers' wages are too depressed to generate sufficient demand. This is a classic underconsumptionist argument, but it is important because Hobson frames the problem as a choice between imperialism and an ethically desirable, more equal distribution of income, or social democracy. If there is social democracy, then there is no oversaving, and the need for capital exports does not arise. As argued earlier, a good distribution of income would in fact solve the problem of underconsumption.

One problem with the classic understanding of social democracy is that it is supposed to work through workers' remuneration and wage improvement. This can no longer be seen as sufficient policy to combat income inequality, for the simple reasons that stable employment for most of the world's workers has become a luxury and wage income for the newer workers of the South has decreased as a proportion of household income. The implications of these developments cast social-democratic policy in a new light. It is much more evident in the case of the countries of the South that new urban populations do not expect to become full-time workers who earn wage incomes sufficient to sustain a livelihood. Instead, they are faced with irregular employment situations that do not offer any stability. A proper wage relationship may last a while, followed by self-employment or informal work in a hidden workshop or on the street or at home doing contract work. All these employment relations are typically precarious, dependent on market conditions, on the whims of regulators and enforcers, on global conditions and transnational commodity chains of networked corporations that might shift their sources of supply according to some calculation in the head office. At the household level as well, there is no expectation that a single wage earner can account for sufficient income for basic reproduction. Household incomes derive from many sources, as members engage in different kinds of work, including domestic production. It is often the case that urban dwellers retain links with their villages, sometimes renting out the land they still own or even having their plots cropped and tended, to go back for the harvest themselves. More recent urban settlers find employment back in the countryside as seasonal agricultural laborers. Recent accounts of newly urbanized workers in Shanghai and Bangkok returning to their villages after losing their jobs in the city are evidence of sporadic wage earners resorting to an extreme strategy when other options have been exhausted. In sum, most urban wage earning is characterized by part-lifetime employment, which, even under the best conditions, is unstable and precarious. From the perspective of the household, it is exceptional (perhaps confined to the emerging "middle class") that wage earnings constitute the decisive preponderance of household income.[22]

This last conjecture may be argued by reference to the increased flow of migrants from the countryside to the megalopolises of the least-developed countries in the South, a migration that gives rise to the newly reidentified phenomenon of slums.[23] The survival of marginal populations in the large cities of the Third World is a question that has been discussed extensively in social science literature since the 1970s, when the dominant modernization paradigm had to give up its optimistic outlook on the absorption of peasants into the modern sector and accept that formal waged employment for the majority of the new urban dwellers was unlikely. That this new population would likely remain in the "informal sector," without ever enjoying steady employment, was the implicit expectation.

There is, however, a growing suspicion that the present conjuncture might be signaling an even more ominous, longer-lasting development. Since the advent of globalized production, liberalized trade, and worldwide supply chains, there have been arguments that the availability of capital and a huge potential supply of low-wage labor in the newly incorporated Asian countries will disturb the balances that have prevailed over the previous decades. What if the introduction of the vast labor resources of China and India into the world economy has irreversibly changed the equation in the rest of the world, where urban populations continue to increase? Not only might wages remain permanently depressed, but there is also the possibility that low-skill manufacturing jobs might disappear altogether except in the exporting countries of Asia. Another structural dimension of the changes in employment patterns is the long-term trend that new jobs are in the motley category of "services." "Services," in the lower, less-education-requiring ranges—personal services such as caregiving, restaurant work, domestic help—mostly offer precarious employment and low wages. This predicament adds to the circumstances in which nonwage income has to be tapped as supplement.

While it is the cities of the South where the insufficiency of wage income to sustain the workers' livelihoods is most evident, the growing share of increasingly precarious service employment is also a feature of employment patterns in the North. The permanent exclusion especially of less-educated young males inhabiting *banlieues* or projects in excluded neighborhoods, often stigmatized as cultural or racial others, has become a well-rehearsed trope of social science.[24] There is also the "end of work" literature that signals a momentous change in the assumption that work will be the principal medium of cohesion in society, with the emerging view that increasing productivity robs the certainty of employment from all but the creative class, or the self-programming, educated, postindustrial workers, with the rest of the population, even in the First World, enjoying only a temporary and uncertain relationship with employment.[25]

For populations in the cities of the North, most of the household income strategies enumerated earlier will not be available in the future: self-employment, for instance, in street vending, is not an expanding job category, there are limits to domestic production in apartment buildings, and home work is not readily available without labor-intensive technology. Nor are any links with villages of origin maintained. There is, however, another component of household income that household budget studies term "transfers," which include informal family or community assistance as well as more formal benefits associated with the state component of the welfare regime. These formal transfers, or social expenditures, which range from housing subsidies, child and elderly care, and unemployment benefits to basic income contributions and old-age pensions, are making up a growing share of household budgets of lower-income populations. It is clear that decreasing employment opportunity and stagnating wage incomes will further highlight the importance of social policy. With the advent of permanent levels of high unemployment, the role that public expenditures play in social reproduction has become paramount and has made social policy into a most contested political field.

Growing demands for social assistance and public transfers on the one hand and fiscal constraints on the other have defined the political parameters of welfare-state restructuring. Despite all the political attempts to reduce the proportion of social expenditures out of GDP, however, it has increased in most countries. Only in the northern European countries, where the proportion was highest prior to the 1980s, have there been small declines; otherwise the trend has been upward. For the OECD as a whole, the average of social expenditures as a proportion of GDP was 20.6 percent in 2005, as opposed to 17.7 percent in 1985; in the countries of the EU, the average was 23 percent in 1985 and 26.9 percent in 2006.[26] There is an impression that the welfare state is in retreat, owing to the fact that the demand for social expenditures has increased much faster, partly because of the employment situation described earlier and partly for demographic reasons. It is indeed true that states cannot afford to be as generous as they once were because there are many more claimants than before; if, however, the share of social expenditures in GDP is taken as the metric, no such retreat is identifiable.[27]

The picture is somewhat different in the South, where the welfare state is only in its infancy.[28] In most countries of the South, rudimentary welfare systems geared to state employees and to the organized working class have been in place; these tend to exclude the least advantaged portions of the working population while rewarding the minority of workers who are formally employed with pensions and health insurance. During most of the developmentalist period, newly urbanized workers had to rely on their families and their connections with the village in order to be able to cope with life-cycle risks. Now, however, a more formal extension of social policy to those who need it most, namely, those who have no hope of steady employment, has to be on the agenda.[29] This was recognized by international policy agencies in the form of the World Bank's relaxing its market orthodoxy and shifting its attention to social assistance and health-care systems and, more generally, to poverty reduction.[30] Universalization of benefits such as health care and the institution of social assistance programs resembling basic income guarantees, especially when they are formulated as citizenship rights (e.g., "conditional cash transfers" and old-age pensions for the poor who have no other social security, in countries such as Brazil, Mexico, Turkey, and South Africa), are signs that point to the growing importance of "transfers" in making up the total household income for the urban poor.[31] The recent institution of universal health care (e.g., in South Korea and Taiwan) is a strong move toward decommodification of needs, as is a commitment to the provision of low-cost housing.

The programs that increase social expenditures funded by the central revenues of the state also constitute measures for redistribution of income. The European welfare state has the impact of making income distribution more equal: social expenditures are calculated to lower the Gini coefficient, the standard measure of income distribution in which zero would denote a perfectly equal distribution, by an average of one-third. When the welfare state is weaker, as in the United States, there is more poverty, and the income distribution is more unequal.[32] Social expenditures in the South, although growing, are not close to the quantitative weight of social expenditures in EU countries: they amount to between 10 and 15 percent of GDP in Argentina, Chile, Brazil, and Turkey.[33] It should be remembered that Greece, Spain, and Portugal had lower ratios at the time of their adhesion to the European Community in the 1980s; they adjusted rapidly, however, and they now have harmonized with their northern partners. In general, social expenditures seem to increase as a proportion of national income as societies get richer—with the consequence that income distribution gets better.

Social protection is instituted to respond to basic needs and to sustain what the society considers to be a decent life. At its most accomplished, it is a way of decommodifying the means of livelihood.[34] It is also, however, a mechanism for income distribution; what it does is to raise the level of the social wage, especially when the private wage (that part of the livelihood that comes from the market) is not amenable to such manipulation because the workers have a weak bargaining position or because there is no prolabor political mobilization. As discussed earlier, globalization has changed the parameters of the class struggle, and conditions now structurally favor capitalists. Unemployment and the threat of outsourcing are factors disciplining labor in even the lower-wage countries. Businesses and states argue that international competition makes it impossible to increase wages. This is the "private" component of wage income. By contrast, the burden of the "social wage" falls not on the employers directly but on public revenues. The cost of the social component of poor people's incomes will be absorbed in taxes, and its impact will be dissipated. Health-care reform and poverty-reduction programs are politically popular; even neoliberal politicians are not viscerally opposed. Once such programs are in place, it is extremely difficult to retract them; they become permanent features of the social terrain.

Social expenditures contribute to the provision of basic needs such as health, education, subsidized housing, and child and elderly care and therefore increase the capacity for private consumption. Since the rich can already access all these services privately, through the market, social expenditures improve the income distribution and counteract the tendency toward underconsumption without resorting to a massive expansion of consumer credit. The stimulus package in China, for example, included both employment creation (in infrastructure projects in the interior of the country, where addressing regional inequality would improve income distribution) and moves toward expanding health services (increasing the social wage).

Social policy permanently raises the real incomes of the target population, and a global predilection in favor of increasing social expenditures in each country would start to heal global income inequality. Messages relating to the desirability of increasing social expenditures are being transmitted through opinion-leading international organizations and advocacy platforms such as social forums. The World Bank and various agencies of the United Nations have contributed to the making of public opinion by launching programs for poverty reduction, public services for the poor, and universal health care. Now that neoliberal ascendancy has come to an end, these programs, initially criticized as palliative measures designed to render neoliberalism more palatable, seem more convincing.[35] Antipoverty policies make a real contribution to livelihoods—especially in places where global markets condemn former peasants to urban joblessness. For these populations of the new slums, state expenditures for delivering basic needs such as paved roads, clean water, transportation, and other urban amenities improve the quality of life immeasurably.[36] Healthcare measures relieve anxiety and improve the quality of life for poor beneficiaries to a greater extent than any other program of comparable cost.

As long as the underlying cause of the crisis, worsening global inequality, is not addressed, the recovery of the economy will likely remain temporary, and any attempt to stimulate the economy will likely create yet more speculation and bubbles. There will be incentives to expand the credit mechanism, and financial engineers will find ways of creating ever-riskier instruments and assets. The risks involved in financial expansion will in turn threaten the real economy. More important, however, is the inability of the real economy to guarantee employment. It may well be that this global crisis will have been the punctuating instance of what many people have feared, that gains in productivity are such that good portions of the labor force are becoming redundant, that the market will condemn larger proportions of the potential labor force to permanent unemployment. The way global capitalism has evolved threatens the livelihoods of masses of people who cannot even hope to be employed; Rosa Luxemburg's aphorism that "there is one thing that is worse than being exploited by capital, and that is not being exploited by capital" seems to have attained transparent validity. For large populations, exploitation through wage employment will likely remain a fervent wish, not to be fulfilled. This is a frightening prospect within the parameters of a system that requires a labor-market-mediated participation in the social world. It will lead to permanent exclusion of marginalized populations and political strife. Against this alternative, social policy emerges as the only platform that has a chance to retain democratic legitimacy for the modern state while addressing the problems caused by unregulated markets. Social policy may improve income distribution within countries and may even create employment outside the logic of "market rationality." Such nation-state-based policy would, of course, be immeasurably strengthened if accompanied by attempts at *inter*national redistribution.

While it is probably naive to expect the constitution of an effective form of global governance directed toward the provision of social services in the foreseeable future, the ravages of the neoliberal era may well have created an environment in which the kind of reaction anticipated by Karl Polanyi to the unregulated market may be emerging.[37] The "double movement," as Polanyi termed it, covers a range of disparate responses to the unregulated rule of the market that tends to upset social balances and "destroy society." Society as a whole defends itself against the domination of the unregulated market. It is this wide range of responses that permits the inclusion of reactions from international technocrats together in the same category with World Social Forum participants, poor people's movements, labor struggles, and slum dwellers' or peasants' resistance, as instances of the double movement.[38] Deliberate political mobilization defining itself on "socialist" or "social-democratic" platforms is only one component of such wide-spectrum defense against the market. Novel forms of resistance and alliances come on the agenda in the new networked and globalized society in formation. France's President Sarkozy's bringing together Nobel laureates Amartya Sen and Joseph Stiglitz to establish a more adequate measure of human welfare than the economists' preferred GNP feeds into UN agencies' attempts to highlight poverty and human development; the World Bank reforms itself to focus on poverty; governments scramble to find ways to limit the damages caused by the financial sector.

Neoliberalism has lost the script after three decades of ascendancy. The new platform emerging in reaction is not yet coherent, nor is there a purposeful leadership. All the reactions, however, bring to light the enormous risks involved in the increasing marginalization of large slices of humanity. Whether from above or below, whether they follow a project or merely offer resistance, whether there is a deliberate attempt at global networking or militant localism, these movements all seek to redirect attention to human needs—and might even manage to save capitalism from the sickly embrace of neoliberalism.

CHAPTER 7

The Crisis of Global Capitalism:
Toward a New Economic Culture?

Manuel Castells

The hypothesis underlying the analysis presented in this chapter is that the crisis of global capitalism that exploded in 2008 is structural and multidimensional. Therefore, even if the free fall of the economy was contained by late 2009, thanks to massive government intervention around the world, it is not likely that we will see a return to the social and economic conditions that characterized the rise of deregulated, global informational capitalism in the preceding three decades. The policies and strategies that are currently in place to handle the crisis may result in a sharply different economic system, just as the New Deal, the construction of the European welfare state, and the Bretton Woods global financial architecture ushered in a new form of capitalism in the aftermath of the 1930s Depression and World War II.[1] Furthermore, the model of Keynesian capitalism of the 1950s was called into question after the crisis of the 1970s and the economic restructuring that took place under the combined influence of three independent but interrelated developments: a new technological paradigm, a new form of globalization, and the new cultures that emerged from the social movements of the 1960s and 1970s. The new system, global informational capitalism, and its social structure, the network society, displayed some historically irreversible features (such as the logic of the global network society based on digital networking of all core human activities), together with some components susceptible to change under the impact of crises arising from the contradictions of this model of economic growth. Thus, the current crisis stems from the destructive trends induced by the dynamics of deregulated global capitalism, anchored in an unfettered financial market made of global computer networks and fed by a relentless production of synthetic securities as the main source of capital accumulation and capital borrowing.[2]

We have reached the threshold of this particular type of capitalism, which entered a process of implosion only halted by the intervention of an old acquaintance, the state, which had already been sent to the oblivion of history by the apologists of market fundamentalism. One of the key measures to stop the free fall of this form of capitalism is the reregulation of financial markets and financial institutions, which is tantamount to drastically restricting lending. Therefore, we are witnessing the end of easy credit. And because easy credit fueled consumer demand, and consumption accounted for three-fourths of GDP growth in the United States and two-thirds in Europe over the past decade, this could signal the transformation of an economy and society based primarily on mass consumption of commodified goods and services. Still, for many, the crisis can be overcome by fine-tuning the regulatory machine and restarting the engine of demand via public spending. Then we would return, in essence, to business as usual. I argue that this is a mirage. And if this is the case, there will be a new economy and, therefore, a new economic culture. As the period of triumphant global informational capitalism was linked to the hegemony of a culture of unrestricted individualism, economic liberalism, technological optimism, and glorified greed, any substantial socioeconomic restructuring of global capitalism implies the formation of a new economic culture. Since culture (a specific set of values and beliefs orienting behavior) is a material practice, we should be able to detect the embryos of such culture in the spontaneous adaptation of people's lives to the constraints and opportunities arising from the crisis. The observation of these protocultural forms of a new economic culture, and of their interaction with the contours and evolution of the economic crisis, constitutes the matter of the reflection proposed in this text. However, to proceed with this exploration as systematically as possible, I first characterize the current economic crisis and explain the process of its formation. I then refer to the multidimensionality of this crisis, as other major crises that were already rampant in this model of social organization came to light when the current patterns of life appeared to be unsustainable. The critical point of the crisis is the gradual undermining of mass consumption, as this was the key mechanism of capital accumulation, social stability, and ideological legitimization.

Next, I examine and evaluate the policies and strategies that governments have set into place to manage the crisis and to restore economic growth. Finally, I attempt to propose an empirically grounded typology of social practices that reconstruct economic activities away from the circuit of commodified consumption-production, which is characterized by working to produce and consume, borrowing to keep up consumption, and artificially generating capital (securitization and derivatives) to expand the lending capacity.

Roots and Characteristics of the Economic Crisis of 2008–...?

The economic crisis that exploded in the last quarter of 2008 developed in four waves.[3] The first originated in the collapse of the financial and real-estate markets, particularly in the United States, which brought some of the leading financial institutions into insolvency and threatened the entire financial system. The second extended the financial breakdown to the economy at large, causing the technical bankruptcy of major manufacturing corporations (e.g., General Motors and Chrysler) and the phasing out of thousands of companies around the world. The third induced massive unemployment (between 9 percent and 20 percent in major developed economies by the end of 2009), as well as underemployment, sharply curtailing income. The fourth drastically shrunk demand as jobs were lost, wages were frozen, and companies and households shifted from borrowing to saving to repay their debts, while financial institutions were compelled to clean their balance sheets and reduce lending. Let us examine the process of crisis formation as a necessary step to understanding the different forms of capitalism that may emerge after the crisis.

The global financial crisis was the direct consequence of the specific dynamics of the global informational economy whose analysis I presented some time ago, together with other analysts.[4] It resulted from the combination of six factors. First, the liberalization and deregulation of financial markets and financial institutions allowed the quasi-free flow of capital across companies and around the world, thereby overwhelming the regulatory capacity of national regulators. Second, the technological transformation of finance provided the basis for the constitution of a global financial market around global computer networks and gave financial institutions the computational capacity to operate advanced mathematical models. These models were deemed capable of managing the increasing complexity of the financial system, operating globally interdependent financial markets through electronic transactions effected at lightning speed. Third, the securitization of every economic organization, activity, or asset made financial valuation the paramount standard to assess the value of firms, governments, and even entire economies. Furthermore, new financial technologies made possible the invention of numerous exotic financial products, such as derivatives, futures, options, and securitized insurance (e.g., credit-default swaps), which became increasingly complex and intertwined, ultimately virtualizing capital and eliminating any semblance of transparency in the markets so that accounting procedures became meaningless. Fourth, because financial markets only partially function according to the logic of supply and demand and are largely shaped by "information turbulences,"[5] the mortgage crisis that began in 2007 in the United States after the bursting of the real-estate bubble reverberated throughout the global financial system. Indeed, although a similar real-estate crash in Japan in the early 1990s had severe effects on the Japanese economy, its impact on the rest of the world was limited because of the lower level of interpenetration of Japanese real-estate markets with global financial markets. Fifth, the lack of proper supervision in securities trading and financial practices enabled daring brokers to pump up the economy and their personal bonuses through increasingly risky lending practices. In 2007, worldwide, the value of financial companies' assets over the value of the securities the companies sold was just 1.5 percent. At an aggregate level, in the United States, the debt of financial companies increased from 39 percent of GDP in 1988 to 111 percent of GDP in 2008. Sixth, the imbalance between capital accumulation in newly industrializing countries, such as China and oil-producing countries, and capital borrowing in the richest economies facilitated a credit-led expansion in the United States and Europe and increased the risk of financial collapse by lending the capital accumulated in these economies to the United States and other countries, so as to sustain the solvency and import capability of these economies while taking advantage of favorable rates. The massive military spending of the US government to foot the bill for its adventure in Iraq was also financed through debt, to the point that Asian countries, and particularly China, now hold a large share of US Treasury bonds, thus intertwining the Asian Pacific and the US budgets in a decisive manner.[6]

The paradox is that the crisis coincided with the rise of the new economy, an economy defined by a substantial surge in productivity as the result of technological innovation, networking, and higher education levels in the workforce.[7] Indeed, in the United States, where the crisis first started, cumulative productivity growth reached almost 30 percent between 1998 and 2008. However, because of shortsighted management policies, real wages increased by only 2 percent over the decade, and in fact weekly earnings of college-educated workers fell by 6 percent between 2003 and 2008. And yet real-estate prices soared during the early 2000s, and lending institutions fed the frenzy by providing mortgages, ultimately backed by federal institutions, to the same workers whose wages were quasi-stagnant or diminishing. The hope was that productivity increases would ultimately catch up with wages as the benefits of growth would trickle down. This never happened because financial companies and realtors reaped the benefits of the productive economy, inducing an unsustainable bubble. The financial services industry's share of profits increased from 10 percent in the 1980s to 40 percent in 2007, and the value of its shares increased from 6 percent to 23 percent, while the industry only accounts for 5 percent of private-sector employment. In short, the very real benefits of the new economy were appropriated in the securities market and used to generate a much greater mass of virtual capital that multiplied its value through lending to a crowd of eager consumers-borrowers. Thus, in the United States, between 1993 and 2008, bank lending accounted for only 20 percent of total net lending. The rest came from money market funds, exchange-traded funds, hedge funds, and investment banks that had transformed into lending agencies in a deregulated environment. Furthermore, most banks also relied largely on securitization, instead of their own deposits, to finance their loans. And they lent to each other, so as to spread the risk. But in fact when their liabilities were exposed, their intertwining spread the crisis. This damaging exposure came as a result of the bursting of the real-state bubble, which revealed the extent of household debt, in both the United States and Europe, and subsequently consumers' inability to repay loans. However, this crisis was in fact the consequence of the liberalizing policies designed to stimulate the financial market by banking on home equity. In 1982, the properties of US households were worth 106 percent of GDP, and their debts amounted to only half of it. Then lending was deregulated by the Monetary Control Act of 1980 and the Garn–St. Germain Act of 1982. It became possible for households to borrow on the value of their homes, which they did eagerly, particularly during the 1990s, when the value of property and stocks increased. When the value of property fell sharply in 2006, the reality of unsustainable indebtedness struck everyone, everywhere. In the 1960s, the savings rate for US households over their disposable income was about 8 percent. In the early 2000s, the savings rate had gone down to 2.7 percent. Though the aggregate worth of households in the United States increased from $42.1 trillion in 2001 to $69.3 trillion in 2007, it fell to $51.1 trillion in the first quarter of 2009 after the decline in property prices. In proportional terms, more household wealth was destroyed in the United States during this crisis than in the crisis of the 1930s. While inflation was kept relatively in check throughout the OECD because of significant productivity growth, the gap between loan size and the ability of both consumers and institutions to repay what they had borrowed widened. In the United States, household debt rose from 3 percent of disposable income in 1998 to 130 percent in 2008. As a result, prime mortgage delinquencies as a percentage of loans increased from 2.5 percent in 1998 to 118 percent in 2008.

Yet no one could do much about it because the global financial market had escaped the control of any investor, government, or regulatory agency. It had become what I called, in 2000, a "global automaton," imposing its logic over the economy and society at large, including its own creators. And so, a financial crisis of unprecedented proportions unfolded around the world, dramatically ending the myth of the self-regulated market, calling into question the predictions of most mainstream economists, and sending governments and businesses into a frantic scramble to tame the wild automaton that went into reverse and devoured tens of thousands of jobs (i.e., family lives) on a daily basis. The total market capitalization of the financial markets fell by more than half in 2008. Many financial companies collapsed (Lehman Brothers being only the most notorious of them), and others were brought to near bank-ruptcy. The IMF evaluates the global loss for financial institutions at about US$4.3 trillion. The losses for the top-twenty American banks in 2009–11 are projected to be as high as $560 billion, while their projected income, under the most favorable conditions, would be just $575 billion. Of course, there is not much left to feed new capital lending. Estimates for the United States in 2009 pointed to the disappearance of six thou-sand out of eight thousand American banks.

Furthermore, the economic crisis accentuates the social and envi-ronmental unsustainability of the current model of economic growth while increasing the visibility of such unsustainability.

A Multidimensional Crisis

The fading model of economic growth based on global financial capital-ism has enhanced a number of destructive trends that, altogether, con-stitute the crisis of a certain model of social organization. Here, I simply remind the reader of the main dimensions of this crisis and emphasize their interrelation.

The environmental crisis, epitomized by the process of global warming, threatens our livability on the planet (not the planet itself, by the way, which would do much better without our presence). It is largely the consequence of a mode of production that treats the environment as a free resource and does not include the environmental, economic, or social costs of production and consumption in its accounting. The automobile industry, the icon of twentieth-century industrial capitalism, is a clear example of ecologically irresponsible productivism.[8]

The environmental crisis is closely related to the urban crisis we are experiencing in most of the world. But the urban crisis is much deeper—it influences the deterioration of everyday life, the downgrading of public health, the structural gridlock of the transportation system, and the rise of the City of Fear, marked by violence and distrust. In its current mani-festation, it is directly related to the specific urban form resulting from a society organized around global networks of wealth, power, and informa-tion. I have shown in my work the spatial architecture of the network society. It is made of nodes and networks that link places throughout the planet depending on the programs of these networks. The nodes of these networks constitute the major metropolitan areas of our world, and these nodes attract capital, talent, and technology, as well as the huddled masses of countries in an endless process of restructuring/destructuring. These metropolitan regions are at the same time the sources of innovation and wealth accumulation, of cultural creativity, of communication, and of power making while sharpening social exclusion and social conflicts among global citizens of the world and surviving locals. Urban space has been submitted to the dynamics of real estate, and real estate became the primary choice for speculative financial investment. Financial markets became intertwined with housing markets, and consumption was primarily fueled by risky lending that used these subprime mortgages as collateral for other financial assets recombined in synthetic securities. Because home ownership was the basis of credit to consumers, as well as the material foundation of their consumption-dominated life, the collapse of the housing market led simultaneously to the bankruptcy of the financial system and to the destruction of the value of household assets that were supporting their borrowing capacity. Thus, after the crisis in the housing market, there is no more borrowing power for consumers and no more credit available from lending institutions. In the United States, in 2008, capital lending from capital markets was reduced by almost one trillion dollars—that is, more than the lending capacity of the entire banking system in 2007. Therefore, the crisis of this particular model of urban growth is the key connecting point between the financial crisis, the environmental crisis, and the crisis of the consumption society.[9]

The current crisis makes more apparent the crisis of everyday life resulting from the incapacity of social services, markets, and institutions to adapt to the crisis of patriarchy. The patriarchal nuclear family has been called into question by the transformation of women's consciousness, coupled with the needs from the expansion of the market to incorporate new, educated, and more vulnerable labor, over the past three decades, in both advanced and developing countries. There is an increasing mismatch between the traditional model of societal self-representation of society, based on patriarchy, and the reality of life for a substantial proportion of households (the majority in developed countries).

Households formed by a heterosexual couple and their underage children account only for between 20 percent and 30 percent of households in advanced societies. New types of families (e.g., extended households formed by networks of single women and their children, same-sex marriages) and new lifestyles (centered on single living) are on the rise everywhere. These trends are in contradiction with the characteristics of the current housing stock, as well as with the structure of service provision inherited from a previous social/cultural structure. The gradual pattern of transformation was proceeding with relative ease because the economic-growth machine was churning out jobs, income, and credit cards to the individual worker. When jobs are lost, income is reduced, and credit is frozen, the absence of a family network to cushion the impact of the crisis aggravates the direct consequences of the crisis for livelihood, particularly for less-paid women and their children. In countries with a well-developed welfare state, some of the impact is absorbed by institutional coverage of basic needs. In less-protected societies, the individualized social structure becomes a landscape of despair. Even in countries with long-term unemployment insurance and universal health care, the length of the crisis may reach a breaking point in terms of minimum survival capacity and budgetary limits to government spending. In other words, as the ties of solidarity of the traditional family structure have been weakened without yet operating the transition to a new form of egalitarian family, the cushion provided by the family structure in periods of economic distress has been seriously undermined, with the obvious devastating consequences for a way of life based on market relationships and commodity consumption.

The communication system, still based on the mass media for the majority of the population, is entering a fundamental crisis at various levels. We must remember it is primarily based on advertising revenue.[10] First, if there is a decisive shrinkage of solvent demand, the effects of advertising on consumption dwindle correspondingly because it becomes almost perverse to stimulate a demand that cannot be realized. Second, corporate austerity (induced by declining profits and financial difficulties) translates into a reduction of the advertising budget to be shared among the same number of media outlets, thus reducing revenue for media corporations. Third, the Internet-based new media, including social media networks, are increasingly taking over much of socialized communication, and corporations have not yet found an effective business model for the Internet. Altogether, there is a trend to diminish the role of mass media in shaping the public mind, a trend that is already present across the majority of people under thirty years of age. It follows a fundamental transformation of the production of cultural patterns in our society, with an increasing separation between communication production and media consumption.

Perhaps the most fundamental crisis is the crisis of the political institutions that are in charge of managing crises. Because if management mechanisms malfunction, the crisis may spiral out of control. Therefore, the crisis of the state is not simply a derivative of the economic crisis but one of its sources. This is because if we accept that this is largely a crisis resulting from the absence of regulation and supervision on behalf of the public interest, the ideological and political demise of the responsibility of the state in the past two decades is arguably at the root of its cause. However, this is not simply a matter of the political class lacking the foresight to manage the new world. It is structural as well. It starts with the often-repeated fact that we live in a globalized world without an effective global governance system, notwithstanding some ad hoc institutional partnerships that I have conceptualized as the network state, a sort of protostate of the global network society.[11] Yet the "proto-" is of essence when a structural crisis causes the walls to crumble, since we still do not have the appropriate instruments to act on the global financial market and the global consequences of the crisis. Furthermore, the role of the state is undermined at two fundamental levels. One is ideological, because the battle of political ideas in the past two decades was won by the so-called neoliberal paradigm emphasizing the role of the market and decrying the intervention of the state in economy and society. Although the extent of the conservative libertarian influence varies among countries, in all cases it put on the defensive, particularly in the media, the traditional supporters of the welfare state. Another, and more fundamental, political factor is the crisis of political legitimacy throughout the world. In fact, it was because of the crisis of political legitimacy that the critics of state intervention were able to delegitimize the intervention of the state on behalf of the public interest. Surveys from around the world show that people do support government responsibility in health or education and would support taxation for this purpose, but they do not trust their political leaders to use their taxes on their behalf. Consistent survey data for the past ten years show that, on average, two-thirds of citizens in the world do not consider their governments to represent the will of the people, and this data holds in the United States and in Europe, with the exception of Scandinavia. The roots of this global crisis of political legitimacy are complex, and so I refer readers to my book on the matter.[12] But its relationship with the other dimensions of the crisis is highly significant. On the one hand, because people do not trust their political representatives, governments have a relatively small margin for daring decisions in a democratic environment in which elections dictate the pace of what citizens can tolerate. On the other hand, the generalized skepticism of citizens vis-à-vis their institutions did not have serious consequences for social stability as long as they could consume and be merry on credit. When the music stops, and they look at their foreclosed habitat filled with the objects of their borrowed consumption, their cynicism may well turn into rage. This is why the key differences between countries in this crisis will depend on the ability of political leaders to establish or restore trust. In this sense, the United Sates is in a better position because, by pure coincidence, a historic election took place at the very same time the crisis exploded, bringing into government a new leader with an explicit mandate to manage a crisis that was not blamed on him. Yet, because the eye of the storm formed in America, Obama has the daunting task of reinventing politics and reinventing capitalism with little cooperation or understanding from the political elites in a world that is objectively interdependent.

In sum, the model of socioeconomic organization associated with the rise of global informational capitalism appears to be unsustainable in multiple, interrelated dimensions, of which I have only mentioned the most salient. However, the technological revolution that unfolded simultaneously induced major gains in innovation and productivity that accelerated capital accumulation on a global scale, expanding consumer markets and labor inputs. Thus, as long as the global financial market, the driver and repository of capital accumulation, was able to proceed, in spite of recurrent financial crises (1992–94, 1997, 1998, 2000–2001), the growth of easy credit for governments, corporations, and households provided a sense of prosperity and security for enough people to have enough faith in the endless valuation of their assets and in the borrowed happiness of their consumed lives. When the unthinkable happened, and the money machine went into reverse, the house of cards on which the model was built began to collapse, revealing the harsh truth behind the myth of endless capital expansion on the vast landscape of an imagined flat world. At this point in the story, people still believe (they have to) in what politicians promise (they have to): happy times will be here again. Maybe. But if so, most likely it will be under a different pattern of economic rules, social organization, and institutional framework.

Out of the Crisis: The Promises and Limits of Remedial Policies

There is no such thing as a social vacuum. Social systems do not collapse as a result of their internal contradictions. The crisis, its conflicts, and its treatment are always a social process. And this social process, as all others, is enacted and shaped by the interests, values, beliefs, and strategies of social actors. This is to say that when a system does not reproduce its logic automatically, there are attempts to restore it as it was, as well as projects to reorganize a new system on the basis of a new set of interests and values. The ultimate outcome is often the result of conflicts and negotiations between the standard bearers of these different logics.

In terms of economic policies, a number of strategies are being considered, and some implemented, by governments, corporations, and international institutions. Gordon Brown may have made his last contribution on his way to early retirement by coining the notion of "the London Consensus" after the April 2009 G20 meeting, thus replacing the notorious "Washington Consensus" trumpeted in the past two decades. In the new policymaking perspective, the state, both as nation-state and network state, recovers its steering role and manages capitalism on behalf of capitalists and, if there are any resources left, for the well-being of the people. (Of course, avoiding collapse—specifically, financial collapse—is a precondition for people to have anything.) This is supposed to be accomplished through the following mechanisms:

- Refloating of major financial institutions and major corporations whose demise would bring havoc to the economy and society. This entails in some cases (e.g., AIG, General Motors) de facto temporary nationalization of corporations to be transformed under the aegis of the government and then returned to the private sector with viable business plans. According to the International Monetary

Fund, by mid-2009, governments around the world had invested US$432 billion to recapitalize their banks and had guaranteed bank debts for a total of US$4.65 trillion.[13] By 2009, the US government owned 34 percent of Citigroup, the British government owned 43 percent of Lloyds Banking Group and 90 percent of the Royal Bank of Scotland, and the German government owned 25 percent of Commerzbank and 90 percent of Hypo Real Estate. State-owned banks in China, India, Brazil, and Russia have increased their decisive share in overall investment and lending in the economy. In the United States, two-thirds of government capital injected in the banks went to the five largest banks, which were those with the lowest capital ratios, that had suffered the biggest loan losses during the crisis. Furthermore, these banks, which represent 63 percent of US market share, have now become de facto guaranteed by the federal government. It appears that no government is willing to repeat the dangerous experiment of letting a major financial company collapse, as was the case with Lehman Brothers. This strategy requires major public funding, and therefore a massive transfer of money from taxpayers to corporations, and a significant indebtedness of governments vis-à-vis global financial markets and major lenders, such as China and the sovereign funds.

- Regulation and strict national supervision of financial institutions and lending practices. This was particularly the case of the major financial overhaul in the United States announced by Obama in June 2009, with an increased role for the Federal Reserve Board and the creation of a federal agency to protect consumers (essentially, regulating the credit-card market, the key problem in credit markets, together with subprime housing mortgages). The G20 countries agreed during their September 2009 meeting on a number of regulatory measures and recommended that all financial institutions increase their assets to reach a level of 5 percent of the value of all securities sold, up from 1.5 percent in 2007. Surveillance measures on offshore financial centers and vague limitations on bonuses for financial executives were also considered.

- Design of a global financial regulator, perhaps using a variation of the College of Central Banks scheme proposed by Brown in the

London G20 summit. It is obvious that there is a long way to go before reaching any effective agreement on such a global regulator because of the redistribution of global power involved in this institutional reform.

- In the meantime, strengthening of international economic institutions, such as the IMF, the World Bank, and the Bank of International Settlements, with a new power-sharing agreement in favor of countries with capital in hand (China, India, Brazil, Russia, the oil-producing countries). In fact, the G20 has already replaced the G8 as the steering club of the global economy.

- At the national level, fiscal stimulus to restart the economy in key sectors, particularly industries that are particularly relevant for infrastructure and employment (e.g., the automobile and energy industries).

- Coverage of social needs in times of crisis (extending unemployment insurance, providing housing allowances, expanding health coverage, subsidizing education, overhauling public services, etc.).

The major variations among the implementation of these common strategies refer to the following differences:

- For some, it is simply a matter of restoring the financial health of the system and letting the market play their way. The problem here is that the same mechanisms that provoked the crisis usually lead to the same consequences. Thus, it is doubtful that the financial system will be reinstated as it was, with its emphasis on the derivatives market and on nonbank lending. The new financial system will probably be a much leaner system, with much less capital and less ability to create virtual capital or avoid regulation.

- For others, all that is needed is a new form of temporary Keynesianism, emphasizing massive job creation in the short term.

- Finally, for others (I would probably include President Obama here), there is an opportunity to induce corporations to produce differently and people to consume differently, particularly in environmental terms. It is also an opportunity to gather public support for an expansion of the welfare state, particularly in health and education, on the basis of public funding and innovation and new technologies.

In all cases, the hope is that within two or three years there will be enough trust restored in the system so that the market will begin processing a new influx of capital and the machine will restart. With increased political trust comes increased patience from citizens eager for results. On the other hand, if governments do not deliver, many citizens will turn to conservative solutions, shun any tax increase, reject corporate bailouts, blame foreigners, and individualize their response to the crisis by breaking networks of solidarity. *Sauve qui peut . . .*

All these strategies have a major flaw: they rely on the belief that the system can be restored with relatively minor changes. This assumption, in my view, is unrealistic. Let us see why.

The Limits of Capitalist Perestroika

As with the Soviet perestroika, which originally aimed to adapt Communism to a new socioeconomic environment, current policies to lift global capitalism out of the crisis face a number of major difficulties.

1. First, the key measures to refloat financial institutions and jump-start demand depend on *massive public spending* in an already critical situation of public debt in most countries. According to the IMF, the budget deficits of the G20 countries altogether have increased from 1.1 percent of their aggregate GDP in 2007 to 8.1 percent in the second quarter of 2009. Government debt for the G20 countries was about 40 percent of their GDP in 1980; it rose to 70 percent in 2000 and is projected to be the equivalent of 120 percent of GDP in 2014. In the case of the United States, its gross debt in 2014 is projected to be 112 percent of GDP. Under these conditions, financing spending without a substantial inflationary surge would depend on the following:

    a. *Increasing economic growth.* This could come later, but not in the early stages of recovery.

b. *Raising taxes.* This is politically difficult, although it may work via selective taxation of the richest segment of the population, although this is not nearly enough to finance the level of spending necessary. Some countries, such as Spain, are raising taxes, and they are finding strong resistance that is already reflected in the reversal of political opinion against the incumbent Socialist government in 2009. Closing fiscal loopholes for corporations would be more effective, but it will be resisted by the very same corporations that are being saved by governments.

c. *Borrowing from China and other capital-accumulating countries.* This is in fact the predominant solution in the United States these days and may become an important option for European countries as the crisis goes on, with Russia eager to play the role of helpful lender to increase its influence in Europe. However, China is also facing difficulties because of declining export markets. During the crisis, between the fourth quarter of 2007 and the second quarter of 2009, US exports fell by $215 billion, and its imports fell even more, by $440 billion, and so its current account deficit was reduced from $804 billion in 2006 (or 6 percent of GDP) to $395 billion (or 2.8 percent of GDP). Most of this improvement of the US trade deficit is at the expense of China's surplus. As a result, thousands of jobs have been eliminated in China, and there is a reverse-migration pattern from the coastal areas to the inland regions. Therefore, China needs to spend more and save less, as its saving rate was over 50 percent of GDP in 2008. In fact, China has embarked on a large program of domestic fiscal stimulus. In November 2008, the Chinese government announced a $585 billion stimulus package in infrastructure, health, and retirement. But only 30 percent of the stimulus will come from the central government. Most of the rest will be financed by Chinese banks happy to see their lending constraints lifted. Lending and spending by government and banks accounted for 75 percent of China's growth in the first quarter of 2009. China has the opposite problem of Western economies. Domestic demand is withheld in China because of the low level of income of most of the population. Real household income has fallen from 72 percent of national income in 1992 to 55 percent in 2007, while employment has only increased by 1 percent. In contrast, corporate profits have increased to 22 percent of GDP in 2007, and most companies use these profits to reinvest, generating higher profits that generate higher savings. In 2009, investment accounted for 87 percent of Chinese growth (whereas US consumer demand accounted for 70 percent). Investment helps China's foreign exports, but it depletes China's domestic demand. In China, overinvestment leads to underconsumption. China solves the problem by undervaluation of its currency (yuan) so that it keeps selling in export markets rather than in the domestic market. However, the situation appears untenable as its trading partners request a revaluation of the yuan to reduce their trade deficit. If this happens, China will reduce the amount of dollars accumulated in its economy and will have less resources to finance the US government and companies at the time it needs to stimulate domestic demand to compensate for lost export markets. In a nutshell, China's lending capacity is not up to the level of what the United States and other governments would need to finance the gigantic overhauling required to restore growth in their economies.

d. *A surge in productivity growth via innovation and entrepreneurship.* However, innovation and entrepreneurship largely depend on research-and-development (R&D) investment and venture capital. Under the current conditions of a credit crunch and cautious investment policies, innovation, without drying out, is slowing down. Companies have cut off long-term R&D, the most important type for new waves of innovation in process and product. According to some OECD estimates, when growth falls by 2 percent, R&D spending drops by 3 percent. Surveys of five hundred big companies in the United States indicated that 34 percent expected to spend less on R&D in 2009, and 21 percent did not expect to spend more in the future. Investment by venture capitalists in the United States in the second quarter of 2009 was down 51 percent in relationship to 2008.

2. The most important issue to be reckoned with in order to restore capitalism as usual is *how to restart demand under new financial conditions that will considerably restrict lending.* US households, because of

their high level of indebtedness and dark prospects in the labor market, are now saving as much as they can and spending as little as they can. In the second quarter of 2009, savings rates rose to 5 percent of disposable income, in contrast to 2.7 percent in 2007. Projections suggest that households may try to save as much as 10 percent once they pay their immediate liabilities, because after a crisis people try to build protection against future misfortune. Households' net assets in 2009 are at 487 percent of their disposable income, down from 639 percent in 2006 and from the historical average of 500 percent. To restore their assets to the 500 percent level, US households would have to repay $1.4 trillion in debt, which under current circumstances, if everything goes well, would take until 2012.

Thus, with lower wages, higher savings rates, and reduced credit availability, consumption is substantially curtailed. Consumer demand accounts for over 70 percent of American spending. And so American spending in 2009 was about $760 billion short to restart the economy at its precrisis level of employment. Because of the role of US consumer demand in the global economy, an alternative will have to be found to sustain exports, and thus growth, in other economies.

3. The fall of demand and the inability of the financial market to sustain investment under the new astringent conditions have induced a *sharp increase in unemployment around the world*, particularly in the United States and in western Europe. According to the IMF, over twenty-five million jobs may be lost in the crisis, and many of them will probably not be recovered. It forecasts high rates of unemployment in Spain, Ireland, the United States, the United Kingdom, Italy, and Germany, with double-digit rates of unemployment that may last for several years. Policies to restore employment, including job-training programs, do not seem to work in the absence of new investment and with the persistence of weak demand. Thus, work-sharing schemes are in place in twenty-two OECD countries (less working hours with an equivalent reduction of salary, partially compensated by the government), and the duration of unemployment insurance may be extended.

4. *The duration of the crisis* may outlast the ability of governments to keep their stimulus packages in place, as they focus primarily on

restoring the viability of financial institutions, which is a daunting task. From early 2008 to spring 2009, the crisis wiped out US$30 trillion from the value of global shares and US$11 trillion from the value of homes. These losses amounted to about 75 percent of world GDP. The problem is not only the destruction of wealth. The issue is that the overpriced assets held by banks and households were accompanied by large debts that have to be repaid.

Thanks to government rescue packages, the largest banks are coming back to life. In May 2009, US regulators announced the results of stress tests of nineteen banks and revealed a shortage of capital of only $75 billion. This rallied markets and lowered the shortfall further. Several of the banks were confident enough by summer to repay the government $63 billion in capital. Banks have regained trust in each other. However, in the United States, the most serious losses are probably in traditional mortgages, losses that are currently evaluated at $185 billion but are probably worse, unless housing prices recover, which is unlikely. Furthermore, as I said earlier, banks only account for 20 percent of lending, and an assessment of the nonbanking financial institutions has not been completed after the crisis. Outside the United States, many banks refuse to face reality. European banks need to raise US$375 billion to restore the capital lost in the crisis. This is equivalent to six months of projected profits. To match US leverage ratios, European banks would need to raise US$2.8 trillion, equivalent to three and a half years of projected earnings. According to several surveys, if banks in Europe and the United States have to spend two or three years balancing their books, they will be reluctant to lend until their financial health is restored. In the meantime, industries that depend on external financing, such as high-tech manufacturing, will find it difficult to invest. In other words, even if banks are restored to financial health by the government, they will be hesitant to resume lending and will not lend as much as they had in the precrisis context.

Furthermore, in Europe and the United States in 2009, companies were only operating at about 66 percent of capacity. So they will use existing capacity before borrowing and investing anew. Therefore, little job creation will take place for an uncertain period of time. Similarly, the self-employed are an important part of growth, and they usually finance their projects by borrowing against their homes and with risky loans. Because this kind of lending is now difficult, the rate of self-employment is likely to drop, thus reducing the likelihood of entrepreneurship and innovation. The fact of the matter is that there will be no return to easy financing. The real cost of borrowing for American companies with a BBB rating in the early 2000s, before the crisis, was 3 percent. In the new context, the cost will be around 4.5 percent, a level similar to that of the 1990s. Thus, there is an environment of reluctant lenders joined by reluctant borrowers. The result is a stagnant economy.

5. Thus, without going further into technicalities, it appears that, even counting on the successful implementation of the range of policies I mentioned earlier (a very optimistic projection), *the pool of available credit will be sharply reduced*; that there will be a shift from market-delivered goods and services to public-sector-delivered goods and services (e.g., in health, education, transportation); that economic activity will stagnate first and then grow slowly for a long time; and that public spending, the current mechanism to keep the economy in suspended animation, will eventually be curtailed because of the coming fiscal crisis of the state and the limits of international lending. The social consequences of this shrinking of global capitalism are unpredictable. But we know some things:

First, there is a dramatic shift of capital accumulation from the United States to the Asian Pacific and oil-producing countries (bearing in mind that China still represents only 5 percent of global GDP, in contrast to the United States' 25 percent, and that US foreign direct investment is thirty times larger than Chinese foreign direct investment). This not only modifies power relationships but also decreases the control of the United States and Europe over decisions regarding their own economic policies—for instance, in terms of monetary policy.

Second, there will be slower job growth and probably higher productivity as technology substitutes for labor to reduce costs and increase efficiency.

Third, there will be reduced income, so there will be less money in consumers' hands.

Fourth, credit will be extraordinarily tight for a long time, and so consumption will be much reduced. In short, there will be less working time and more living time; less exchange value and—potentially—more use value in the economic transactions among people; less possibilities for consumption and greater possibilities of doing something else; more reliance on government programs and thus more citizen watch on public services; and a change of power relationships in the family, as men more often than women are impacted by job loss and pay reduction in this crisis.

Under these conditions, a new set of economic transactions, less dependent on credit and consumption, may develop. *What is emerging is a three-layer economy*:

a. A revamped informational capitalist economy for a much smaller segment of the population, most likely the sector dominated by the professional class. It should require a new wave of technological and organizational innovation, a kind of new, new economy unfolding, with new products and new processes in fields such as energy, nanotechnology, bioinformatics, telecommunications, and digital new media and entertainment. However, because there is a reduced pool of venture capital and of R&D investment, this new round of innovation does not have the potential of increasing the consumption of the majority of the population.
b. A much enlarged public and semipublic sector and a smaller market sector, with tighter regulation of financial institutions.
c. A use-value economy (not necessarily excluding for-profit production) whose characteristics I identify in the next section.

If people cannot consume as much as they would like, they will have to find something else. But they cannot find something else unless they value this something else—that is, if they generate from within a new economic culture, actually a variety of economic cultures unified under the common pattern of superseding consumerism. Since new values do not generate in a vacuum, this nonconsumerist culture may only grow on the basis of actual social practices that exist in societies around the world, often first enacted by dropouts of the current economy because of their rejection of what they consider a destructive way of life. These are not neohippies. They come in all formats and in some cases under very innovative forms (e.g., ethical hackers, as per the concept elaborated by Pekka Himanen,[14] such as the creators of the Internet and the World Wide Web). I expand on this subject in the next section. But the critical remark is that the rise of a new economic culture may result from the historical convergence between a cultural vanguard searching for a different way of life and the disoriented masses of ex-consumers who no longer have the opportunity to consume anything but themselves, people who have nothing to lose except their canceled credit cards.

A Use-Value Economy? A Typology of Observed Economic Practices

There have always been economically marginalized people who transform their condition into the centrality of a new value system.[15] When the movement accelerates, it is a sign of the obsolescence of the predominant economic system. It usually starts in the minds of young people, those with the time and energy to imagine something else and to invest in the value of their lives rather than in the value of their stocks. They are sometimes followed by people who cannot live any longer according to the market logic, such as the workers who refuse to quit when their company closes and instead form a self-managing cooperative, as has been the case for a number of companies in the United States, Canada, and Europe, as reported by Naomi Klein. And there is a mass experience of use-value social practices by the millions in the world who take care of our natural environment or try to transform their cities in their daily practice while putting pressure on their local governments to achieve a sustainable city. This landscape of social transformation is as vast as it is often ignored by the media and derided by politicians. There is also a growing literature that is gradually setting the record of these social practices.[16] For the sake of simplicity of my argument, I propose a typology:

- *Consumer cooperatives,* usually motivated by consuming organic produce and using environmentally safe products. They are based on trust, voluntary work, joint financing, fair pricing, and collective decision making.

- *Producer cooperatives,* often connected to consumer cooperatives as their trusted suppliers. Their nucleus is in the realm of agroecological production, but they have extended to a wide range of production of goods and services. Some of these cooperatives are for-profit production cooperatives operating on different principles of traditional market accounting (e.g., increasing the value of the share of a worker depending on his or her contribution to the cooperative).

- *Urban farming.* There is an explosion, particularly in the United States and in France, of people cultivating their own produce, to escape from industrial food, to improve their own health and the environment at large, to exercise, and to save money. The example set by Michelle Obama's cultivating tomatoes and vegetables with her children on the White House lawn has been hailed all over the United States and has been imitated by hundreds of schools around the country while also legitimizing self-cultivation to the point that the American Food Association sent Michelle Obama a letter protesting the implications of her action. Urban farming also aims to reduce the transportation of food around the world, a major source of environmental destruction.

- *Barter networks and time banks.* People exchange services and goods on a small or large scale using the Internet to create a sort of non-monetary eBay market or Craigslist. In some cases, as in the outskirts of Barcelona, these networks have created and printed their own currency, only to be used within the network. In most cases, the exchange is based on the time invested in doing something for someone else. This is exchanging life time for life time.

- *Communal living,* using habitat to share space and everyday life, most often without the countercultural and sexual connotations of the 1960s communes. This is actually a mass solution for youth, who share a housing unit to escape the constraints of the housing market and then to build on their housing solution to expand to other shared activities (cooking, taking care of kids, helping each other in work or study, etc.). They often provide free services to the neighborhood, for instance, free repair of bicycles. In some cases, communal living starts with squatting, but most often this is not the case.

- *Transformation of transportation systems in cities.* This is already a mass practice, focused on transportation by bicycle, skateboard, or foot instead of automobiles. It is a way to fight atmospheric pollution, to improve one's health, and to improve urban quality. Critical Mass and other bicycle-based collective practices are a mixture of social movements and grassroots-generated urban policies that are transforming cities around the world. They are most effective when they succeed in connecting with innovative local governments.

- *Community banking,* taking over local financial institutions, sometimes with the help of government, to collect necessary funding to save neighbors from foreclosure.

- *Volunteer-based social services,* from medical clinics to psychological counseling and legal support.

- *Counseling networks* (under professional guidance) of public health practice to drastically diminish people's consumption of pharmaceutical drugs by their being in good health as a result of better living habits. This includes, for example, support groups for escaping the chemical dependency on junk food, as has been the practice for quitting smoking. The self-help health movement has extraordinary economic consequences, as people's consumption of drugs, pushed by pharmaceutical companies and their doctors, is a significant part of total household consumption.

- *A revival of voluntary associations* (particularly among the youth), often in a networking form, that emphasize the switch from paid activities (entertainment shows, discos, bars) to local celebrations, open concerts, performances shared over the Internet, and a whole range of innovative cultural activities adapted to people's choices (street theater, storytelling in schools and working places, not-for-profit recitals by musicians and singers).

- *P2P digital cultural sharing and open-source innovation in the computer world,* which is contesting the for-profit production of culture, music, and technology. The passion to create and share, in Himanen's approach, substitutes for commercialization of creativity, inducing the commons of the Information Age and engaging in the battle for free culture and a free Internet. This is tantamount to decommodifying the major space of communication of our time.

Of course, the entire economy cannot be based solely on these practices. This is why there is still a need for the reconstruction of a form of innovative, global capitalism, based more on the culture of innovation than on the technology of financial/real-estate speculation. However, I contend that the size of these decommodified economic activities is already significant, in terms of the millions of people involved and the time that they take to do it. Furthermore, in a context of massive shrinking of monetized consumption capacity, the whole range of economic practices based on a different principle may well provide access to goods and services to millions of people using their time, their minds, and their personal networks, rather than their scarce money and limited credit, while reducing their need to consume what in fact they hardly need (e.g., expensive drugs that are either placebos or only needed to compensate for the lack of elementary self-care, such as daily exercise).

So there is a whole world already out there, a world that could become a significant share of the new world when and if the practices embedded in the now-crumbling model of financial capitalism are no longer viable. Yet this is not my manifesto or my proposal, in spite of my obvious interest in these emerging practices rooted in a different economic culture. As a researcher, my primary goal is to observe in the coming years how new social practices may emerge to deal with the contradictory situation of a consumption-led capitalism that is no longer able to provide the means of consumption. It looks like, in the last resort, the decisive battle against capitalism may not be about the means of production but about the means of consumption. Therefore, it is primarily a confrontation between different economic cultures.

CHAPTER 8

The Convolution of Capitalism

Gopal Balakrishnan

Introduction: The Limits of Capital in a Historical Perspective

What does today's slow-motion meltdown of markets indicate about the historical viability of capitalism? Looked at in a longer-term historical perspective, the latest round of global turbulence might open up new perspectives on its outer boundaries of development. Indeed, properly understood, it brings to light an epochal shift concealed over the preceding decades of financialization. In what follows, I argue that the world's most advanced societies have been heading to what the classical economists once called "the stationary state" of civilization, a potentially insurmountable condition of stagnation. After a quarter century of ever-greater dependency on debt and speculation, both the developed and developing worlds are entering a new historical period in which the ongoing problem of warding off the deflation of bubbles has converged with secular trends that have diminished their capacities for further development through the classical path of technological innovation. The future is often conceived in terms of the arrival of a new, dynamic phase of capitalism: the advent of this stationary state, or what has been called "grey capitalism," points to a more uncertain future, beyond capitalism.

Frederic Jameson once wrote that it was easier for contemporaries to imagine the end of the world than an end of capitalism.

"Postmodernism" was, in his view, a cultural condition in which the experience of history, of vast multidimensional transformations in modes of life, had devolved into a linear modernization story of advancing markets, elections, and human rights. Alternate futures and unsubsumable pasts were threatened with extinction, as contemporary social experience collapsed into a static present projected back and forth in time. According to this view, contemporaries of earlier phases of capitalist society could contemplate its ultimate fate in terms of classical narratives of decline and fall, but in its late or postmodern phase, such precedents have become increasingly unpersuasive. Reflecting this wider experience of the irrelevance of the remote past, contemporary variants of social theory are no longer "historicist" in the explicit or implicit way that the classics of this tradition were.

Although the term is sometimes used more narrowly, there were several variants of "historicism" in this sense. Karl Marx once held that contradictions between static property forms and dynamic forces of production erupted in periodic crises that stripped the existing order of things of its apparent naturalness. These momentary denaturalizations opened up perspectives on the origins and declines of past modes of life, highlighting the relativity and transience of one's own. Amid the depression of the late nineteenth century, Friedrich Engels and Karl Kautsky dwelt on perceived parallels between the spread of primitive Christian communities and the rise of modern socialism. But encounters with historicity were far from being the exclusive province of the Left. From Nietzsche to Spengler and Toynbee, the experience of decadence seemed to invite comparison to comparable episodes from ancient and even non-European pasts.

Arguably, all such philosophies of history have long since ceased to offer any promising analogies for thinking about the future of late, or postmodern, capitalism. Assuming for the moment that capitalism actually could come to an end, as all older forms of society have, we still might lack any relevant historical analogies of how this might unfold, for the contours and transitional forms of its descent would likely bear little resemblance to the ways in which older agrarian civilizations collapsed or changed into some other form of life. In contrast to these rigidly traditional Malthusian worlds, capitalism is supposed to be able to renew itself indefinitely through crises of creative destruction.

Nearly all commentators on today's worldwide slump assume that another age of expansion lies somewhere in the future, despite the lack, at present, of any convincing scenarios of how this might come to pass. Crises of creative destruction are supposed to be the way in which capitalism renews itself. Is the current state of financial emergency laying the foundations for a future round of accumulation? Most commentators on today's slump assume that a more or less long and painful restructuring eventually will release a new period of expansion based on the growth of emerging markets and new technologies.

There are some reasons to be skeptical about this assumption. Hegel once remarked that for an ending or a beginning to be understood historically, it had to happen twice, so to speak. It might be instructive, then, to recall that at the end of the 1970s, the USSR was thought to be at the height of its power, shortly before its final collapse. By most accounts, the terminal phase of stagnation that overcame it demonstrated the inability of command economies to match the discipline and transparency of free-market mechanisms. We should now be in a position to reconsider the ideologies of the market that have dominated the political and intellectual scene since the 1980s, in light of the recent implosion of large parts of the financial system, at massive public expense. In fact, the need for a wholesale reconsideration of our historical situation, its overall direction, should now be obvious. However great the gap in the respective levels of development of the United States now and the USSR then, there is an irony in the fact that we confront this challenge less than twenty years after the collapse of the USSR. A period of triumphant capitalist globalization has culminated in systemic disorders that have put capitalism's future into question. Although this is hardly a 1989 moment for capitalism, there is compelling evidence to suggest that we are entering into a long era of perestroika whose final prospects are unclear.

After the disappearance of the Soviet bloc, narrative schemas of a convergence with or transition to socialism were replaced with diametrically opposed ones of a transition from socialism toward a modernity of liberal democracy, markets, and human rights. These neomodernization paradigms have made it nearly impossible to address the significance and depth of the problems that the capitalist system is now facing.[1] From the 1980s and gaining ever-wider credence after the fall of Communism, the narrative of globalization seemed to provide an integrated account of the main economic, political, and cultural trends of the future. As a result, the bursting of the speculative bubbles that have powered the turbulent economics of globalization could lead to an interpretive vacuum regarding the overall evolutionary direction of the world system. The crisis of a paradigm that until recently structured a vast array of perspectives on developments in economics, politics, and culture may give rise to a disquieting loss of overall intelligibility.

After all, more than two decades have passed during which the power and legitimacy of capital have stood nearly unchallenged. It is understandable, then, that recent setbacks have yet to occasion a shift of paradigm, as there is a very strong desire in many quarters to believe that nothing fundamental is changing. In the current politico-ideological atmosphere, the suggestion that the history of capitalist expansion might be coming to an end is likely to elicit resistance, if not outright dismissal. Indeed, the very idea that capitalism could be in the tightening grip of what Marx called a contradiction between its relations and forces of production appears like a hoary relic from a bygone era. Across the ideological spectrum, "the market" is still almost universally regarded as a quasi-natural condition of growth without limit, checked only by the exogenous threat of ecological disaster.

One might go so far as to say that there is currently a taboo on thinking about the possible ends of capitalism, an exercise that invariably recalls older false prophesies. In Europe, fascism's defeat of the Left in the midst of a catastrophic depression seemed to convey an object lesson in the futility of expecting economic crises to generate support for socialist alternatives. Superimposed on this traumatic experience was the subsequent stupendous post–World War II recovery of capitalism under American leadership, on a Keynesian basis that seemed to neutralize the economic contradictions and crisis tendencies of the system. Other unexpected reversals of fortune were to follow. When the world economy entered a long slump in the 1970s, US hegemony briefly seemed to be in danger, as "antisystemic" forces overwhelmed client states in Saigon, Managua, Kabul, and Teheran. Of course, instead of leading to any breakthroughs to a new order, the crisis of the 1970s galvanized a momentous neoliberal counteroffensive. These various comebacks have made even Marxists wary of the idea that the latest capitalist crisis could be deep and long enough to put a question mark over the future of the system.

There are several plausible conceptions of capitalism. Adam Smith, Max Weber, Karl Polanyi, and Joseph Schumpeter all offered persuasive historical and structural accounts of modern economic dynamics. The writings of Karl Marx gave rise to a number of competing accounts. Some variants of Marxism understand capitalism in terms of class structures and struggles, others, in terms of the socioeconomic compulsions of "the value form." The account presented here does not exclude the insights of these understandings of the defining dynamics and main historical features of an undoubtedly multidimensional socioeconomic modernity. But I argue that a certain strain of the most old-fashioned Marxism now provides one decisive advantage over these other accounts: it conceived of capitalism in epochal terms and sought to peer into its "structural" future, the ultimate limits of its capacity to reproduce its own material preconditions. The deflation of neoliberalism should provide an occasion for raising some of these long-forgotten, older questions. Where are we in the history of capitalism—midstream or somewhere closer to the outer limits of its capacity to reproduce itself through the intensive and extensive expansion of the productive forces? We should not waste the opportunity that the onset of a crisis provides for thinking about these questions.

Adam Smith on the End of Capitalism

The following is a brief restatement of the conception of economic development shared by the political economists of the classical school before Marxism. This classical account opens up a window on the possible futures of the world system. According to this view, growth takes place through increases in productivity that lead to an ongoing diminution in the cost of social reproduction. Ongoing per-capita growth of income through the reduction of costs provides the key to understanding capitalism's unique expansionary pattern of historical development. Over the course of its history, capitalism has had to overcome a succession of internal and external obstacles to the continued unfolding of this dynamic of growth. It is interesting to note that earlier theorists of the wealth of nations were uniformly more pessimistic than Marx about the long-term prospects of commercial civilization. Smith, Malthus, and Ricardo all assumed that the productivity gains from specialization and the division of labor eventually would be checked and reversed by the running down of soil fertility and by population increase that would lead, inevitably, to rising rents and food prices and thus lower real wages. The historian E. A. Wrigley writes, "For reasons cogently argued by Smith and his successors, the momentum of growth was expected to peter out after a time, arrested by changes endogenous to the growth process itself, and giving rise in due course to the supervention of the stationary state."[2]

Marx wrote at a time when such barriers seemed to have been overcome by explosive advances in productivity, as the industrial revolution entered into the phase of "machines producing machines." But his thoughts on the various ways in which economic growth under capitalism might be self-undermining can be seen in the light of the concerns of this older tradition, that is, as an attempt to reconceptualize the limits presumed by an older Malthusian pessimism: what were the possible, endogenously generated obstacles to accumulation that a vastly more innovative industrial mode of production might confront?

While all capitalist crises stem from anarchic, self-undermining processes of expansion, this process does not unfold according to the same pattern each time. Indeed, every generalized economic crisis going back to the nineteenth century has assumed a novel form. What, then, are the most important specific characteristics of the current slump? I propose that the coming era of socioeconomic shakeout and contraction is the result of the convergence of two developments: it is the latest and so far most extreme resurfacing of unresolved economic problems going back to the 1970s, a "conjunctural" crisis of overproduction that has been compounded by an "epochal" drift in the economically most advanced regions toward a postindustrial stationary condition. I will wait until the end of this chapter to identify the causes of the advent of the postindustrial stationary state, or grey capitalism, as distinct from the preindustrial one foreseen by the classical political economists.

The Long 1970s

Before I provide an account of how the transition to a stationary state could lead to an indefinite prolongation of the current "financial crisis," I will attempt to show that the latter is the culmination of a long downturn in the world economy going back to the 1970s. It is important to establish that the current meltdown in the world economy did not come after a period of dynamic expansion but after a decades-long downturn in the advanced capitalist zone. Indeed, the past three decades of neoliberalism can be characterized as a protracted effort to surmount the world economic crisis of the seventies. Today's slump is the latest manifestation of a long deceleration in the growth rates of the advanced economies.[3] This slowdown is the result of a reduction in the rate of return on capital investment in the advanced capitalist economies that never fully recovered after the 1970s. Many have argued that the economic crisis of the seventies was caused by the excessive power of unions and by overregulation that diminished the incentive to invest. This view cannot account for the fact that even though the share of national income going to wages and benefits fell after the 1970s, the profit rate did not return to its previous level. This faltering profit rate, countered by an unsustained upswing, can be explained primarily in terms of a mounting overcapacity in global manufacturing and is therefore the persisting cause of the economic deceleration of the period. Overproduction means production in excess of what could yield the previously going rate of profit. This reduced rate of profit generated smaller surpluses for reinvestment in the advanced economies and thus a slowdown in the growth of plants and equipment. Investment in plants and equipment is what makes sustainable income growth possible, because it is the main source of the growth of productivity.

In the largest advanced capitalist economies, this slowdown led to either stagnation in wage growth or higher unemployment. Over the period in question, the main response of employers was to hold down the wage and benefit level, while governments attempted to check the growth of social expenditures. But such cutbacks only reinforced the stagnation caused by overproduction in the first place by holding down the growth of demand. This prolonged deceleration and stagnation of demand occasioned a counteracting, systemwide expansion of government, firm, and household debt. Over this period, an increasingly large part of this world pool of savings has been recycled into unsustainable debt and speculation, lacking an outlet in investments that would increase productivity. But the manufacturing sectors of the world's leading export economies have been just as dependent on this buildup of debt and speculation as have been the finance and real-estate sectors of the debtor countries. Their surpluses are, of course, the flip side of US and other countries' deficits, but they do not cancel each other out, in the sense of not being a problem for the world economy, as they both emanate from the same impasse of accumulation.

Antonio Gramsci described a similar problem during an earlier episode of economic crisis:

> Observation of the 1929 crisis has spotlighted exactly this point: that there exist unstoppable speculative phenomena which have brought down even the "healthy" firms, on account of which one can say that "healthy firms" do not exist anymore. In consequence, one can use the word "healthy," only in coupling it with a historic reference—"in the sense it once had."[4]

This formulation nicely captures the real, if always tenuous and relative, distinction between the so-called real economy and speculation. Marx memorably theorized the bewitching relationship of exchange to use value, but he correctly held that the wealth of society consisted of its accumulated use values and that this wealth had to assume forms that would make the whole process materially reproducible on expanding scales for actually existing human beings.

How is this problematic but real distinction between the so-called real economy and "speculative phenomena" asserting itself in the current financial crisis? The latest meltdown should be viewed as the result of mounting pressure for a large-scale shakeout of overproduction that has been kept at bay over the past three decades, despite ongoing downsizing and the flight of capital from overcrowded manufacturing lines to lower-cost regions and into uncontrollable speculative phenomena. An age of gravity-defying accounts imbalances, asset inflation, and the runaway growth of household debt is coming to an end.

One way of looking at the recent crisis is to see it as movement back to Keynesianism or perhaps even "state capitalism," the latest swing of a pendulum movement in the history of capitalism between the more- and less-regulated organizations of accumulation.[5] Putting aside the question of whether some viable form of crisis management might be emerging, the idea that after full-blown neoliberalism, capitalism can shift back to Keynesianism as a solution is based on a false analogy to the 1930s, a time when capitalism was supposedly saved by various forms of deficit spending. The reason why the analogy does not work is that neoliberalism was not just a break with postwar Keynesian deficit spending but a continuation of it by other means, that is, by a long-term macroeconomic stimulus that drove up the value of financial assets and, in many countries, real estate, with little regard for hard budgetary constraints, in either the private or public sectors. Neoliberal austerity in exporter countries directly depended on America's new form of promarket, prorich, and variably militarized Keynesianism. The ballooning surpluses of the most successful export-oriented economies have been made possible by deficits augmenting the private and public debt of the world's main importer economy, the United States.

Impending public-solvency crises might bring an end to the capacity of governments in the advanced economies to smooth out business cycles and dampen recessions through demand creation, the preferred strategy during the postwar "golden age" as well as in the subsequent neoliberal period. This has begun to happen to smaller countries such as Greece, but the fallout may soon spread to the largest ones. The past thirty years have witnessed a continuing expansion of the money supply, the steady buildup of public and private debt compensating for a deceleration in the real economy: is it realistic to assume that the United States can now indefinitely stimulate market rallies by taking on vastly more debt through public expenditure? If it cannot, then the economies of the rest of the world that rely on exports to the US market are also in danger of sinking. In the 1930s, civilian and military deficit spending stimulated output by creating demand in economies that had already bottomed out. Today, very large stimulus packages could prevent debt-laden economies from plunging into a deleveraging depression, but they cannot surmount the impasse of accumulation that led to the problem in the first place. More American debt simply prolongs the problem of massive global misallocation and imbalances that led to the current wipeout.

Would it have been possible after the 1970s for the advanced capitalist economies to endure a crisis on a scale sufficient to liquidate the vast quantities of marginal and inefficient capital holding down the rate of return, thereby restoring the necessary conditions for a more dynamic capital accumulation? According to Schumpeter, this is what capitalist crises periodically do—this is what he meant by "creative destruction." It would follow from this view that if these societies had been purged by a thoroughgoing depression after the 1970s, expansion could have resumed on a basis less dependent on the buildup of debt and the blowing up of speculative asset bubbles. The early 1980s Reagan-Volker shock of 21-percent interest rates was a brief experiment in this direction, but the immediate effects of the ensuing recession were so catastrophic that the US government shifted course and began pumping the prime with a massive bout of military Keynesianism, inaugurating the subsequent pattern of American debt and deficits as the main source in the growth of world demand. The buildup of debt over this period has certainly prevented the kind of cathartic purging of the vast overproduction, the excess of less efficient producers holding down the rate of return, that a true depression would have brought about. But would such harsh medicine have worked, or would it have simply killed off the patient? Much of Latin America underwent savage bouts of austerity during this period and reemerged, however unsteadily, through a vast realignment of its economies to exporting. Of course, if the advanced economies had succumbed to a depression on a comparable scale, this export path of growth would simply have been impossible, for there would have been no one to export to. More or less this is what happened in the thirties, and it took the full-scale wartime mobilization of belligerent economies, followed by the massive destruction of productive capacity of the defeated, to blast through this impasse.

In order to understand why the capitalist system after the seventies went down the path it did as a way of holding off a depression, with all the attendant long-term consequences of these modes of crisis management, one has to take into account changes outside the economy, from geopolitics to culture, that set the system down this path. After World War II, a complex of institutions emerged—mass university education, free or assisted health care, unemployment compensation, social security, and the like—that anchored a social contract based on rising expectations. Even as the postwar golden age gave way to a period of slower growth in wages and benefits, these expectations could still be satisfied, as household consumption was bolstered by the entry of women into the workforce, then growing debt levels, and finally property bubbles. Again, those economies that did not go through all the steps in this sequence depended on exporting to those that did, the United States first and foremost.

The political systems of the OECD were geared to protecting parts of this social contract even as growth slowed and inequality moved to levels that had not been seen for half a century. Fortunately for most of these populations, there are no higher powers to impose the kind of structural adjustment programs that heavily indebted countries with weak political systems were forced to endure. The return to lower growth rates of consumption characteristic of earlier eras of capitalism would likely have reignited a legitimation crisis in advanced capitalist states, as would any massive scaling back of health care, education, and welfare. Perhaps if there existed a powerful bloc of far-wealthier societies, Western populations might have accepted such a fate, in the hope that by following dictates imposed from above and outside, they might one day move up the ladder again. But except for the bottom layers of the US population, significant disentitlements did not take place anywhere in the advanced capitalist world. In a context of economic deceleration, growing levels of debt were needed to make up for the potential falloff in consumption, health care, and, in the United States, increasingly expensive university degrees. In a sense, it is these institutions that have locked in the necessity of higher rates of growth in one form or another. Over the long term, these commitments may become unsustainable on a capitalist basis. The countries that experienced depression-like collapses in the 1980s and early 1990s, from Mexico to Russia, were able to come back from the brink by hitching their economies to export markets, although popular living standards in many of the societies that underwent this transformation never returned to earlier levels. Advanced capitalist economies will not be able to export their way out of the crisis if their economies, altogether making up nearly two-thirds of the world GDP, begin to contract.

The Rise of China?

But has the period not witnessed the rise of the East, counteracting decline elsewhere? The globalization narrative, for all its Western triumphalism, is often understood to involve a shift of the center of the world economy toward East Asia, with massive political and cultural shifts to come. In the 1980s, Japan was at the center of this story, before it succumbed soon after to a national version of the stationary state, a pioneer of a more generalized condition. China from the mid-nineties has taken its place as the horizon toward which the world system is supposed to be moving. But despite its extraordinary rates of growth and still-immense untapped domestic potential for continued growth, China cannot become the center of a new phase of world capitalist expansion.

From the nineteenth century, the history of capitalism has often seemed to unfold in the form of rise-and-fall narratives, with the decline of the British Empire setting the stage for the ascent of warring rivals, the United States, Germany, and in its own region, Japan. After World War II, the military dimensions of capitalist competition disappeared and gave way to struggles over market shares, mainly between these same three powers. (The fall of the USSR in 1991 came so soon after the extent of its stagnation had become broadly apparent, and was tied up so directly with the collapse of an ideology, that somehow it did not seem at the time to be entirely explicable in these terms.) Up until the late eighties, the narrative of rising and falling powers seemed to offer a persuasive framework for tracking the main trend line and vicissitudes of the world system.

But even from the onset of the period that supposedly witnessed the roaring comeback of the United States under Reagan, this plotline has become increasing erratic, and one might say that, finally, the thread has been lost. Over the past thirty years, US hegemony rose and declined in a bewildering sequence of turnarounds, topped off by the recent deflation of plans for yet another American century. Japan's seemingly inexorable ascent up through the 1980s suddenly went into reverse and was followed by two decades of stagnation. Germany's parallel rise from defeat and occupation appeared to culminate in its reunification as a Great Power, shortly before it became the sick man of Europe, although now—so hopeful commentators would have it—perhaps it is ready to show the way again, after many years of virtuous belt tightening. Even long-sclerotic Britain experienced a decade in the sun as a junior partner in war and bubble economics. Finally, it remains to be seen whether the European Union itself, recently declared the safe haven of a more civilized variant of capitalism, will survive the centripetal logic of fending off the consequence of sinking employment and sovereign defaults. Over the past three decades of postindustrializing capitalism, sudden spins in the wheel of fortune have resulted in what could be called a comedy of great powers.

The rise of China in the last phase of full-blown neoliberalism and continuing into the present moment of relative stabilization, of ad hoc "regulatory liberalism," appears to have given this narrative of hegemonic succession yet another lease on life. But while its vast, still-undeveloped potential makes it seem more plausible that it could eventually surpass the United States (unlike the merely medium-sized economies of Germany or Japan), it is unlikely that China's future will unfold in the form of an indefinite extension of its current economic performance. From the nineteenth century, capitalist powers with a half or even a fifth of the per-capita income of the leading economy caught up and even surpassed the hegemon through imitative and innovate processes of modernization. Is it possible that this process could be repeated today by an economy that is vastly poorer, at a qualitatively lower level of development, with barely a tenth the per-capita income of the richest economies?

One might reflect on how economic development might have proceeded in Europe or the United States from the nineteenth century if they had been locked into a world market dominated by economies with more than ten times their income level. The massive relocation of technologically lower-rung manufacturing to China is not replicating the classically expansionary phases of the capitalist system. This end of the value-added chain is already too crowded to sustain development along these lines indefinitely. Although the world economy as a whole has grown very rapidly along these exact lines, it has grown too slowly and disproportionately for even this to be sustainable. A new China-centered era of world economic growth could only happen on the basis of more advanced, new productive forces. The US industrial technique that spread to Europe and Japan after the war was at the cutting edge, allowing for a great equalization of levels of development between leader and follower economies. A vastly poorer China will not catch up by comparable processes, especially as the cutting edge is no longer embodied in relatively easily replicable manufacturing processes but in far more complex and costly techno-scientific infrastructures. The prospects for further technological revolutions in the advanced capitalist economies are dim, but China is presently very far from the existing higher echelons.

In the not-so-distant future, China's rate of growth will soon slow down as export markets dry up. Before the financial crisis hit, many observers foresaw that the world economy could not indefinitely continue to depend on an American demand sustained by growing deficits and debt. Many predicted that growth would come to depend on the

expansion of domestic consumption in China and other emerging markets. This shift, or "delinking," as it was called, was expected to unfold
smoothly, without wrenching shutdowns and the deindustrialization of
whole regions, as production for export would be redirected by the invisible hand toward rising, untapped disposable income in the home market.
But however desirable China's rulers might find such a scenario, they
are more aware than economists in the West of the enormous dislocations that such a transformation would involve and have so far made no
attempt to break out of a dependence on exports, a competitively deval-
ued currency, and the low level of domestic purchasing power that follows from these macroeconomic commitments. They have stuck to the
path of least resistance, for changing course would entail unforeseeable
sociopolitical transformations, and this will not happen until they are
forced to do so by circumstances. The current stimulus plan based on
enormous infrastructural investment is simply an intensification of the
capital-intensive, low-wage path the economy was on before, with little
prospect of the redirection to domestic consumption that was supposed
to prevent the world economy from entering into a protracted slump
by opening up new untapped markets. There are few reasons to believe
that as the economies of Japan, the United States, and much of Europe
contract, China not only will avoid going down with them but somehow
will be able to continue to grow so fast as to open up opportunities for
their export-based recovery. China's GDP is simply too small to carry the
weight of the world economy on its shoulders, however well its unusual
political system, more capable of major reversals of course than most,
might manage to somehow weather the storm.

The Decline and Fall of Fossil-Fuel Capitalism

The other great hope of the political season is that renewal might come in
the form of green capitalism, although vague declarations of purpose have
proven to be easier than the implementation of concrete measures. Fossil-
fuel capitalism is deeply entrenched, and a protracted slump will not necessarily make its disentrenchment easier. A decline in world output and consumption will lead to an ongoing reduction in the price of oil and gas and
therefore of the market incentive of the shift to alternate energy sources.

It is possible that the political will could emerge to restructure the largest economies along ecologically sustainable lines, opening up enormous opportunities for investment—although how many people would find employment through investment in such technologies is another matter. But at present, it seems unlikely that such a politics could also be harnessed to a narrow project of stimulating floundering markets. The scale of public support that would be needed to establish a new energy infrastructure would immensely exceed the capacities of private capital. This was the case in the past, and it is all the more so now.

Of course, if populations in the largest economies were exposed to emergency conditions resulting from an accelerated deterioration of their environment, they might become more open to the forms of total mobilization that would be needed to bolster the floodgates. In the past, major war has been the only context in which modern states have gone this far, bypassing the market either wholly or in part. Even if one were to presume a very dynamic future for market societies, they are now heading toward ecological challenges that far exceed their capacities of effective response.

Looked at in a longer-term perspective, the financial crisis can be explained in terms of an inability of advanced capitalist societies to generate a new sociotechnical infrastructure to supersede the existing grid. The current one is the midcentury culmination of the second industrial revolution and entrenches a now sixty-year-old interconnected bloc of productive forces at the heart of the world economy. This inertia of declining Fordist infrastructures has created obstacles to a renewal of the wavelike patterns of economic development that go back to the mid-nineteenth century. As a result, it has become increasing difficult to understand the past quarter century of capitalism in terms of past cycles.

The Advent of the Stationary State

Market rallies from the mid-1980s were often seen by contemporaries as indications of a historically unprecedented capitalist dynamism. Little could be further from the truth. Although US central bankers initially hoped that "irrational exuberance" might conjure up animal spirits from heroic eras of entrepreneurialism, the resulting bubbles enabled unsustainable minibooms of new technological investment. In contrast to the information-technology boom and bubble of the 1990s, the speculative manias out of which America's railway infrastructure emerged provided a foundation for a long period of output and employment growth. Alan Greenspan and other architects of the neoliberal financialization may have initially had such historical precedents in mind. But at some point, it may have become apparent to them that there was, in fact, little evidence that a New Economy was emerging to justify the grandiose projections of the market. Nonetheless, they were confident that something would materialize eventually as long as foreigners continued to buy American debt with their mounting surpluses. As so much nominal wealth was being created in the meantime, after a while they lost sight of what distinguishes it from what it is supposed to represent. In any event, they may have concluded, there now seemed to be few alternatives to this form of wealth creation.

At this point, we can return to the question of why this prolonged downturn failed to create the conditions for a renewed upswing: why did a New Economy not come to replace the Old? The economic history of the past thirty years is like the Sherlock Holmes tale of the dog that didn't bark. What did not happen, but was supposed to, was a Third Industrial Revolution, a great leap forward in the productive forces. The economic downturn that began in the 1970s seemed to many people to presage the coming of a nuclear-cybernetic New Age of capitalism. Instead, as we have seen, the coming phase was propelled by the pseudodynamism of asset bubbles, the epic adventure of a flight forward into finance.

Many people will find this stagnationist account implausible. After all, did not a "post-Fordism" of information technology and containerization—the two signature breakthroughs of the period—bring enormous advances in productivity? These developments undoubtedly powered a huge increase in world trade, but in vast excess of the growth of the world economy itself. The main consequence of technological change in this form has been to enable an epic relocation of manufacturing, from rich countries to countries with lower labor costs. Since the latter's growth is so heavily dependent on exporting to the advanced economies, this relocation has led to a steadily increasing volume of world trade—goods crossing oceans and national borders.

The problem is that since the seventies, world markets have been weighed down by overproduction, and the arrival of one after another

Asian exporting economy has compounded this world economic pileup. But the attrition of higher-cost manufacturing in the advanced economies may not be on a sufficient scale or occur rapidly enough to clear a path for the continuation of their high rates of growth on the current export-dependent path. The reason why this may not be sustainable for long is that it reproduces the conditions that have led to a slower overall growth of the world economy. Over the past quarter century, the surpluses that accrue to exporters were poured back into buying the US government debt that has made this whole circuit sustainable until now, instead of funding investment in whole new lines of production.

Is there some longer-term change at work causing the unprecedented protraction of a cyclical downturn and the global convolutions through which it has unfolded? Marx was a theorist of the ultimate limits of capitalism: did he offer an account that would explain its present and future situation? Yes and no. He seems to have foreseen that the explosive productivity growth of machines making ever more productive machines would result in the employment of ever fewer workers, although he did not have a very good idea of the time frame of this process. It is reasonable actually to assume, though, that over the long term, overall productivity growth will be thwarted by its tendency to reduce employment and, thus, the aggregate demand to purchase the expansion of output. The advances in the forces of production that reduce the amount of labor time needed to produce the output of society would collide with social relations that dictate that individuals must work forty or more hours a week to be able to live, generating growing structural unemployment and a stagnation of aggregate demand.[6]

But even if this process unfolded over the long term, it is not clear that it is the direct structural cause of the economic deceleration of the advanced economies. I would argue that it may be manifesting itself in an indirect way, as the decline of industrial employment gives rise to ever larger service sectors. For the story of sustainable productivity growth through industrial revolutions cannot continue in the era of "the service sector." These processes once reduced the agricultural populations of industrializing societies to single digits and have begun to do the same to their industrial workforces. (Total global manufacturing employment has, of course, not sunk, as its decline in the advanced economies has been made up for by outsourcing to cheaper labor zones, where the tendency to replace capital for labor is weakened.) It is more than unlikely that this pattern of economic development will be repeated in large parts of what is called the service economy. Whereas Marx seems to have thought that the "internal" cost of capital borne by firms would go up, bringing down the profit rate, I argue that certain "external" costs of reproducing society go up over the long term that cannot be counteracted by productivity gains elsewhere in the economy. The increasingly intractable problem that advanced capitalist societies confront is that there are no ways to hold down the burgeoning costs of health and age care without reducing the level and quality of provision. Simply put, as industrial employment declines, growth slows down because most services cannot be subject to the productivity growth through replacing human beings with machines and nonhuman energy sources. This is the main reason why capitalist economies are heading toward the stationary state.

> Some services which are impersonal, as in telecommunications, have attributes similar to manufacturing and hence can be technologically progressive. However personal services, such as certain types of medical care, cannot be easily standardized and subject to the same mass production methods used in manufacturing. These types of services will be "technologically stagnant." In general, if there are two activities, one of which is technologically progressive and the other technologically stagnant, then in the long term the average rate of growth will be determined by the activity in which productivity growth is slowest.[7]

Postindustrial capitalism will not be able to reduce the costs of social reproduction because of an almost insurmountable technological stagnation in core aspects of services such as health care. Moreover, the shift to a slow-growth service economy overlaps with a demographic transition to aging populations that will need to be supported by relatively smaller numbers of productive workers. These "biopolitical" problems are insurmountable within the framework of capitalism. Capitalist growth has been dependent on an age structure that may not be sustainable over the long term. The conjunctural crisis of neoliberalism has converged with an epochal one brought on by a transition to a grey capitalism of slow-growth service sectors and aging populations. While advanced capitalist societies are pioneers of this historical shift, their stagnation will lead to immediate slowdowns in currently developing regions and will generate currently unforeseeable patterns of longer-term development.

Over the neoliberal period, the flagging powers of the market were sustained by an ever-greater level of public support. Marx thought that capitalism would give rise to a socialization of productive process, and in an entirely unanticipated fashion it has. This socialization has unfolded not through a centralization and concentration of an expanding means of production but through the emergence of an increasingly costly, publicly supported social and material infrastructure on which the fortunes of the for-profit economy has come to depend. How long will capitalism in this form survive, and what lies beyond its horizon? Unlike the last era of capitalist catastrophe in the 1930s, advanced capitalist societies will probably not have to confront anything like the horrors of war and fascism, although the drift toward worldwide ecological fatality continues unabated. The danger is compounded by the fact that the transition to the stationary state has unfolded in a historical context of atomization and the paralysis of the self-determining powers in both these societies and in many other sectors of the world system. If the politics of the coming period stays within the mold of an untenable project of status quo maintenance, disasters will become all the more likely, as populations fail to comprehend and respond to the historical situation they are in. Everything depends on whether the current morbid phase of this irreversible civilizational change will be overcome, releasing new forms of collective response or even new modes of life with different measures of wealth.

CHAPTER 9

The Future in Question:
History and Utopia in Latin America (1989–2010)

Fernando Coronil

> A map of the world that does not include Utopia is not worth even
> glancing at, for it leaves out the one country at which Humanity is
> always landing. And when Humanity lands there, it looks out, and,
> seeing a better country, sets sail. Progress is the realisation of Utopias.
> —Oscar Wilde, "The Soul of Man Under Socialism" 1891

The year 1989, world historical for many reasons, marked the close of
a long period of military dictatorships in Latin America. It also initiated novel approaches to progress through democratic procedures and
the reconceptualization of democracy as not only a means to achieve
progress but also one of its central ends. At that time, the defeat of
Augusto Pinochet in a plebiscite brought to an end a dictatorship that
had imposed on Chile a harsh neoliberal "shock treatment" that inaugu-
rated neoliberalism's ascendancy in Latin America. Pinochet's victorious
opponent in 1989 was the *Concertación*, an electoral alliance of seventeen
political parties, committed to promoting political democracy as well as
social welfare and thus to binding together political and social rights.
Only two decades later, several Latin American countries are governed by
presidents who seek to deepen democracy by rejecting neoliberalism and
proclaiming ideals commonly associated with socialist principles; more
than three hundred million of the over five hundred million people who

live in Latin America are governed today, in 2010, by such leaders. To a large extent this change at the level of the state has been propelled by new social movements, indigenous communities, and political organizations that have struggled to construct a more equal and just society. Politics in Latin America during this period has veered from the familiar path. Despite visible as well as submerged continuities, novelty, apparent by the introduction of new actors, innovative agendas, and original ideals, has been its birthmark. Encompassing a wide range of heterogeneous processes in many of Latin America's twenty nations, this unprecedented transformation escapes conventional categories. What are we to make of this complex political change, one commonly referred to as Latin America's "turn to the left"?

In this chapter, I explore this broad question by focusing on a particular topic: the image of the ideal future that animates these changes. I examine this imagined future, the present-day future imaginary, not the Left's potential or likely future, however important these questions may be. While this is already a bounded topic, I draw even more precise boundaries around it. Given these nations' diversity and their internal heterogeneity, I limit my exploration by directing attention to the ways imaginaries of the future inhabit the state, the nation's central representative and main agent of "progress." This future imaginary can be glimpsed in everyday political actions and discourses as well as through concrete cultural artifacts such as plans, projects, and constitutions. Yet, since fundamental conceptions of history—not their specific content but their framing temporal structure—are often implicit or taken for granted, I focus on how ineffable imaginaries of the future inhabit the present, how the "what is to be" saturates the "what is" or, in Reinhardt Koselleck's terms, how the "horizon of expectation" relates to the "space of experience during this leftward turn."[1]

The polemical notion of the "Left" has historically been given changing and contested meanings. Norberto Bobbio has provided a parsimonious conceptual grid for classifying political orientations in terms of the dual axis of equality/inequality and liberty/authoritarianism. According to him, *left* and *right* are not absolute but relative terms that represent shifting positions within an always historically specific political spectrum. For him, the Left is basically defined by a movement from inequality to equality; liberty can be associated with it, but it is not its defining criterion.[2] Building on his insightful discussion but avoiding its rather sharp separation between equality and liberty, I use the notion of "left" as a fluid sign to identify actions directed toward universal equality and well-being and thus toward forms of political life without which these goals cannot be achieved, including democracy, diversity, justice, and freedom. The meaning of each of these terms depends on the meanings of the others, so that they form a conceptual ensemble. Rather than being fixed or given, the particular significance of these terms individually and as an ensemble is the product of historical contests over their significance.

Since left and right are relational categories defined through mutual interaction, the changing meanings of leftist projects have been produced by struggles to overcome the ever-changing relations of domination exerted by specific "rights." The Left stands in opposition to the Right because it pursues general well-being in ever more domains, ever more comprehensively. Conceptualizing it thus as an expansive democratizing political project, the "Left" can be identified with discrete achievements, such as the recognition of the rights of ethnic communities or of "nature" as a political actor, as established in Ecuador's 2008 constitution, as well as with the general process that encompasses them, such as the pursuit of an alternative social order guided by the indigenous concept of *el buen vivir*—living well (*sumak kawsay* in Kichwa).

As a political project, the pursuit of well-being for all—and all now includes non-human entities—is now less than ever the monopoly of the "West," of its dominant conceptions and logics. In effect, these struggles in Latin America are part of a decolonizing process that challenges the ethnocentrism of Western modernity and opens up spaces for other imaginaries based on different histories, epistemologies, aesthetics, and ethics. Since the Left/Right distinction is a Western scheme, it is understandable that its use has been contested in Latin America; current struggles entail defining what the "Left" is and whether it is still a relevant category. Perhaps more than in other periods (at least in Latin America), there are now multiple "leftist" ways of imagining an ideal society, entailing competing notions of well-being, justice, and rights. Some seek to expand material prosperity and individual rights to all, often entailing contests over the definition of collective and individual forms of property; others are based on conceptions of harmony among populations, with each other and with their common natural surroundings; "nature" is now represented in political discourse in some Andean nations not as an entity to be controlled or exploited by human beings but as a sentient being with rights of its own. For some, "right" and "left" are no longer relevant political categories. This proliferation of movements and positions erodes Western hegemony without necessarily entailing the rejection of the West or the establishment of an exclusive alternative hegemonic center. At this time, it no longer seems viable, or perhaps even desirable, to grant historical leadership to a privileged political agent or to postulate a universally valid political standpoint. Through exchanges among universalizing practices and ideals coming from within and outside the West, from centers as well as margins, these changes in Latin America have made it possible to question parochial universalisms and to pursue a more open universality.[3] Not without a sense of its inadequacy, in this essay I use the term "Left" to refer to these changes.

My central argument is that a puzzling paradox has marked this leftward turn. On the one hand, there is a proliferation of political activities inspired by socialist or communitarian ideals aiming at fundamentally changing society. On the other, there is a pervasive uncertainty with respect to the specific form of the ideal future. While there is an intense desire to change the nation, it is not clear *what* to desire—what are realistic aspirations, how to connect desire and reality. It has become common in Latin America to entertain the belief that actually existing capitalism is unviable for the long term while recognizing that socialism as it has actually existed offers no viable models for the future. Indeed, the project to build a "socialism of the twenty-first century," as proposed in Venezuela, Ecuador, and Bolivia, entails an implicit critique of the historical socialisms of the twentieth century, but its various national expressions thus far do not seem to have provided an alternative to them. Under the stewardship of leftist states, economic activity continues to unfold on the basis of capitalist relations, yet standing in tense relation to the expectation of an indefinitely deferred postcapitalist future. The entanglement between utopian aspirations and pragmatic or opportunistic accommodation has had tumultuous and contradictory effects on everyday life, personal relations, and national politics.

During this leftist turn, the present—the experience of the here and now—seems to be pulled by conflicting forces. On the one hand, it is animated by numerous struggles for a better society. On the other, it is trapped by formidable barriers that block these struggles. The hope of bringing about fundamental change is often displaced by the debilitating sense that human society cannot be improved. This double vision generates a split world, one that appears to oscillate between the malleable landscape of utopian imaginaries and the immutable ground of recalcitrant histories. From the fissure between these worlds there emanate contradictory dispositions and incentives that stretch the present forward and push the desired future toward an uncertain horizon. The Left pursues a just future, but its particular content eludes it. It has a sense of direction but no clear destination.

With the title "The Future in Question," this chapter seeks to evoke the distinctive presence of the future in Latin America during this turn to the left, the contradictory ways in which the coming time saturates the here and now and affects the current political imaginary. On the one hand, the future enters the public stage as an open horizon of expectation, as potentiality, offering a hopeful sense of possibility characteristic of liminal phases or revolutions. On the other, the future imposes its presence as a receding historical horizon, a future in doubt, inducing a sense of despondency typical of periods of decline or historical depression. I explore in two parts the question of this future. In the first, I discuss briefly the context in which the current Latin American Left has emerged. In the second, I examine the Left's future now, the paradoxical mode in which it has come to inhabit the present.

Emergence

I restrict my discussion of the rise of the Left to a brief outline of three conditions that affect its development at this time. These conditions have to do with the changing fate of the two major modernizing paradigms in the twentieth century, capitalism and socialism, and the crisis of neoliberalism, a model of capitalist development that at the end of the twentieth century promised to offer the key to progress.

The End of Socialism
The first condition is the global crisis and collapse of actually existing socialism at the end of the twentieth century (one could also say, the

collapse of "actually nonexistent socialism"—or of various forms of state capitalism), symbolized by the fall of the Berlin Wall in 1989, the dissolution of the Soviet Union in 1991, and the rapid immersion of China in capitalist markets and logics. This collapse has been widely interpreted not just as the end of particular historical socialisms but as the historical end of socialism.

The Victory of Capitalism

The second condition is the apparent global triumph of capitalism. As soon as one of the two rivals in the twentieth-century struggle for world supremacy vanished, it seemed not just that the other antagonist was victorious but that its victory was permanent. Moreover, as if blinded by success, ideologues of capitalism also claimed that its promise of universal progress was soon to be universally realized. At the close of the century, neoliberalism had achieved globally the status of a sacred dogma. Conceptualized as the triumph of economic science over political ideologies, it proposed the dominion of technocracy in social affairs and the demotion of politics to the domain of the partisan and the emotional. In 1989, John Williamson coined the term "the Washington Consensus" to refer to a decalogue of policy prescriptions that would ensure that all nations that followed it, even those with serious economic problems, would achieve economic growth. These policies reflected the integration of geopolitical concerns with a technical version of neoclassical economics that reduces social life to an individualistic calculus of utilities or a game of expectations. This fantasy of universal progress was famously articulated in Francis Fukuyama's paradigmatic 1989 article (and 1992 book) in which he proclaimed the "end of history." In these texts, he argued that the worldwide generalization of the free market would dissolve ideological struggles, bring about progress, and create global harmony.

The Crisis of Neoliberalism

The third condition concerns the negative impact of free-market policies: growing polarization within and among nations, ecological destruction, exclusion of vast sectors of the population, the subordination of production to financial speculation, and pervasive individualism and consumerism. These effects have been felt in the capitalist system as a whole but earlier and more intensely in the Global South.

Because Latin American countries in most cases obtained their political independence in the first quarter of the nineteenth century—rather than after World War II, like most new nations in Africa and Asia—they have had extensive experience with various forms of modernization projects, from liberal ones in the nineteenth century, before the recent neoliberal phase, to state-centered ones during most of the twentieth century, ranging from state-promoted import substituting industrialization (ISI) to state-supported export promotion. Some Latin American countries sought to modernize through distinct models of socialism or of socialist-inspired political projects: Chile under Salvador Allende (1971–73), Nicaragua under the Sandinistas (1979–89), and Cuba under Fidel Castro and, since 2006, his brother Raul (1959–current).

In response to the global hegemony of neoliberalism, during the last two decades of the twentieth century most states in Latin America reduced the role of the state in the economy, dismantled welfare institutions, deregulated the economy, and promoted the pursuit of comparative advantages according to free-market principles. These changes brought about aggregate economic growth but at the cost of a more polarized society and severe social dislocations. In response to these problems, the region saw the rise of a large variety of social and political movements focusing on specific demands, often inspired by socialist ideals, such as the Zapatistas in Mexico, the Landless Workers' Movement in Brazil (MST), the Piqueteros (unemployed) in Argentina, and the indigenous movements in the Andean nations. In part because of neoliberalism's polarizing effects, but also as a result of the activism of social movements and political organizations, the ideological supremacy of neoliberalism did not last long in Latin America. Even Fernando Henrique Cardoso, the acclaimed *dependentista* scholar who as president of Brazil (1995–2003) endorsed neoliberal policies and helped to integrate Brazil further into the structures of global capitalism, made it clear that he held no illusions about globalization's future: in his own lapidary expression, "Within globalization, no alternative, outside globalization, no salvation."[4]

Through regional meetings, the political organizations and social movements that opposed neoliberalism developed alliances and common projects. After a series of such meetings, representatives of these movements joined with kindred activists from all over the world in the World

Social Forum, a gathering that met for the first time in 2001 in Porto Alegre, Brazil. Ever since, the World Social Forum has sought to articulate these disparate organizations in a common alliance against neoliberalism and for social justice and democracy. Indeed, for these movements and organizations, it has been clear that neoliberal globalization offers no real alternative. And yet, because "actually existing socialism" has not offered salvation, it has been easier for them to criticize neoliberalism than to articulate a viable alternative to it. Their concrete proposals typically address particularly harsh aspects of capitalism, not capitalism itself as a whole system.

With no visible redemption outside or within capitalism, utopian dreams have not so much vanished as taken the form of a rather raw hope for a remote future; the Left has centered its critique on acute forms of domination by capital rather than on capitalism. As historian John French has perceptively noted, a focus on the critique of neoliberalism obscures an acceptance of capitalism. At the same time, it also serves to unite disparate sectors in the longstanding struggle for national development:

> If opposition to neoliberalism, not to capitalism, marks the fundamental boundary of the contemporary left, as I would argue, the terminology could be said to obscure the essential capitalist and imperialist enemy, if viewed in orthodox Marxist terms. Yet the emphasis on neoliberalism is especially appropriate to Latin America, where autonomous or semi-autonomous national development (be it capitalist or socialist) has long been a shared goal across the political spectrum. While anti-capitalism has had its place in the discourse of the region's left, the practical emphasis has more often been on the incapacity of capitalism to achieve the autonomous national development being sought, while the bourgeoisie has long been criticized for failing to spark a bourgeois democratic revolution or deliver prosperity to the masses.[5]

This insightful comment helps us see the current dilemmas of the Left in the context of Latin America's recurrent struggle to achieve some variant of Western progress. The region's long postcolonial experience has made it familiar with the shortcomings of different development projects and rather accustomed to the interplay between renewed promises and deferred achievements. At this time, however, the combination of widespread engagement in transformative politics with intensified uncertainty about the future has created particularly intense tensions between grand expectations and quotidian practices.

When neoliberalism was promoted as a reigning ideology in the United States and England, Latin America became the experimental ground for the implementation of neoliberal "shock treatments," most notably in Pinochet's Chile (1973–89) under the tutelage of the infamous "Chicago Boys" and during the ruthless rule of Argentina's military junta (1976–83). Through less repressive means, these policies were also implemented by democratic regimes, such as those of Carlos Andrés Pérez during his second presidency in Venezuela (1989–93) and Fernando de la Rúa in Argentina (1999–2001). In both cases, these presidents were removed from power largely as a result of the effects of these policies, Carlos Andrés Pérez in 1993, Fernando de la Rúa in 2001.

Given this history of truncated modernizing projects, it is understandable that Latin America became the region with some of the earliest and strongest protests against the current phase of neoliberal structural adjustments. Needless to say, the strongest opposition to them came as part of the struggles against the dictatorships in Chile and Argentina that had implemented these policies as a package, or "shock treatment," that was at once economic, cultural, and political. In other contexts, protests were largely a spontaneous response to a particular set of policies, such as Venezuela's 1989 *Caracazo*, the largest and most violently repressed anti-IMF uprising in the world, in reaction to food shortages and increased gasoline and transportation costs, or Argentina's massive movement in 2001 to oust President Fernando de la Rúa under the slogan *que se vayan todos* (away with them all), an unexpected protest in a country considered until then a model of the Washington Consensus but suddenly torn by a financial crisis and devastated productive structures resulting from the implementation of this model. In other cases, protests were carried out by social movements that had long organized toward this end, as during the 1994 Zapatista uprising in Chiapas, coinciding with the implementation by the Mexican state of NAFTA, the North American Free Trade Agreement.

As one would expect, despite neoliberalism's negative effects in the Global South, its limitations became globally visible only when they impacted the North. When its policies did not work in the South, the dominant view attributed this failure not to the free market but to these backward nations, not to the cure but to "patients" unprepared to undergo the whole policy prescription. It was only as a result of the 2008 financial meltdown in the United States that the free market lost its sacred aura. As if a veil had been lifted, the whole world could now see the unregulated free market not as a self-regulating natural principle but as an all-too-human invention gone wild that needs to be disciplined and supported by the state. While the election of Barack Obama was to a large extent a response to the effects of neoliberalism in the United States—of the housing crisis and the financial meltdown resulting from deregulation—the election of many leftist presidents in Latin America was a much earlier response to the multiple effects of neoliberalism in the region.

Several genealogies and typologies have been produced to account for this leftward shift in Latin America. Most journalists and academics, despite their differing interpretations, see the election of Hugo Chávez in 1998 as the beginning of this shift, as his campaign was marked by an identification of democracy with the welfare state, a strong rejection of neoliberalism, and the promise of radical change. This makes sense, insofar as his election initiated a cycle of electoral victories of presidents who pledged to undertake fundamental social transformations. I prefer to mark the source of this shift with the electoral defeat of Pinochet in 1989 in order to highlight what I regard as central to this change: the value attached to democracy as the political form through which to pursue collective welfare and as a value in itself. But there is a difference. In Chile at that time, a society marked by intense political conflicts and torn by a brutal dictatorship, the establishment of political democracy was the major challenge faced by the multiparty alliance that sought to overturn the Pinochet regime; this alliance proposed to ameliorate the negative effects of neoliberalism, not to replace it. Now, in a period when neoliberalism has been in decline if not in crisis, all leftist presidents elected after Chávez have promised to deepen democracy by limiting neoliberalism and implementing fundamental social welfare measures: in 2002, Lula da Silva in Brazil; in 2003, Nestor Kirchner in Argentina; in 2004, Tabaré Vasquez in Uruguay; in 2005, Evo Morales in Bolivia; in 2006, Michelle Bachelet in Chile, Daniel Ortega in Nicaragua, Rafael Correa in Ecuador, and Hugo Chávez reelected in Venezuela; in 2008, Fernando Lugo in

Paraguay; in 2009, José Mujica in Uruguay; and in 2010, Dilma Roussef in Brazil. Despite their differences, the pursuit of a deeper democracy has been their common ground.

Perhaps the most influential typology about these left regimes was a rather early scheme devised by Mexican scholar and politician Jorge Castañeda, who divided their leaders into reasonable reformers and backward populists—implicitly, into the good and the bad Left. At one end he placed the "open-minded and modern left," represented by Brazil's Lula da Silva, and at the other end, the "closed-minded and populist left," represented by Venezuela's Hugo Chávez.[6] Even those who criticized Castañeda's argument have tended to repeat its dichotomous structure, often making opposite evaluations—Lula as the compromising reformist and Chávez as the true revolutionary. Of course, from conservative perspectives, often expressed through the mainstream media, all these leftist governments are seen in a negative light; in the United States, the media tends to oscillate between setting the "good" Left against the "bad" one or treating them all as an undifferentiated negative force.

Under leftist rulers, political contests over different visions of society have stimulated public debate but have also tended to polarize political discourse, turning often useful simplifications into flat caricatures that block rather than stimulate understanding. In the context of heated political confrontations, this flattening of reason and heightening of emotions have affected political representations both in Latin America and abroad, including those produced in academic and artistic circles. For instance, Oliver Stone's documentary on the rise of the Latin American Left, *South of the Border*, forcefully challenges blatant distortions produced by the US media but presents an inverse mirror image of the Left that reproduces the media's flat vision of history. The demonization of the Left cannot be countered by its deification; the reduction of politics to a battle between Good and Evil must be challenged by accounts that develop the public's capacity to make sense of the world and of the history that produces it. If the mainstream media numbs people, we need accounts that help un-numb them.

Seeking to avoid flat dichotomies, or at least to turn them into meaningful distinctions, I offer a scheme that helps explore the Left's futures in Latin America by focusing on the conditions of possibility of historical change facing each nation. This scheme connects historical experience and political expectations by noting how distinct sets of economic and political conditions affect different modalities of leftist politics.

Political conditions. In countries that have experienced recent dictatorships and severe political repression, the Left tends to underplay the notion of revolution or socialism, to emphasize formal democratic procedures, to establish broad alliances and political compromises, and to project socialist principles into the distant future. The tone of politics is moderate. Here the clearest examples are Chile, Argentina, Brazil, Uruguay, and Paraguay. On the other hand, in countries that come from conditions of economic and political turmoil and periods of political and social instability, involving the insurgency of excluded indigenous populations or popular sectors, the Left tends to promote basic constitutional changes, to be confrontational, and to take up openly the banner of revolution and socialism. The tone of their politics is radical (or immoderate). Here the paradigmatic examples are Venezuela, Bolivia, and Ecuador.[7]

Material conditions. A twin set of core economic conditions fundamentally affects the relations between state and society during this shift to the left: how a nation's economic surplus is produced and how it obtains foreign exchange. While the generation of a surplus depends on the relation between capital, land, and labor (a central concern for both classical liberal and Marxist theories), the capture of foreign exchange depends on the relation between the national and international economies. When analyzed together, these two factors make visible the critical but insufficiently recognized role of ground rents in Latin America as "nature-intensive" or resource-based economies.[8] Agricultural and mineral rents play different roles and have distinct social implications as elements of specific ensembles of social relations. Whereas agricultural lands are typically privately owned and are thus the foundation of landowning classes that benefit directly from them, mines are generally controlled by the state, and their rents help give the state central political and economic importance. In the Latin American context, the dominance of agricultural rents at the national level generally goes together with a dispersion of economic power, a relatively diversified economy, a strong business sector, and a structural conflict between exporters and consumers over the allocation of agricultural goods either as sources of foreign exchange or as domestic consumer goods. Mineral rents, in contrast, tend to promote the concentration of power in the state, the creation of a subsidized and dependent business sector, and a structural conflict over the distribution of collective rents among citizens with equal rights over these rents but with unequal influence over the state that distributes them. Although ground rent is important in all societies, it plays a dominant role in nations in the Global South because of their subordinate position in the international division of labor and of nature. While I highlight the importance of natural resources, my argument counters the notion of the "resource curse," for resources do not do anything by themselves but through the social relations that make them significant.

During this leftward swing, where agricultural rents are central in a national economy, they have tended to support the forging of alliances between classes and interest groups, the negotiation of policies between the state and major sectors, and the promotion of a moderate political style, as occurs in Brazil, Argentina, and Chile. On the other hand, where mineral rents are the dominant locus of a national economy, they have promoted the concentration of power in the state, the dependence of the private sector on the state, and the development of a radical or immoderate political style that has intensified conflicts between classes and regions, as occurs in Venezuela, Ecuador, and Bolivia. In all Latin American nations, primary products (mineral or agricultural) remain the fundamental export commodities and sources of foreign exchange; in many countries, labor power, an unusual primary "export commodity," has increasingly become, transformed into remittances, a major source of international currency. Despite the rejection of neoliberalism, the pursuit of comparative advantage in this domain continues to be the core economic policy of all Latin American states.

Of course, this simple scheme only begins to apprehend the complexity of each situation, not only because other factors also contribute to define each national context, but because these two conditioning factors may have complementary as well as conflicting effects. For instance, in Chile, even at the height of Pinochet's neoliberal project, the copper industry remained in the hands of the state, free from the free market, and copper income (and foreign exchange) granted the state extraordinary financial resources and domestic political leverage; this situation has not changed, except that the steady increase in copper prices in the past few years has given the state even more financial power. In this respect, Chile, despite its more diversified economy and post-Pinochet conciliatory political style, shares with mining countries the presence of a strong state. In Argentina, despite a tendency to establish alliances during the post-dictatorship turn to democracy, there has been historically a chronic conflict between agricultural producers interested in exporting their products in order to maximize their profits and consumers interested in keeping them in the domestic market in order to improve their welfare. The state must negotiate between these conflicting demands, which often become explosive, as was the case in 2008, during Cristina Fernández de Kirchner's presidency.

In addition, other forms of foreign currency must also be taken into account, such as international loans, which typically come together with coercive "collateral" political obligations. For instance, during the second presidency of Fernando Henrique Cardoso, when Brazil was facing severe financial needs and Lula was the likely candidate to win the 2002 presidential election, the IMF granted President Cardoso a US$30 billion loan but stipulated that only US$6 billion would be delivered to him and that the rest would be given to the new president under the agreement that all candidates would accept the IMF's prescriptions. Lula's Workers' Party (PT), through its "Letter to the Brazilian People," agreed to this condition.[9] This incident shows that the international financial community *no vota pero sí veta* (does not vote, but it does veto).[10] Whether resulting from rents, profits, or loans, foreign exchange is a major force in the dynamics of what I have called "national" and "global" postcolonial imperialisms—modes of imperial dominion mostly exerted through economic control and political influence yet backed by the largest territorial and extraterritorial armed forces in human history.[11]

Since I find most labels commonly used to differentiate these leftist regimes inappropriate, I refer to the two groupings of this simple scheme by acronyms formed by the initials of three typical representatives of each: VEBo, for Venezuela, Ecuador, and Bolivia; and BrAC, for Brazil, Argentina, and Chile. Despite their differences, one thing is clear: far from facing the end of History, all these nations face its return; for them, History is back. But what kind of history is this, and what future inspires it?

The Left's Futures

It is remarkable but not exceptional that this leftward turn has entailed the return of History. National histories in Latin America have been typically represented as inscribed in a global historical journey toward Progress. What is rather exceptional about this juncture is not the reinscription of Latin America into History as a grand process but that now it is not clear where History is going.

Ever since the conquest and colonization of the Americas, the region's ruling elites have had a certain sense of its ideal future, or, perhaps more accurately, substantial models of ideal futures have heavily inhabited the region's quotidian life. Insofar as these elite imaginaries have been hegemonic, Latin America has lived the present under the shadow of the future; as Susana Rotker noted, "Latin America is...an action without past or present, only a future."[12] Under the burden of imperial futures, the present has appeared as a transitional period, a stage of history to be left behind, if not simply rejected as an embarrassing reality. These ideal futures have always already been known because they have always been the present of metropolitan centers: first, of the "civilized" colonial empires and, after independence, of the major modern industrial nations.

The legitimacy of elites in Latin America has depended on their ability to be messengers of the future. As political and cultural leaders, their task has been to be brokers between Latin America and the "civilized" or "modern" world, in effect, between past and future. In order to perform this historical alchemy, they have to become, in their very beings, embodiments of the future. They incarnate the future through myriad techniques of the self, including socialization at home, selective consumption, education, travel, and language learning. One could identify which "future" has been imagined by these elites by tracing their travels and, most of all, by noting in which nation they have been educated and what languages and literatures they read. Historically, their crucible for self-making was first Spain and Portugal, but soon afterward it was France and England, and since World War II it has been the United States. For some leaders of the Left, of course, the Soviet Union and East Germany played this civilizing function. In Latin America, the main languages of civilization have been Spanish for Spain's postcolonies, Portuguese for Brazilians, and for all, first French and now English.

This mode of historicity saturates political life with the syndrome of the "non-yet," a perspective that depicts some societies as always already not yet civilized, not yet industrial, not yet modern. It also classifies and ranks contemporary societies by transforming space into time, geographical contiguity into temporal distance, and cultural difference into evolutionary hierarchy. As a result, while existing at the same time in contiguous spaces, some societies are defined as civilized and others as primitive, representing an earlier and inferior stage of humanity. Given the dominance of this viewpoint, in Latin America's relation to the modern world, simultaneity has not meant contemporaneity, for to be contemporaneous, as Ernst Bloch argued for other regions, is to be fully modern. Anthropologist Johannes Fabian has called this framing "the denial of coevalness," that is, the construction of an "allochronic temporality" whereby simultaneously existing societies are given different evolutionary value and placed into different historical periods; while those treated as barbarous are displaced into the past, those viewed as civilized are kept in the present and presented as the apex of humanity.[13] When they are all placed on the same progressive arrow of time, non-Western societies are seen as representing the past of civilized societies and civilized ones as embodying the future of the non-West. When non-Western peoples are excluded from Western history, they are treated as radically other, more creatures of nature than creators of culture.

This historicist vision presents the West as the apex of civilization and the Rest as backward regions occupying a previous stage of development. In terms of this worldview, the area that has become Latin America has been variously depicted as both different and inferior at different times according to changing dominant typologies: as savage, primitive, backward, traditional, underdeveloped, developing, the Third World, emerging, failed—all different labels that identify it as less than, as living in what historian Dipesh Chakrabarty has called, for other postcolonial societies, "the waiting room of History."[14] From this imperial perspective, Latin America is seen and sees itself as always catching up, never catching up, always not quite, permanently looking at history from the backstage, never sufficient, always never enough.[15]

In the twentieth century, particularly after the decolonization of European colonies in Africa, Asia, and the Caribbean following World War II, "modernization"—commonly understood as a process of development through industrialization, urbanization, democratization, and secularization—became the key to achieving the long-cherished ideal of civilization. Like most nations in the Third World—a category created at that time—Latin American countries continued to seek modernity, despite efforts at originality or at being nonaligned, by pursuing one of two established models: capitalism, the familiar track of the First World, or socialism, the experimental trajectory of the Second World. But after a long battle between these antagonistic models, neither one achieved a real victory. At the end of the twentieth century, although actually existing socialism was defeated, capitalism's triumph has been shown to be pyrrhic. While this system has been a transformative historical force that has offered substantial benefits to large sectors and reduced poverty in some areas, it has done so at the expense of the exclusion of majorities and the degradation of the material foundations of humanity. Almost half the world's population is living under the poverty line; the wealthiest 20 percent consume 82.5 percent of all the riches on earth, while the poorest 20 percent live on 1.6 percent. Facing the bankruptcy of both models, Latin American cultural and political elites, as well as the population at large, long accustomed to viewing the present as a stage toward an ideal future, now confront the lack of guiding models; they face a crisis of futurity.

Now that History is back, the Left faces a similar future in all Latin American nations, even if embodied in different national dreams and under different political and economic conditions. Here I explore the gestalt of this future, this common "future form," through five interrelated themes.

1. Agitated Present, Spectral Future

I name this rubric "Agitated Present, Spectral Future" in order to evoke a modality of historicity, of being in the world, in which the future appears phantasmatic, as if it were a space inhabited by ghosts from the past and ideal dreams, and the present unfolds as a dense field of nervous agitation, constantly entangled in multiplying constraints, a conglomeration of contradictory tendencies and actions leading to no clear destination. Despite constant activity inspired by high hopes, despite even significant achievements, a nightmarish sensation of being trapped saturates the present, as if it were jammed or moved without advancing or in the wrong direction. Even when states manage to promote economic growth and public welfare, the ideal future remains elusive, threatened by chronic problems and newly emerging obstacles.

Under this modality of historicity, the present time seems not only agitated but expansive; it prolongs itself within lasting constraints. While it occupies the space-time of what may be measured as the chronological future, it does not become the Future itself, insofar as the future is imagined not just as the homogeneous time that lies ahead but as the anticipated epoch of historical fulfillment. As this historical future is identified not with empty calendric time but with the meaningful time of fulfilled history, it comes to embody both renewed hopes and repeated deferrals. As if held back by recalcitrant circumstances, this anticipated future keeps appearing and receding like a mirage, a haunting promise that threatens to always be a deferred presence.

Nationalist leaders in Latin America, including those on the left, have commonly defined the promised future as a "second independence": the achievement of economic and cultural autonomy, of real, as opposed to formal, political independence. In the past, this goal typically had a specific historical foundation: the wars of independence, which broke the colonial link and established Latin American nations as formally independent republics (with significant exceptions, such as Brazil, whose independence was achieved by political means in 1822, when it became a monarchy, and Cuba, which became a US protectorate in 1898 after thirty years of war against Spain and was finally granted conditioned independence in 1902). Reflecting differences in political trajectories and goals, leftist regimes now have established more diverse foundational genealogies for the still heralded goal of "the second independence."

In an insightful discussion of the turn to the left in Latin America, Claudio Lomnitz notes the tendency for all left regimes now to establish a particular foundational past for their current struggles: Evo Morales places it in Bolivia's five hundred years of anticolonial resistance; Hugo Chávez defines it through the heroic leadership of Bolívar in the wars of independence (on occasion he looks to the sixteenth-century indigenous leader Guaicaipuro's battle against the Spanish colonizers); Cuauhtemoc Cárdenas sees himself as continuing the struggle of his uncle Lázaro Cárdenas for social justice in Mexico; Michelle Bachelet hails Allende's struggle for democratic socialism; Nestor Kirchner claims as his own Argentina's Peronist culture; Lula links himself to Brazil's transition to democracy in 1983; and Tabare Vásquez highlights Uruguay's social-democratic legacy of the 1920s. Juxtaposing temporal scales and historical epochs, Lomnitz states,

> Bolivia, Venezuela, Mexico, Uruguay, Argentina, Brazil, Chile: 500 years, 200 years, 90 years, 80 years, 60 years, 40 years, 30 years. But also the pre-colonial era, the early republican moment, the popular regimes, and democratic socialism. These are some of the ghosts that haunt the new foundationalism.[16]

In the face of a history of partial achievements and constant deferrals, the ghosts of epic rebellions, revolutions, and republican nation-building continue to animate the ongoing process of nation-building—of constructing the nation and reconstructing its foundations. It is evident that the more varied repertoire of founding moments at this time reflects the Left's diverse nature. While the appeal to such founding moments may express an old political habit, its anxiously reiterative character reveals a distinctive anxiety concerning the future. In the past, claiming as foundational certain historical moments had served less to establish the basis for continuous development than to legitimate the ongoing pursuit of familiar goals in the face of continually deferred achievements. Despite more varied foundations now, a similar exchange between past glories and deferred triumphs is at work, except that now it is not just that the desired future remains unfulfilled but that its very being has become ethereal. Facing a groundless future, the Left must repeatedly ground itself in the past.

The invocation of a memorable past fixes certain times and places in the current national imaginary. This form of imagining the nation, by territorializing a history and historicizing a territory, helps frame the relation between past, present, and future.[17] As the uncertain long term shrinks, the short term expands, digging into the past to resurrect its icons and extending into the calendric future as it pushes the anticipated historical future beyond an ever-receding horizon. In a lucid discussion of the current turn to the left in Latin America, Boaventura de Sousa Santos notes the peculiar relation assumed at this time in Latin America between the short and long terms. Whereas the long term has historically been the horizon of the Left, the overwhelming dominance of capitalism has now restricted the domain of the Latin American Left to the short term.[18] Without clear alternative images of the future, its struggles must focus on the here and now. According to him, this concentration on the short term also makes less relevant classical debates about reform and revolution. While he attributes this situation to a lack of integration between theory and praxis, I see it as reflecting also the extraordinary structural constraints within which the Left has emerged.[19]

In my view, these constraints have produced a rather peculiar articulation between practices and ideals in the short and long terms; while leftist governments proclaim socialist ideals for the long term, they promote capitalism in the short term. And while they promote capitalism in the short term, they regard capitalism as unviable for the long term. Thus we have capitalism for a present without a future, and socialism for a future without a present.

When these tensions prevail, they make quicksand of the present. We must keep moving to stay on top, torn between the desire to find a secure footing for all and the instinct of self-preservation that compels individuals to desert collective projects. The ever-present talk of corruption within the current Left suggests that this tension leads many to use the language of the common good to conceal self-interested pursuits.

Of course, different countries embody this paradoxical historicity in different ways. Following my typology, while the VEBo countries (typified by Venezuela, Ecuador, and Bolivia) more openly endorse socialism and promote policies associated with it, such as the nationalization of enterprises and constitutional reforms, BrAC countries (exemplified by Brazil, Argentina, and Chile) take more moderate positions and focus on redistributive policies and social reforms. Since an original leftist economic project cannot be equated either with nationalizations (reducing it to a form of state capitalism) or with redistributive policies (reducing it to a version of a social-democratic state), the task remains to develop a viable project for the long term. While VEBo countries seem to have more innovative political projects and BrAC countries appear to be following a rather familiar track, both groupings are still seeking to define an original path toward a postcapitalist future.[20] While these leftist states may be moving in that direction, their reliance on the pursuit of comparative advantages suggests that so far they have not been able to meet this fundamental challenge.

2. Beyond Reform and Revolution

The rather familiar rhetoric of reform and revolution continues to be commonly employed in Latin America, even if it is increasingly unclear what these terms mean. In light of the typology I have proposed, it is evident that the VEBo countries—whose states control abundant mineral rents and are not the product of recent experiences of dictatorship— invoke more frequently the notions of revolution and of socialism. The BrAC nations—with diversified economies and coming from recent military dictatorships—follow the lead of Chile and Brazil in pursuing a politics of rhetorical moderation and class alliances.

During the twentieth century, "revolution" became the mantra of nationalist discourse. Revolution signified radical change. Most governments in Latin America, whether moderate or radical, claimed to be revolutionary. Often the label "revolution" was used not to promote but to contain radical change; the archetypical example of this usage is Mexico's PRI, the Partido Revolucionario Institucional (the Institutional Revolutionary Party), a party that took for itself the name of the Mexican revolution in order to domesticate its radical potential, making its oxymoronic name an apt descriptor of the party's normalizing ethos.

For the radical Left, "revolution" has historically meant the overturning of the capitalist system; it has claimed revolution for itself, reform for all others. But since overturning capitalism requires conquering the state, "revolution" came to identify two processes and to have two distinct meanings: taking over the state through armed struggle and unleashing radical change from the state. As the Cuban revolution became the model of this view of "revolution," one that was emulated in many countries in the 1960s, these two meanings were seen as part of one process. The military victory of the Sandinistas against the Somoza dynasty in 1979 and the electoral defeat of the Sandinista revolutionary regime a decade later seem to have closed this cycle of armed revolutionary struggle.

The Chilean model, under Salvador Allende (1971–73), proposed an alternative view: "revolution" not as the violent seizure of state power, which should be captured by electoral means, but as the radical transformation of society. During the current leftward turn, this view has become dominant. As the World Social Forum proposes, revolution, including the seizure of power, should be carried out by democratic means. In Mexico, the Zapatista movement began an armed uprising of symbolic dimensions in 1994 but soon abandoned arms and made clear that its path was political struggle, in order not to seize the state but to create a space for a different kind of politics at the local and national level. On the basis of the Zapatista political project, which aims to change society by changing social relations without seizing the state, John Holloway has claimed that true revolutionary politics involves creating a new world by changing society from within, rather than through the state.

For most leftists, however, the state continues to be at the center of revolutionary politics. But even in this case, there is no common agreement about what makes politics radical. Chávez has converted the state into the main agent of the revolution, first through state-produced reforms inspired by a sui generis model of the Third Way and after 2005 through what he has called "Socialism of the twenty-first century." But while the state is the main agent of revolutionary change in Venezuela, Chávez is the center of the state, unabashedly making its basic decisions and contradicting his own goal to promote "participatory democracy." Just as in 2005 he proudly declared in Porto Alegre that he alone decided that Venezuela should be socialist, in 2007 he boasted that he single-handedly wrote the socialist-inspired constitutional reform that he presented to the National Assembly, the product, as he said, of his *puño y letra* (written in his own hand).

At the other end of the left political spectrum, in Chile, the Concertación governments have sought to achieve consensus on basic developmental goals. José Insulza, who served the Concertación government for ten years, calls this approach, one that avoids ideological labels and focuses on particular policies, "socialism by enumeration." As he explained to me, "We prefer to focus on housing, education, health, and so on. We don't need to use the label 'socialism.' We call this 'socialism by enumeration.'"[21] This helps explain why President Michelle Bachelet could not transfer her great popularity (84 percent) to Eduardo Frei, the Concertación's candidate, and why the election of conservative billionaire Sebastián Piñera in 2010 has been widely perceived as a more "efficient" way of continuing Chile's "modernization," rather than as a change of developmental models.

These differing strategies for change blur the boundaries between reform and revolution. According to Boaventura de Sousa Santos, in Latin America now "there are reformist processes that seem revolutionary" (his example is Venezuela under Chávez), "revolutionary processes that seem reformist" (his example is the Zapatista movement), and also "reformist processes that don't even seem reformist" (his example is Brazil's PT).[22] Independent of the validity of his examples, the point is that in the present context the concepts of reform and revolution, however indispensable in ideological struggles, have become increasingly inadequate as guides for action and as analytical categories.

One may read these circumstances as reflecting the closure of radical options but also as offering openings for new ways of imagining the ends and social logics of fundamental change. It is now less acceptable to justify questionable means in the name of superior ends. Instead, there is a growing demand to make everyday political actions correspond to ultimate values, to make the present prefigure the future. Democracy is increasingly valorized not as the protective shell of political life but as its foundation, not just as means of revolution but as its end. In tension with historicist teleologies, it is now more possible to imagine the present not as a stage toward history's pre-ordained future but as its necessary ground, if not as the history we want, then as the history we have.

3. Beyond the Single Revolutionary Subject

The recent turn to the left in Latin America has taken place through the actions of a rather large diversity of actors who have become recognized as icons of the "Left." This contrasts with a historical tradition in which the Left was identified with political parties or organizations that claimed to represent workers and peasants as the main agents of revolutionary change. While this is true for all countries during this turn, in VEBo countries certain sectors or individuals have assumed the main or sole leadership of the process, whereas in the BrAC countries the tendency has been to establish a politics of alliances among competing sectors.

In the past thirty years, as chronic and new problems proliferated in Latin America—in part resulting from the closing of protected enterprises, the expansion of informal economies, and severe migrations and displacements—there took place in Latin America a general disenchantment with traditional political parties and with politics itself. In this context, new social movements came to play a significant role in politics, such as the Zapatistas in Mexico, the Landless Workers' Movement (MST) in Brazil, the Piqueteros (unemployed) in Argentina, and the indigenous and Afro-descendant movements in Ecuador, Bolivia, Colombia, and Peru. While these movements have struggled for specific demands, such as land, work, and recognition, and have reactivated the existing political system, they have also challenged politics as usual. At the same time, while most traditional political parties lost power, new parties became so important that in two cases they gained the national presidency through elections: the PT (Workers' Party) in Brazil and the MAS (Movement Toward Socialism) in Bolivia. Although these parties have at their core a particular social sector (workers and coca growers, respectively), they are socially heterogeneous and do not regard this core as a universal class. They have come to power through multiclass alliances in both regional and national politics; it should be remembered that before Lula won Brazil's presidential election in 2002 through alliances with business sectors, the PT had won important regional electoral victories through broad political alliances, as in São Paulo and Porto Alegre.

The new leftist presidents, elected with the support of these movements and organizations, represent a wide range of personalities, social origins, and political experiences. Including two women, an indigenous leader, a trade-union organizer, a former priest, and a lower-class and low-ranking military officer, this set of presidents reflects an exceptionally broad spectrum of the Latin American population. Their conceptions of rule vary, from the attempt by Chávez to create a uniform society through the monological voice of the state to the heteroglossic project announced by José Mújica, the new president of Uruguay. The product of a divided society, Chávez has built on this division and turned it into a chasm between *revolucionarios* and *escuálidos* (revolutionaries and "squalids," the term Chávez applies to his critics). Since 2005, he has turned this division into a struggle to the death between two systems: socialism and capitalism. His slogan for the revolution during this new phase is *patria, socialismo o muerte* (fatherland, socialism, or death).[23] In contrast, Uruguay's Mujica proclaimed in his inaugural speech the goal of *una patria para todos y con todos* (fatherland for all and with all), pointedly rejecting his earlier radical position as a Tupamaro leader (Tupamaros were an urban guerrilla organization active in the 1960s and 1970s) but maintaining the ideal of a just society.

While the search for a single revolutionary subject has declined, some leftists have transferred this role from the proletariat to the *pobretariado*, a concept developed by Brazilian liberation theologist Frei Breto to refer to the largest sector of Latin America, the marginalized and excluded[24] (*pobretariado* is a clever play on words, as *pobre* in Spanish means "poor"). But the tendency in the region, particularly in BrAC countries, is to recognize a plurality of agents of change, as if there were an implicit agreement that changing the world now requires an alliance among all those who suffer hardships in the world. In all countries, in a context where the majority of the population is excluded from the formal economy, the exploitation of labor is no longer considered the main factor in the formation of revolutionary subjects. Alliances are now sought among subjects affected by multiple forms of domination, not just economic exploitation but also cultural and political subordination and discrimination.

New political actors now participate in and even define public debate in Latin America. For Marisol de la Cadena, "what is unprecedented" in this turn to the left is "the presence of regional indigenous social movements as a constituent element of these transformations"; for her, these processes entail "plural politics in a political pluriverse."[25] Carlos de la Torre's lucid analysis of new populisms in Latin America has illuminated specific tensions inhering in this "plural politics," such as the conflict between the centralizing policies of Rafael Correa and the demands for autonomy of Ecuador's indigenous communities.[26]

Pluralizing the agents of change, particularly when these include indigenous sectors, has expanded conceptions of historical progress and eroded the hegemony of liberal conceptions of the nation as either a monocultural mestizo community or a multicultural polity. Now it has become possible to propose plurinationalism and interculturality as national ideals, particularly in Andean nations with large indigenous populations. These changes have expanded the domain of the political and brought into the public arena discussions about the legitimacy of cultural diversity that were previously confined to intellectual circles. The 2008 constitutions of Ecuador and Bolivia define these nations as plurinational societies, grant multiple rights to their diverse communities, recognize the value of intercultural dialogue, and in the case of Ecuador, establish for the first time constitutional rights to nature as a political actor. During this turbulent period, competing principles and visions of life generate acute political tensions but also open politics to unprecedented possibilities.

4. Double Historical Discourse

It is common to think of double discourse in the political realm as involving duplicity and expressing a gap between claims and practices, between what is said and what is meant. Current leftist politics in Latin America are certainly not exempt from this rather common form of deceptive political discourse. In any historical context, principled claims are at times contradicted by self-seeking practices. In neocolonial contexts, however, there are specific forms of double discourse that reflect the tension between formal national independence and international dependence. This tension generates "a double discourse of national identity that expresses and organizes the split between the appearance of national sovereignty and the continuing hold of international subordination."[27] But what is distinctive now, in my view, is a peculiar modality of double discourse in which narratives about the present and the future produce accounts that are mutually contradictory but true, since they refer to different temporal horizons. Because it is constituted by the tension between the two temporal narratives of the short and long terms, I call this a double historical discourse.

My concern here is not the sincerity of beliefs or their relation to practices but the specific structural relations that make it possible for conflicting beliefs and practices to coexist without necessarily reflecting bad faith or deception. In an insightful analysis of the current turn to the left in Latin America, Atilio Borón notes a "disjunction" between the "consolidation of neoliberalism in the critical terrain of the economy and policy making" and its visible "weakening in the domains of culture, public awareness [*conciencia pública*] and politics."[28] He sees this disjunction as a reflection of the lack of an alternative economic program. I would modify this acute observation by suggesting that neoliberalism's "consolidation in the critical terrain of the economy" occurs mostly in the short term, for it is also rejected as an economic project for the future. This disjuncture is first between temporal frames and then between domains.

The perception that there is no immediate alternative to neoliberalism with respect to the economic core has led to the proliferation of this type of double discourse formed by narratives that contradict each other but are all true in terms of their respective historicities. The 2010 inaugural presidential speech of Uruguay's José Mújica clearly expresses this temporal disjuncture: "We'll be orthodox in macroeconomics. We'll compensate this extensively by being heterodox, innovative and daring in other aspects" (my translation). In an earlier statement, he had asserted, "We have many things to do before socialism" (*tenemos muchas cosas que hacer antes del socialismo*).[29] Mujica was perhaps more candid than other leftist presidents who also claim that capitalism is ultimately unviable but who seek to maximize income through capitalist production in the here and now. This conflictual interplay between different temporal scales makes the present particularly agitated and murky; it is a space of creative undertakings but also of nefarious forms of duplicity and corruption. There is probably no more emblematic example of this mixture of immorality and deception than the discovery in Venezuela in June–July of 2010 of around four thousand containers with over one hundred thousand tons of imported food rotting all around the national ports, the result not just of ineptitude but of the profit-seeking actions of business networks operating at various levels of the Venezuelan state.

At the risk of simplifying a complex phenomenon, I suggest that the short and long terms are articulated differently in these countries. In VEBo countries, where socialist ideals are constantly proclaimed, there is a close articulation between the short and long terms in the political domain but a sharp disjuncture between them in the economic realm. In BrAC countries, where socialist ideals are understated, politics and economics tend to reinforce each other in the short term, pushing the long term toward an ever less visible future.

This double historical discourse expresses a perverse paradox. As I have already indicated, given the location of Latin America in the twin international division of labor and of nature, at the present time the pursuit of foreign exchange has meant that, in practice, all Latin American states—whether on the right or the left—promote comparative advantages within a neoliberal framework. Since the main comparative advantage of Latin America now is its vast natural resources, the maximization of foreign exchange places all Latin American states on the same economic plane—one of dependence on primary products.

This fundamental economic grounding threatens to erode the radical potential of the left turn and to make all states in Latin America, whether identified with the Left or the Right, converge around a set of rent-seeking economic policies. For example, Colombia, which had a relatively diversified export structure based on agricultural products, under conservative president Alvaro Uribe became a mining nation—oil and minerals now represent over 60 percent of its total exports. While analysts generally place Brazil and Venezuela at opposite ends of the reformist and the revolutionary spectrum, these countries are equally intent on expanding oil production. Under Chávez, Venezuela has become ever more dependent on oil rents and on the imports of consumption goods. Under Lula, despite its rather dynamic economic structure, Brazil has continued to be a nation reliant on its vast natural resources, now magnified by newly discovered oil reserves. Chile, once the paradigmatic neoliberal model in Latin America, offers an instructive example: while the economy has indeed achieved significant rates of growth measured by conventional standards, this expansion has taken place at the cost of a skewed productive structure that relies on the exploitation of a few natural resources. As the 2010 election of Sebastian Piñera in Chile indicates, consensus among competing political parties around this economic foundation has diminished the difference between right and left policies. If this analysis is correct, in a perverse twist of fate, in pursuit of fortune, leftist states may be doing now the work of capital.

Still, since this double historical discourse is part of a plural discursive field, it is modified and challenged by other voices. This is a moment of heteroglossia. Some of these voices, including that of the state on occasion, propose models of the economy that are more ecologically sound and socially harmonious. While the proliferation of multiple voices in the political field may be confusing and conflictual, it offers the possibility of unexpected imaginings and original visions of the future.

5. Radical Democracy

In the past, equality has been the key word in global struggles for democracy: the pursuit of equality of citizens before the law. Marxists have criticized bourgeois democracy as being universal in form but partial in content. As Marx argued, it is not enough to be equal before the law—a universal law that posits that no one can sleep under a bridge only affects those who have no proper housing. Socialist democracy has sought to move from formal equality toward substantial social equality. Yet the socialist democracy of actually existing socialisms has produced its own state-centered inequalities and has imposed a single voice on society.

The current struggles in Latin America build on the global achievements and limitations of bourgeois and socialist democracies. In some respects, they represent a continuity of these past battles and reproduce familiar modes of power and conceptions of development. But it would be a mistake to reduce this complex period to politics as usual, to the familiar; politics now takes a range of forms in different locations. While their effects may be short-lived or be co-opted, the agency of new political actors and the force of new imaginaries have already changed the political scene in Latin America. This leftward turn has reactivated the public sphere and transformed politics itself.

Its most significant achievement, in my view, has been the value now placed on democracy as a political form that requires constant expansion and transformation; in different ways, this has been the joint accomplishment of the various Latin American Lefts in all countries, both through domestic struggles and regional initiatives and institutions, such as ALBA, an alliance that seeks to counter the free-trade association. As it has come to encompass ever-new areas of social life, democracy names now a process rather than a political shell or set of institutions; as a "permanent democracy," it has displaced "revolution" as the key term for the Left at this time.[30] While this achievement is the result of many struggles, perhaps its most significant expression has been the recognition of difference as a political principle. In many countries, particularly in VEBo nations, people now struggle for the recognition not only of citizens' equal rights before the law but of different conceptions of citizenship and of the law. These demands are often cast from different epistemological and cosmological positions and involve a critique not just of Western liberalism but also of Western modernity itself; as such, they involve the struggle not just over distinct sets of rights but over the right to have different conceptions of life. This has been the major contribution of the indigenous movements, from the Zapatistas in Mexico to those in the Andean nations. After a long century of homogenizing projects led by cultural and political elites who endorsed Western notions of progress, these movements have helped redefine the national imaginary, incorporating values of indigenous communities and conceptualizing the nation as plurinational community, as sanctioned in the new constitutions in Bolivia and Ecuador. Even in countries where the struggle for the recognition of difference has played a lesser role, as in Chile, Brazil, or Venezuela, the value of diversity has nevertheless changed the political field.

These struggles have expanded the agents, agendas, and conceptions of democracy. They draw strength from many local experiences. Just as no single social actor can now be represented as the agent of History without meeting significant resistance from other actors, no one conception of democracy can establish its hegemony without debate. The struggle *for* democracy now entails a struggle *about* democracy. As Boaventura de Sousa Santos has phrased it, political battles now pursue not an alternative to democracy but an alternative democracy.[31]

The Currency of the Current

If in the past the Left claimed to have a monopoly on the future, now it can offer but uncertain images of the future. Yet this very lack has opened spaces for the imagination and experimentation. Although the future is not open, it offers openings. And although the final destination may not be clear, the sense of direction is: toward justice, equality, freedom, diversity, and social and ecological harmony. The Left has no map, but it has a compass.

Latin America's crisis of futurity involves yet a more fundamental challenge. It is not just that the Left's imagined future is uncertain but that its real future existence is in question. This turn to the left already may turn out to be only temporary—a passing moment rather than a permanent achievement. At least at the level of the national state, the region seems to be shifting toward the right. A critical election suggests a change of direction: the victory of billionaire Sebastian Piñera in Chile in 2010, despite Michelle Bachelet's 84-percent popularity. Even Fidel Castro, certainly an astute observer and one not prone to offer negative forecasts, has stated that "before Obama completes his term there will be from six to eight right-wing governments in Latin America that will be allies of the empire."[32]

On the other hand, even if the Right may achieve electoral victories in the near future, my sense is that the Left has managed to redefine the terrain on which all political sectors must move. In Latin America, as in Europe, opponents of the Left now frequently endorse many of the Left's principles and policies. As Steven Erlander reported in the *New York Times*,

Europe's center-right parties have embraced many ideas of the left: generous welfare benefits, nationalized health care, sharp restrictions on carbon emissions, the ceding of some sovereignty to the European Union. But they have won votes by promising to deliver more efficiently than the left, while working to lower taxes, improve financial regulation, and grapple with aging populations."

He cites historian Michel Winockas, who argues that "the use of Socialist ideas...ha[s] become mainstream" by leaders, such as Nicolas Sarkozy of France and Germany's Angela Merkel, "who condemn the excesses of the 'Anglo-Saxon model' of capitalism while praising the protective power of the state."[33] In Latin America, the opposition to the Left now has also embraced its fundamental principles. While clearly there remain antagonistic poles in politics that reflect profound social inequalities and ideological differences, the boundaries between the traditional "Right" and "Left" are less sharp. In Latin America, it would be hard to be elected now—and to remain in power—without recognizing *el pueblo* as sovereign and paying more than nominal attention to the increasingly diverse demands of the popular sectors for which the Left has fought.

Some of these demands are very basic and could be addressed by governments of different political orientations, but others are quite radical. Although some of the most utopian demands may be unrealistic at this time, they express hopes and desires that affect the unfolding of current politics. As moderate a thinker as Max Weber recognized utopian strivings as indispensable in political life. As he said, "It is perfectly true, and confirmed by all historical experience, that the possible cannot be achieved without continually reaching out towards that which is impossible in this world."[34] Recently, philosopher Alain Badiou has argued for the need to reach for what seems impossible. Given that capitalism, understood as a self-expanding system propelled by profit maximization, is globally unviable since it excludes majorities, degrades communal life, and erodes the natural habitat of humanity, fighting for an alternative world is absolutely indispensable. He responds to this need by proposing what he calls "the communist hypothesis." For him, this hypothesis is not a utopian ideal but a set of "intellectual practices always actualized in a different fashion" in diverse historical situations. In another register, he also presents this hypothesis as "what Kant called an idea with a regulatory function, not a programme."[35] It is significant that for Badiou this hypothesis has been present in fragmentary form in struggles for equality since antiquity but need not be identified with any model from the past, including those that have claimed to embody the communist ideal.

It is this historical dimension that Slavoj Žižek regards as essential. While enthusiastically endorsing Badiou's core argument, he rejects the notion of the communist hypothesis as a Kantian regulative idea and emphasizes its "precise reference to a set of actual social antagonisms which generate the need for communism."[36] As if echoing Weber, for Žižek this entails constant struggle, moving beyond models that have not worked and fighting to realize new ones, "again and again."[37] From a rather different theoretical perspective but following a similar radical impulse, David Harvey offers in the appendix to *Spaces of Hope* a boldly imaginative image of what one such model of a just and egalitarian society could look like based on cooperative forms of production and more flexible arrangements of work, family, and residence.[38]

Embers of the Past, Poetry of the Future

Throughout this chapter, I have argued that during this leftward turn the reiterative appeal to icons from the past is a symptom that reveals anxiety over an uncertain future and the desire to provide a stable foundation for an agitated present. Yet the appeal to past icons, when it arises organically from ongoing struggles toward a better world, may also express their lasting significance as vital embodiments of ideals of justice and equality. It is in this sense that Javier Sanjinés has used the notion of "embers of the past" to evoke history's capacity to energize and illuminate present struggles: "'Embers' is, above all, a concept of sociocultural temporality: the persistence in the present of 'embers of the past,' buried, flickering, but still capable of igniting new conflagrations."[39] In the introduction to Sanjinés's book, Xavier Albó comments that the image offered by Sanjinés is more apt than Walter Benjamin's notion of "ruins," for "it refers to embers covered by ashes that never were really extinguished and which new winds will make burn again with vigor."[40] Although this is an acute observation, Benjamin viewed the past not just as ruins but as traditions that must be rescued, saved for present struggles. As Susan Buck-Morss argues, his conception of the dialectic involves not just the two familiar moments of negation and supercession (as the transcendence of negation in synthesis) but also the neglected notion of "saving." As she puts it, "the verb *aufheben* has a third meaning as well. It is the German expression for 'to keep, to save,' as in saving a material trace, a memento of the past. I would like for us to keep, to save *this* meaning. It bears affinities with Walter Benjamin's idea of *rescuing* the past."[41] In a similar spirit, the notion of "embers" is used by Sanjinés to recognize how the past can be awakened in the present in order to rescue the future.

Still, it is not clear how past flames can be made to endure and to illuminate present struggles. In a stern analysis of the crisis of modernity in the Global South, David Scott argues that the emancipatory struggles of the past provide inadequate models for the impasses of the postcolonial present.[42] In dialogue with Scott, Gary Wilder revisits the conceptual worlds of thinkers associated with the "Negritude" movement and demonstrates the value of inhabiting their untimely thoughts and exploring their ongoing relevance. Building on insights on "reified objects, emancipatory potentiality and historical temporality" in the work of Walter Benjamin, Theodor Adorno, and Ernst Bloch, Wilder makes a compelling case for examining "futures that were once imagined but never came to be, alternative futures that might have been and whose not yet realized emancipatory possibilities may now be recognized and reawakened as durable and vital legacies."[43]

The quest for sources of emancipatory imaginings was one of Marx's central concerns. While he was intent on freeing radical imaginings from the burden of the past, he recognized the past's capacity to illuminate present struggles. In his examination of the revolutions of the nineteenth century, his call for a poetry drawn from the future was not meant to discard the past, only to open the future to radical novelty. For him, the past could be brought to life if it was invoked to animate struggles to transform the world rather than to adorn its dramas. As he famously argued, while the bourgeois revolutions of the eighteenth century "awakened the dead" for "glorifying new struggles" and "magnifying the task in reality," the social revolutions of the nineteenth century did so for "parodying the old" and for "fleeing from [the task's] solution in reality."[44]

Carried along by winds of history that fan old flames and rouse new struggles, Latin America has become a diverse fabric of collective utopian dreams. The dialogue between past and future informing current struggles has, despite constraints, challenged place-bound, parochial conceptions of universality and has generated global exchanges about reimagined worlds. The search for equality goes beyond the struggle against forms of domination based on region, class, gender, ethnicity, religion, race, or age. Particularly in the Andean region, indigenous movements are proposing to move from anthropocentric struggles toward biocentrism as an expression of a planetary universality. As a result of recent struggles, it is now more possible in Latin America to value difference and to recognize that one does not dream the same in Spanish or in Aymara, as a woman or as a man, as an adult or as a child, from a bed or from under the bridge. Perhaps it has also become possible to engage different cosmologies, to recognize particulars in universals and universals in particulars, and to be open to the call "to see a World in a grain of sand, / And a Heaven in a wild flower."[45]

Of course, given the unequal structures of power within which this leftward turn has taken place, it is possible that its new imaginings may be co-opted or crushed. But given that these imaginaries now unite South and North in a politics that fuses the pursuit of well-being and sheer global survival, it is likely that a counterpoint between the embers of the past and the poetry of the future will continue to conjure up images of worlds free from the horrors of history.[46] Politics will remain a battle of desires waged on an uneven terrain. But as long as people find themselves without a safe and dignified home in the world, utopian dreams will continue to proliferate, energizing struggles to build a world made of many worlds, where people can dream their futures without fear of waking up.

Notes

Notes to Series Introduction

1. Robert Shiller borrowed Alan Greenspan's phrase, with some irony, when he pointed to many of these as early as 2000; see Shiller, *Irrational Exuberance* (Princeton, NJ: Princeton University Press, 2000).

2. Carmen M. Reinhart and Kenneth S. Rogoff, *This Time Is Different: Eight Centuries of Financial Folly* (Princeton, NJ: Princeton University Press, 2009).

3. See Daniel Chirot's account of transformations at Washington Mutual in volume 1. Chirot, "A Turning Point or Business as Usual?" in *Business as Usual: The Roots of the Global Financial Meltdown*, ed. Craig Calhoun and Georgi Derluguian (New York: NYU Press, 2011), chapter 4.

4. If the motive of mortgage salesmen and the corporations behind them was simply greed, their actions were made possible by the long centrality of homeownership to the "American Dream" of integration into the middle class. This connected private profits to government policy designed to make homeownership more accessible. Ironically, the mortgage industry had long used the infamous policy of "redlining" to restrict loans to minorities on the ground that they lived in high-risk neighborhoods. Now it found ways to profit from the riskiest of mortgages—loans to consumers without a reasonable basis for repaying them—and justified its actions as an effort to extend homeownership more widely. Sadly many of those who were sold these mortgages ended up paying more than if they had rented and lost their savings as well as their houses. Like the

mortgage salesmen with whom they worked, developers generally pocketed their profits before this happened.

5. The Federal National Mortgage Association (Fannie Mae) was created in 1938 as part of the New Deal by which the US government under Roosevelt responded to the Great Depression. In 1968, it was privatized (partly in response to financial pressures generated by the Vietnam War) and began to operate as a "government-sponsored enterprise" (GSE)—essentially a corporation making profits for its investors but benefiting from tax exemption. The Federal Home Loan Mortgage Corporation (Freddie Mac) was created as a GSE in 1970, with a mandate to further expand opportunities for homeownership by making it easier for those making loans to home purchasers to sell them on the secondary market, largely by offering guarantees, subsidies, and liquidity. By supporting the secondary market for mortgages, both Fannie Mae and Freddie Mac played important roles in the current crisis. In 2008, they were placed under government conservatorship when their finances became extremely shaky and they required large infusions of cash from the US government. Taxpayers also pay for the legal defense of their managers against fraud charges.

6. As James K. Galbraith says in volume 3, it was like counterfeiting. Galbraith, "The Great Crisis and the Financial Sector: What We Might Have Learned," in *Aftermath: A New Global Economic Order?* ed. Craig Calhoun and Georgi Derluguian (New York: NYU Press, 2011), chapter 10.

7. Tom Wolfe, *The Bonfire of the Vanities* (New York: Farrar, Straus and Giroux, 1987).

8. There is a substantial literature charting the rise of traders and their gambling culture, from Michael Lewis's *Liar's Poker: Rising Through the Wreckage on Wall Street* (New York: Penguin, 1990) through Gillian Tett's *Fools Gold: How the Bold Dream of a Small Tribe at J.P. Morgan Was Corrupted by Wall Street Greed and Unleashed a Catastrophe* (New York: Free Press, 2009). Not only were most traders men, women were paid less and more likely to lose their jobs when crisis hit.

9. A version of this danger appeared earlier in the debacle of Long-Term Capital Management. This hedge fund made spectacular gains in its first few years, then lost US$4.6 billion in less than four months after the Russian financial crisis of 1998 made for a sudden contraction in liquidity. Its board members included two economists, Robert C. Merton

and Myron Scholes, who had shared the 1997 Nobel Prize for their work on just this issue of pricing derivatives. LTCM was closed in 2000.

10. See her chapter in volume 3. Sassen, "A Savage Sorting of Winners and Losers, and Beyond," in *Aftermath*, chapter 1.

11. See respectively the chapters by Daniel Chirot, Beverly Silver and Giovanni Arrighi, Gopal Balakrishnan, and Manuel Castells in volume 1. Chirot, "A Turning Point or Business as Usual?" in *Business as Usual*, chapter 4 ; Silver and Arrighi, "The End of the Long Twentieth Century," in *Business as Usual*, chapter 1; Balakrishnan, "The Convolution of Capitalism," in *Business as Usual*, chapter 8; and Castells, "The Crisis of Global Capitalism: Toward a New Economic Culture?" in *Business as Usual*, chapter 7.

12. See Silver and Arrighi, "End of the Long Twentieth Century."

13. We should not underestimate other cases, such as the bloody French debacle in Algeria, which among other things helped shape confrontations throughout the 1960s.

14. See the chapter by Immanuel Wallerstein in volume 1. Wallerstein, "Dynamics of (Unresolved) Global Crisis," in *Business as Usual*, chapter 2.

15. Wallerstein calls this "the world-revolution of 1968." See Wallerstein, "Dynamics of (Unresolved) Global Crisis"; and *World-System Analysis: An Introduction* (Durham, NC: Duke University Press, 2002). Whether or not one accepts his metaphor, this calls attention to the coincidence of protest and upheaval around the world, including in the Soviet bloc, where repressing discontent may have exacerbated the regime's long, terminal decline.

16. Ivan F. Boesky, commencement address, School of Business Administration, University of California, Berkeley, May 18, 1986.

17. It is informative as well that at the same time Wall Street was celebrating a culture where "greed is good," the phrase "to get rich is glorious" was circulating in China, attributed to Deng Xiaoping.

18. See the chapters by David Harvey in volume 1 and by Galbraith in volume 3. Harvey, "The Enigma of Capital and the Crisis This Time," in *Business as Usual*, chapter 2; and Galbraith, "Great Crisis."

19. Black and Scholes, "The Pricing of Options and Corporate Liabilities," *Journal of Political Economy* 81, no. 3 (1973): 637–54.

20. Merton, "Theory of Rational Option Pricing," *Bell Journal of Economics and Management Science* (The RAND Corporation) 4, no. 1 (1973): 141–83.

21. Thomas Pikkety and Emmanuel Saez, "Income Inequality in the United States, 1913-1998," *Quarterly Journal of Economics* 118, no. 1 (2003): 1-39; Frank Levy and Peter Temin, "Inequality and Institutions in 20th Century America," NBER Working Paper No. 13106 (May 2007); and Timothy Noah, "The United States of Inequality," *Slate*, September 16, 2010, http://img.slate.com/media/3/100914_NoahT_GreatDivergence.pdf.

22. Arguably, a version of the same process helped railroads and associated innovations in the nineteenth century; see Naomi R. Lamoreaux and Kenneth L. Sokoloff, eds., *Financing Innovation in the United States, 1870 to the Present* (Cambridge, MA: MIT, 2007). For a broader, longer-term investigation of similar phenomena linking possibly "irrational" investments to economic growth, see Carlotta Perez, *Technological Revolutions and Financial Capital: The Dynamics of Bubbles and Golden Ages* (Cheltenham: Edward Elgar, 2002).

23. This theme is developed by several chapters in volume 1, *Business as Usual*.

24. See the chapters by Caglar Keyder and Nancy Fraser in volume 1. Keyder, "Crisis, Underconsumption, and Social Policy," in *Business as Usual*, chapter 6; and Fraser, "Marketization, Social Protection, Emancipation: Toward a Neo-Polanyian Conception of Capitalist Crisis," in *Business as Usual*, chapter 5.

25. Phillips, *After the Fall: The Inexcusable Failure of American Finance* (New York: Penguin, 2009).

26. See the chapter by Piotr Dutkiewicz and Grzegorz Gorzelak in volume 3. Dutkiewicz and Gorzelak, "Central and Eastern Europe: Shapes of Transformation, Crisis, and the Possible Futures," in *Aftermath*, chapter 8.

27. This is alas one of the biggest issues for possible global futures not to receive significant attention in these first three volumes. There is, however, a large literature. One starting point is Alejandro Portes and Josh DeWind, eds., *Rethinking Migration* (New York: Berghahn, 2007).

28. See the Ravi Sundaram chapter in volume 2. Sundaram, "Global Governance after the Analog Age: The World after Media Piracy," in

The Deepening Crisis: Governance Challenges after Neoliberalism, ed. Craig Calhoun and Georgi Derluguian (New York: NYU Press, 2011), chapter 8.

29. See the chapter by Mary Kaldor in volume 2. Kaldor, "War and Economic Crisis," in *Deepening Crisis*, chapter 5.

30. See the chapter by Adrian Pabst in volume 2. Pabst, "The Paradox of Faith: Religion beyond Secularization and Desecularization," in *Deepening Crisis*, chapter 7. See also Craig Calhoun, Mark Juergensmeyer, and Jonathan VanAntwerpen, eds., *Rethinking Secularism* (Oxford: Oxford University Press, forthcoming).

31. Reinhart and Rogoff, *This Time Is Different.*

32. See Karen Ho, *Liquidated: An Ethnography of Wall Street* (Durham, NC: Duke University Press, 2009).

33. In this, they may have acted more like the world's rich countries themselves during their periods of growth; see Ha-Joon Chang, *Kicking Away the Ladder* (London: Anthem, 2002); and, in this Possible Futures series, "The 2008 World Financial Crisis and the Future of World Development," in *Aftermath*, chapter 2.

34. See Erik Reinert, *How Rich Countries Got Rich and Why Poor Countries Stay Poor* (London: Constable and Robinson, 2007).

35. See the chapters by Ha-Joon Chang, Dani Rodrik, Jomo Kwame Sundaram and Noelle Rodriguez, and Manuel Montes and Vladimir Popov in volume 3. Chang, "2008 World Financial Crisis"; Rodrik, "Growth after the Crisis," in *Aftermath*, chapter 3; Jomo and Rodriguez, "Structural Causes and Consequences of the 2008–2009 Financial Crisis," in *Aftermath*, chapter 4; and Montes and Popov, "Bridging the Gap: A New World Economic Order for Development?" in *Aftermath*, chapter 5.

36. This became a theme for a variety of more popular futurists, such as Alvin Toffler, but a partially similar argument was laid out in an intellectually richer and more serious (but still misleading) way in Daniel Bell's *The Coming of Post-Industrial Society: A Venture in Social Forecasting* (New York: Harper, 1973).

37. See Immanuel Wallerstein's account, published well before the current financial crisis and in an earlier phase of America's engagement in two intractable wars, *The Decline of American Power* (New York: New Press, 2003).

38. On both the choices open to China and the way Chinese thinkers are considering global change and possible futures, see R. Bin Wong's chapter in volume 3. Wong, "Chinese Political Economy and the International Economy: Linking Global, Regional, and Domestic Possibilities," in *Aftermath*, chapter 6.

39. See the chapter by Georgi Derluguian in volume 3. Derluguian, "The Post-Soviet Recoil to Periphery," in *Aftermath*, chapter 9.

40. See Vadim Volkov's chapter in volume 2. Volkov, "From Full to Selective Secrecy: The Offshore Realm after the Crisis," in *Deepening Crisis*, chapter 9.

41. See the chapter by Vincent Della Sala in volume 2. Della Sala, "A Less Close Union? The European Union's Search for Unity amid Crisis," in *Deepening Crisis*, chapter 6.

42. Again, see the chapter by Pabst in volume 2, "The Paradox of Faith."

43. It echoes something of what Max Weber saw the Protestant ethic generally contributing to the spirit of capitalism. See David Martin, *Pentacostalism: The World Their Parish* (New York: Wiley, 2008); and Birgit Meyer, "Pentecostalism and Globalization," in *Studying Global Pentecostalism: Theories and Methods*, ed. Allan Anderson, Michael Bergunder, André Droogers, and Cornelis van der Laan (Berkeley: University of California Press, 2010); and "Aesthetics of Persuasion: Global Christianity and Pentecostalism's Sensational Forms," *South Atlantic Quarterly* 109, no. 4 (2010): 741–63.

44. We may extend Barrington Moore's powerful point that injustice in itself does not explain rebellion against injustice. Moore, *Injustice: The Social Bases of Obedience and Revolt* (White Plains, NY: Sharpe, 1982). Neither does inequality on its own explain when it becomes intolerable or whether people have and use the capacities to change it. But, of course, there are many responses between obedience and successful revolt.

45. See the chapters by William Barnes and Nils Gilman and by Michael J. Watts in volume 2. Barnes and Gilman, "Green Social Democracy or Barbarism: Climate Change and the End of High Modernism," in *Deepening Crisis*, chapter 2; and Watts, "Ecologies of Rule: African Environments and the Climate of Neoliberalism," in *Deepening Crisis*, chapter 3.

46. See the chapter by David Held and Kevin Young in volume 2. Held and Young, "Crises in Parallel Worlds: The Governance of Global Risks in Finance, Security, and the Environment," in *Deepening Crisis*, chapter 1.

47. See the chapter by Kaldor in volume 2, "War and Economic Crisis."

48. See Fraser's chapter in volume 1, "Marketization, Social Protection, Emancipation." See also Keyder's chapter, "Crisis, Underconsumption, and Social Policy," for an indication that this is an issue in not only rich countries but middle-income developing countries. This involves what the Marxist tradition has analyzed as a crisis in social reproduction—the renewal of the social conditions required to sustain a capitalist society.

49. See Coronil's chapter in volume 1 for a brilliant account linking this to the specific crisis of the idea of a socially transformative project of the Left in Latin America. Coronil, "The Future in Question: History and Utopia in Latin America (1989–2010)," in *Business as Usual*, chapter 9.

50. See Piotr Dutkiewicz and Dmitri Trenin, eds., *Russia: The Challenges of Transformation* (New York: NYU Press, 2011).

51. See the chapters by Watts in volume 2 and Alexis Habiyaremye and Luc Soete in volume 3. Watts, "Ecologies of Rule"; and Habiyaremye and Soete, "The Global Financial Crisis and Africa's 'Immiserizing Wealth,'" in *Aftermath*, chapter 7.

52. See the chapter by Rogers Brubaker in volume 2 and Derluguian in volume 3. Brubaker, "Economic Crisis, Nationalism, and Politicized Ethnicity," in *Deepening Crisis*, chapter 4; and Derluguian, " Post-Soviet Recoil."

53. A further problem is the extent to which prosperity and development seem nearly everywhere to be measured by the acquisition of material commodities. This means that human well-being is not as directly the focus as it might be. Health, education, and levels of inequality are at best indirectly related to aggregate levels of GDP. This is, of course, the point made by the UN's Human Development Index; see Mahbub ul Haq, *Reflections on Human Development* (New York: Oxford University Press, 1995), and extended by Amartya Sen in *Development as Freedom* (New York: Knopf, 1999).

54. See especially the discussion by Barnes and Gilman in volume 2, "Green Social Democracy."

Notes to Introduction

1. Joe Nocera, "Still Stuck in Denial on Wall Street," *New York Times*, October 2, 2010.

2. Gillian Tett, *Fool's Gold: How the Bold Dream of a Small Tribe at J.P. Morgan Was Corrupted by Wall Street Greed and Unleashed a Catastrophe* (New York: Free Press, 2009); William D. Cohan, *House of Cards: A Tale of Hubris and Wretched Excess on Wall Street* (New York: Doubleday, 2009); and Lawrence G. McDonald, *A Colossal Failure of Common Sense: The Inside Story of the Collapse of Lehman Brothers*, with Patrick Robinson (New York: Three Rivers, 2009).

3. Arrighi sadly died in June 2009 with this chapter in draft; his wife and longtime collaborator Beverly Silver completed it. His theory is laid out in *The Long Twentieth Century: Money, Power, and the Origins of Our Times*, rev. ed. (New York: Verso, 2010); and *Adam Smith in Beijing: Lineages of the 21st Century* (New York: Verso, 2009).

4. See Arrighi, *Long Twentieth Century* and *Adam Smith in Beijing*.

5. The first volume of Wallerstein's *The Modern World-System* was published by Academic Press in 1974; the fourth and final volume will appear, from the University of California Press, in 2011 (together with a new edition of the first three). As Arrighi puts it, Wallerstein's 1974 book launched a "radical reorientation of social research" by advancing "a theoretical and historical account of the origins, structure, and eventual demise of the modern world-system." This was something very different from simply studying international relations or economic globalization, and it formed part of the basis for Arrighi's own subsequent work as well as others'. Arrighi, "Capitalism and the Modern World-System: Rethinking the Non-Debates of the 1970s," *Review* 21 , no. 1 (1998).

6. See Robert E. Wright, *Bailouts: Public Money, Private Profit* (New York: Columbia University Press / Social Science Research Council, 2010).

7. One reflection of this was the juxtaposition within academic economics of an explosion of exciting work in microeconomics while macroeconomics became something of an intellectual backwater.

Macroeconomics is, of course, back in the mainstream as the world's economic leaders struggle to cope with massive trade imbalances, nagging unemployment, problems of sovereign debt, and uncertainties in the global currency system.

8. Craig Calhoun and Georgi Derluguian, eds., *Aftermath: A New Global Economic Order?* (New York: NYU Press, 2011).

9. Calhoun and Derluguian, *Aftermath.*

Notes to Chapter One

1. Eric Hobsbawm, *The Age of Extremes: A History of the World 1914–1991* (New York: Pantheon, 1995), 558–59.

2. In this chapter we present a summary of some of the main findings of our previous research. We have refrained here from extensive citations to the wealth of historical and theoretical material on which our analyses are built. For a full version of the arguments presented in this chapter (including extensive bibliographic references), see Giovanni Arrighi, *The Long Twentieth Century: Money, Power and the Origins of Our Times*, 2nd ed. (London: Verso, 2010); Giovanni Arrighi and Beverly J. Silver, *Chaos and Governance in the Modern World System* (Minneapolis: University of Minnesota Press, 1999); Arrighi and Silver, "Capitalism and World (Dis)Order," *Review of International Studies* 27 (2001): 257–79; Silver and Arrighi, "Polanyi's 'Double Movement': The *Belle Époques* of British and U.S. Hegemony Compared," *Politics and Society* 31, no. 2 (2003): 325–55; Silver, *Forces of Labor: Workers' Movements and Globalization since 1870* (Cambridge: Cambridge University Press, 2003); and Arrighi, *Adam Smith in Beijing: Lineages of the Twenty-first Century* (London: Verso, 2007).

3. Fernand Braudel, *Civilization and Capitalism, 15th–18th Century*, vol. 3, *The Perspective of the World* (New York: Harper and Row, 1979).

4. Braudel, *Civilization and Capitalism*, 3: 157, 164, 242–43, 246, 604.

5. Greta R. Krippner, "The Financialization of the American Economy," *Socio-Economic Review* 3 (2005): 173–208.

6. Marx's general formula of capital is MCM', where M is money capital invested in C (commodities including labor, machines, and raw materials) and M' is the money capital accruing to the capitalist once the commodities produced are sold. If M' is greater than M, then the

capitalist has made a profit. If M' is consistently less than M, then there would be no profit and no incentive for capitalists to invest in production either as individuals or as a class. Karl Marx, *Capital*, vol. 1 (1867; repr., Moscow: Foreign Languages Publishing House, 1959).

7. Marx, *Capital*, 1: 755–56.

8. We can imagine this process as a set of overlapping S-curves. The overlap depicts the fact that a new systemic cycle of accumulation emerges at the same time that the still dominant regime is reaching its limits.

9. For a detailed historical account of the evolutionary patterns summarized in this section, see Arrighi, *Long Twentieth Century*; and Arrighi and Silver, *Chaos and Governance*.

10. For more on this point, see Arrighi, *Long Twentieth Century*; and Arrighi and Silver, *Chaos and Governance*, chapter 2 and conclusion.

11. Quoted in Ramachandra Guha, *Environmentalism: A Global History* (New York: Longman, 2000), 22.

12. For reasons to think that China may be able to draw on both the legacy of the Communist era and the legacy of "industrious revolution" from imperial times to fashion a new hybrid model that constitutes such an alternative path, see Arrighi, *Adam Smith in Beijing*.

Notes to Chapter 2

1. Samir Amin, Giovanni Arrighi, Andre Gunder Frank, and Immanuel Wallerstein, *Dynamics of Global Crisis* (New York: Monthly Review Press, 1982), 7.

2. Ilya Prigogine, *The End of Certainty* (New York: Free Press, 1996), 187–88.

Notes to Chapter 3

1. H. Schneider, "'Systemic Risk' Is the New Buzz Word as Officials Try to Prevent Another Bubble," *Washington Post*, July 26, 2010.

2. D. Harvey, *The Enigma of Capital: And the Crises of Capitalism* (London: Profile Books, 2010).

3. A. Maddison, *Contours of the World Economy, 1–2030 AD: Essays in Macro-Economic History* (Oxford: Oxford University Press, 2007).

4. D. Harvey, *Paris: Capital of Modernity* (New York: Routledge, 2003).

5. R. Bonney, ed., *The Rise of the Fiscal State in Europe, c. 1200–1815* (Oxford: Oxford University Press, 1999).

6. R. McKinnon, *Money and Capital in Economic Development* (Washington, DC: Brookings Institution, 1973).

7. J. O'Connor, *Natural Causes: Essays in Ecological Marxism* (New York: Guilford, 1997).

8. G. Arrighi, "Towards a Theory of Capitalist Crisis," *New Left Review* 1, no. 111 (September–October 1978): 3–24.

9. J. Bellamy Foster and F. Magdoff, *The Great Financial Crisis: Causes and Consequences* (New York: Monthly Review Press, 2009).

10. G. Arrighi, *The Long Twentieth Century: Money, Power and the Origins of Our Times* (London: Verso, 1994).

11. H. Cleaver, *Reading Capital Politically* (Austin: University of Texas Press, 1979).

12. R. Luxemburg, *The Accumulation of Capital*, 2nd ed. (New York: Routledge, 2003).

13. G. Debord, *The Society of the Spectacle* (Detroit, MI: Black and Red Books, 2000).

14. A. Bardhan and R. Walker, "California, Pivot of the Great Recession" (Working Paper Series, Institute for Research on Labor and Employment, UC Berkeley, 2010).

15. The following argument, now updated, was first laid out in early 2009 in D. Harvey, "Why the Stimulus Package Is Bound to Fail," unpublished paper, available at http://DavidHarvey.org.

16. What follows is based on Harvey, *Enigma of Capital*, chapter 8.

17. T. Friedman, *The World Is Flat: A Brief History of the Twenty-first Century*, rev. ed. (New York: Farrar, Straus and Giroux, 2006); J. Diamond, *Guns, Germs, and Steel: The Fates of Human Societies* (New York: Norton, 1997); P. Hawken, *Blessed Unrest: How the Largest Movement in the World Came into Being and Why No One Saw It Coming* (New York: Viking, 2007); J. Holloway, *Change the World without Taking Power* (London: Pluto, 2005); and D. Held, *Democracy and the Global Order: From the Modern State to Cosmopolitan Governance* (Cambridge, UK: Polity, 1995).

18. D. Harvey, "Organizing for the Anti-capitalist Transition," unpublished paper, 2010, available at http://DavidHarvey.org.

19. E. Ostrom, *Governing the Commons: The Evolution of Institutions for Collective Action* (Cambridge: Cambridge University Press, 1990).

20. In a recent critical assessment of some of my theses, several commentators readily accepted my diagnoses but fiercely criticized my comments on organizational forms. See D. Harvey, "Debating David Harvey," *Interface* 2, no.1 (May 2010), http://www.interfacejournal.net/.

Notes to Chapter 4

I would like to thank my colleagues Tony Lucero, Sunila Kale, and Wolf Latsch for their helpful comments. Also, I owe thanks to an anonymous reviewer and to Craig Calhoun for their suggestions.

1. I did not speak with highly placed WaMu employees or former employees, who in any case did not feel free to speak, but with bank executives in the region who saw how that giant bank was operating.

2. Mike Carter, "Top Feds Scouring WaMu Files for Evidence of Fraud," *Seattle Times*, March 18, 2009, http://seattletimes.nwsource.com/html/businesstechnology/2008878031_wamu180.html.

3. Killinger's biography is a classic tale of a straight-laced, smart, hardworking midwestern boy who made good. He is from Iowa and got an MBA at the University of Iowa, started off in finance in Nebraska, and worked his way to the top of WaMu, which he turned into one of America's leading banks. Some who know him well complain that in his last years as head of his bank he got carried away, changed his lifestyle from one that was relatively modest to one that was extravagant, and stopped paying close attention to what WaMu was doing. Perhaps he began to feel he needed the fourteen million dollars plus that he made in his last good year as CEO, and so much of that was based on stock options that the stock price had to be kept up. As this chapter is not designed for people interested in gossip columns, there is no point in going into personal details of how his life changed in his last years as the head of WaMu. Anyway, the larger system in which he was enmeshed did not rise or fall on the accidental vagaries of any individual's personal lifestyle choices; however, Killinger's own personal transformation perhaps reflected a wider "bubble" cultural transformation that enveloped

high officials in the financial world and even more widely throughout American society.

4. Robert J. Shiller, *Irrational Exuberance* (Princeton, NJ: Princeton University Press, 2000), 71, 245.

5. Robert J. Shiller, *The Subprime Solution* (Princeton, NJ: Princeton University Press, 2008).

6. Charles P. Kindleberger and Robert Aliber, *Manias, Panics, and Crashes*, 5th ed. (Hoboken, NJ: Wiley, 2005).

7. See, for example, the March 20 issue, which reviews five new books on this topic. "Blame Game" and "All Geek to Them," *Economist*, March 20, 2010, 91–92.

8. Carmen M. Reinhart and Kenneth S. Rogoff, *This Time Is Different: Eight Centuries of Financial Folly* (Princeton, NJ: Princeton University Press, 2009); and Paul Krugman, *The Return of Depression Economics and the Crisis of 2008* (New York: Norton, 2009).

9. Karl Marx, *Capital*, vol. 3, abr., ed. David McLellan (Oxford: Oxford University Press, 1995), 447–57.

10. Ibid., 456.

11. Simon Johnson "The Quiet Coup," *Atlantic*, May 2009, http://www.theatlantic.com/doc/print/200905/imf-advice.

12. Paul Krugman, "The Market Mystique," *New York Times*, March 27, 2009.

13. Scott Malone, "GE Profit Drops on Finance, NBC but Tops Forecasts," Reuters, April 18, 2009, http://www.reuters/com/article/ousiv/ idUSTRE53G24W20090417.

14. Ned Eichler, *The Thrift Debacle* (Berkeley: University of California Press, 1989), 46–49.

15. Charles Ponzi, an Italian immigrant in the United States per-suaded many people in 1920 to invest with him, promising huge returns. Rather than investing, he simply paid off old participants with money from new ones. This worked only as long as the inflow of money was greater than his obligations. The scheme collapsed within months, and he went to jail. Bernard Madoff's vastly larger scheme ran for much longer before being exposed in 2008, but it was based on the same principle.

16. Hyman Minsky, "The Financial Instability Hypothesis: Capitalistic Processes and the Behavior of the Economy," in *Financial Crises*, ed. Charles P. Kindleberger and J. P. Laffargue (Cambridge:

Cambridge University Press, 1982); Kindleberger and Aliber, *Manias, Panics, and Crashes*, 25–37.

17. Kindleberger and Aliber, *Manias, Panics, and Crashes*, 6–7, 294–303.

18. Kindleberger and Aliber, however, point out that the collapse of investment opportunities in Japan caused Japanese capital to flow into Southeast Asia, creating a new bubble that burst with the Southeast Asian economic crisis of 1997, and eventually money "sloshed" into the US economy and contributed to the stock-market bubble that burst in 2000 (see *Manias, Panics, and Crashes*, 142–64). So, in a sense, they suggest that collapsing bubbles that do not provoke major economic crashes may well have longer-term effects that show up in later crashes.

19. Mark Carlson, "A Brief History of the 1987 Stock Market Crash with a Discussion of the Federal Reserve Response" (Washington, DC: Federal Reserve, November 2006), http://www.federalreserve.gov/Pubs/feds/2007/200713/200713pap.pdf.

20. Kindleberger and Aliber, *Manias, Panics, and Crashes*, 263.

21. Eichler, *Thrift Debacle*, 86–146.

22. Alvin H. Hansen, "Economic Progress and Declining Population Growth," in *Readings in Business Cycle Theory*, ed. American Economic Association (Philadelphia: Blakiston, 1944), 379.

23. Joseph A. Schumpeter, "The Analysis of Economic Change," in American Economic Association, *Readings in Business Cycle Theory*, 14–15; and Nikolai D. Kondratieff, "The Long Waves in Economic Life," in American Economic Association, *Readings in Business Cycle Theory*, 20–42.

24. Richard Swedberg, "Introduction: The Man and His Work," in *Joseph A. Schumpeter: The Economics and Sociology of Capitalism*, ed. Swedberg (Princeton: Princeton, NJ: University Press, 1991), 28.

25. Alfred Kleinknecht, Ernest Mandel, and Immanuel Wallerstein, eds., *New Findings in Long-Wave Research* (New York: St. Martin's, 1992); and Joshua A. Goldstein, *Long Cycles* (New Haven, CT: Yale University Press, 1988).

26. Walt W. Rostow, "Kondratieff, Schumpeter and Kuznets: Trend Periods Revisited," *Journal of Economic History* 35, no. 4 (1975): 719–53.

27. Simon Kuznets, "Schumpeter's Business Cycles," *American Economic Review* 30 (1940): 257–71; and Swedberg, "Introduction," 58–59.

28. Solomos Solomou, *Phases of Economic Growth, 1850–1973: Kondratieff Waves and Kuznets Swings* (Cambridge: Cambridge University Press, 1987), 169–71.

29. Bert de Groot and Philip Hans Franses, "Stability through Business Cycles," *Technological Forecasting and Social Change* 75 (2008): 301–11.

30. Simon Kuznets, "Modern Economic Growth: Findings and Reflections" (Nobel Prize lecture, 1971), http://nobelprize.org/nobel_prizes/economics/laureates/1971/kuznets-lecture.html.

31. Six papers from the 1980s and 1990s by Kydland and Prescott together and by Prescott alone on what came to be called "real business cycles theory" can be found in James E. Hartley, Kevin D. Hoover, and Kevin Salyer, eds., *Real Business Cycles* (London: Routledge, 1998).

32. Lawrence H. Summers, "Some Skeptical Observations on Real Business Cycle Theory," in Hartley, Hoover, and Salyer, *Real Business Cycles*, 97–101.

33. N. Gregory Mankiw, "Real Business Cycles: A New Keynesian Perspective," *Journal of Economic Perspectives* 3, no. 3 (1989): 89.

34. The disorganized state of macroeconomic theory is shown by the insistence of two of the foremost Chicago School economists, Gary Becker and Robert Lucas, that the development of stronger and more widespread property rights, the realization among people that knowledge is important, and the consequent rational decline in birth rates were the main factors in producing the Industrial Revolution's great spurt of economic progress. With secure property rights and a rational expectation among families that spending more time training their smaller number of children would pay off, birth rates fell, workers became more capable, and economic growth took off. After proving this with a set of elegant, abstract mathematical models, Lucas concludes, "Defined as the onset of sustained growth, the industrial revolution was not exclusively, or even primarily, a technological event." See Robert E. Lucas, *Lectures on Economic Growth* (Cambridge, MA: Harvard University Press, 2002), especially 169. In an article on business cycles, Lucas stated that technological changes are so common in modern economies that they do not cause meaningful cycles. For him, fluctuations in the business cycle, following the monetarist "Chicago" model, are caused by changes in the money supply. See Robert E. Lucas, "Understanding Business Cycles," in

Business Cycle Theory, ed. Finn E. Kydland (Aldershot, UK: Elgar, 1995), 85–107. This relegation of technological progress to a minor position as a cause of the Industrial Revolution might strike many people, including me, as the ultimate in absurd reasoning by economists who refuse to let facts get in the way of their elegant theoretical models. This school's insistence that unemployment is caused by the wrong incentives, which reward idleness over work, and that market forces make involuntary unemployment impossible is even more contrary to reality. See Mankiw, "Real Business Cycles," 82, 85, 89.

35. Milton Friedman and Anna J. Schwartz, *A Monetary History of the United States, 1867–1960* (Princeton, NJ: Princeton University Press, 1963). For a short, updated version, see Anna J. Schwartz, "Understanding 1929–1933," in *The Great Depression Revisited*, ed. Karl Brunner (Boston: Martinus Nijhoff, 1981).

36. "The Other-Worldly Philosophers" and "Efficiency and Beyond," *Economist,* July 18, 2009, 65–69.

37. Charles P. Kindleberger, *The World in Depression 1929–1939* (Berkeley: University of California Press, 1973).

38. John K. Galbraith, *The Great Crash of 1929* (New York: Avon Books, 1980), 157.

39. George A. Akerlof and Robert J. Shiller, *Animal Spirits* (Princeton, NJ: Princeton University Press, 2009).

40. Peter Temin, "Notes on the Causes of the Great Depression," in Brunner, *The Great Depression Revisited*, 108–24.

41. Daniel Chirot, *Social Change in the Modern Era* (San Diego, CA: Harcourt Brace Jovanovich, 1986), 61–63, 223–226; and more generally, David Landes, *Unbound Prometheus* (London: Cambridge University Press, 1969).

42. Kindleberger, *World in Depression 1929–1939*, 31–198, 294; and Paul Bairoch, *Economics and World History* (Chicago: University of Chicago Press, 1993), 5.

43. Kindleberger, *World in Depression*, 177; Bairoch, *Economics and World History*, 8–14; and W. G. Beasley, *The Japanese Experience* (Berkeley: University of California Press, 1999), 241–45.

44. Eric Hobsbawm, *The Age of Extremes* (New York: Vintage, 1996), 257–86.

45. Ibid., 403–32.

46. For example, Paul M. Sweezy and Harry Magdoff, *The Irreversible Crisis* (New York: Monthly Review Press, 1988); Immanuel Wallerstein, *The End of Liberalism* (New York: Norton, 1995), 210–51; and, more generally, Immanuel Wallerstein, *The Decline of American Power* (New York: New Press, 2003).

47. Godfrey Hodgson, *More Equal than Others* (Princeton, NJ: Princeton University Press, 2004), 249–76.

48. Krugman, *Return of Depression Economics*, 182.

49. Editorial, "G20 ou G2," *Le Monde*, July 31, 2009, www.lemonde.fr.

50. Dan Eggen and Tomoeh Murakami Tse, "Wall Street Shifting Political Contributions to Republicans," *Washington Post*, February 23, 2010, http://www.washingtonpost.com/wp-dyn/content/article/2010/02/23/AR2010022305537.html.

51. Robert Z. Aliber, "The Global Savings Tsunamis," *Wilson Quarterly* 33, no. 3 (2009): 56–58.

52. Joseph E. Stiglitz, *Freefall: America, Free Markets, and the Sinking of the World Economy* (New York: W.W. Norton, 2010).

53. For a very short synopsis of my view of what happened, see Daniel Chirot and Clark McCauley, *Why Not Kill Them All?* (Princeton, NJ: Princeton University Press, 2006), 135–39.

Notes to Chapter 5

1. Karl Polanyi, *The Great Transformation*, 2nd ed. (Boston: Beacon, 2001).

2. Karl Marx and Friedrich Engels, "The Communist Manifesto," in *Selected Writings* (Indianapolis, IN: Hackett Publishing, 1994), 161.

3. Here I paraphrase Jürgen Habermas, *Moral Consciousness and Communicative Action* (Cambridge, MA: MIT Press, 1990), 207.

4. Nancy Fraser, "Struggle over Needs: Outline of a Socialist-Feminist Critical Theory of Late-Capitalist Political Culture," in *Unruly Practices: Power, Discourse, and Gender in Contemporary Social Theory* (Minneapolis: University of Minnesota Press, 1989).

5. Nancy Fraser, "Rethinking the Public Sphere: A Contribution to the Critique of Actually Existing Democracy," in *Habermas and the Public Sphere*, ed. Craig Calhoun, 109–42 (Cambridge, MA: MIT Press, 1991).

6. Nancy Fraser, "Social Justice in the Age of Identity Politics: Redistribution, Recognition and Participation," in *Redistribution or Recognition? A Political-Philosophical Exchange*, by Nancy Fraser and Axel Honneth, trans. Joel Golb, James Ingram, and Christiane Wilke (London: Verso, 2003).

7. Nancy Fraser, "Reframing Justice in a Globalizing World," *New Left Review* 36 (2005): 69–88.

8. Polanyi, *Great Transformation*, 183.

9. John G. Ruggie, "International Regimes, Transactions, and Change: Embedded Liberalism in the Postwar Economic Order," *International Organization* 36, no. 2 (1982): 379–415.

10. Nancy Fraser, "Feminism, Capitalism, and the Cunning of History," *New Left Review* 56 (2009): 97–117.

11. Hester Eisenstein, "A Dangerous Liaison? Feminism and Corporate Globalization," *Science and Society* 69, no. 3 (2005): 487–518.

12. Luc Boltanski and Eve Chiapello, *The New Spirit of Capitalism*, trans. Geoffrey Elliott (London: Verso, 2005); and Fraser, "Reframing Justice."

Notes to Chapter 6

1. Karl Polanyi, *The Great Transformation* (1944; repr., New York: Rinehart, 1957).

2. M. F. Bleaney, *Underconsumption Theories: A History and Critical Analysis* (New York: International Publishers, 1976); and Walden Bello, "The Capitalist Conjuncture: Over-accumulation, Financial Crises, and the Retreat from Globalization," *Third World Quarterly* 27, no. 8 (2006).

3. Vicente Navarro, John Schmitt, and Javier Astudillo, "Is Globalization Undermining the Welfare State?" *Cambridge Journal of Economics* 28 (2004).

4. International Labour Office, *World of Work Report 2008: Income Inequalities in the Age of Financial Globalization* (Geneva: International Institute for Labour Studies, 2008).

5. David Harvey, *A Brief History of Neoliberalism* (New York: Oxford University Press, 2005).

6. John B. Foster, "The Household Debt Bubble," *Monthly Review* 58, no. 1 (2006).

7. International Labour Office, *World of Work Report*.

8. Harvey, *Brief History of Neoliberalism*.

9. Giovanni Arrighi, "Towards a Theory of Capitalist Crisis," *New Left Review* 1, no. 111 (1978).

10. Robert Boyer, ed., *The Regulation School: A Critical Introduction* (New York: Columbia University Press, 1990).

11. Michel Aglietta, "Capitalism at the Turn of the Century: Regulation Theory and the Challenge of Social Change," *New Left Review* 1, no. 232 (November–December 1998).

12. For a discussion of topics relating to global governance, see the essays in David Held and Anthony McGrew, eds., *Governing Globalization: Power, Authority and Global Governance* (Cambridge, UK: Polity, 2002).

13. Robert Hunter Wade, "The Rising Inequality of World Income Distribution," *Finance and Development* 38, no. 4 (2001); and Robert Hunter Wade, "Is Globalization Reducing Poverty and Inequality?" *World Development* 32, no. 4 (2004).

14. Emanuel Saez, "Striking It Richer: The Evolution of Top Incomes in the United States (Update with 2007 Estimates)" (paper, Department of Economics, University of California, Berkeley, 2009), http://www.econ.berkeley.edu/~saez/saez-UStopincomes-2007.pdf.

15. The studies that attempt to directly estimate changes in this index rely on household-survey data from countries where these are available. The economist Branko Milanovic, who has worked on available household data, has found a slight increase in inequality through the 1990s, but with reversals in the trend. See Milanovic, "True World Income Distribution, 1988 and 1993: First Calculations Based on Household Surveys Alone," *Economic Journal* 112, no. 476 (2002).

16. Ben Funnel, "Debt Is Capitalism's Dirty Little Secret," *Financial Times*, June 30, 2009.

17. In the United States, middle-income households earned less in 2008 than in 1999. See, for example, Neil Irwin, "Aughts Were a Lost Decade for U.S. Economy, Workers," *Washington Post*, January 2, 2010, http://www.washingtonpost.com/wp-dyn/content/article/2010/01/01/AR2010010101196.html.

18. "The Debt Trap," *New York Times*, July 20, 2008, http://www.nytimes.com/interactive/2008/07/20/business/20debt-trap.html.

19. Rosa Luxemburg, *The Accumulation of Capital* (New York: Modern Reader, 1968); and Rosa Luxemburg, *The Accumulation of Capital—An Anti-critique* (New York: Monthly Review Press, 1973).

20. James K. Galbraith, "Global Keynesianism in the Wings?" *World Policy Journal* 12, no. 3 (Fall 1995); and Gernot Köhler, "Global Keynesianism and Beyond," *Journal of World Systems Research* 5, no. 2 (1999).

21. J. A. Hobson, *Imperialism: A Study*, 3rd ed. (London: Allen and Unwin, 1938).

22. Jan Breman, "Myth of the Global Safety Net," *New Left Review* 59 (September–October 2009).

23. Mike Davis, *Planet of Slums* (London: Verso, 2006).

24. Loïc Wacquant, "Urban Marginality in the Coming Millennium," *Urban Studies* 36, no. 10 (1999).

25. Jeremy Rifkin, *The End of Work* (New York: Putnam, 1995); and José Nun, "The End of Work and the 'Marginal Mass' Thesis," *Latin American Perspectives* 27, no. 1 (2000).

26. These figures are from the OECD database of social expenditures and include health expenditures out of the public budget but not education outlays. See W. Adema and M. Ladaique, "How Expensive Is the Welfare State? Gross and Net Indicators in the OECD Social Expenditure Database (SOCX)" (OECD Social, Employment and Migration Working Papers no. 92, 2009), www.oecd.org/els/social/expenditure.

27. Walter Korpi, "Welfare-State Regress in Europe: Politics, Institutions, Globalization, and Europeanization," *Annual Review of Sociology* 29 (2003); and Philip Genschel, "Globalization and the Welfare State: A Retrospective," *Journal of European Public Policy* 11, no. 4 (August 2004).

28. Ian Gough, Geof Wood, et al., *Insecurity and Welfare Regimes in Asia, Africa and Latin America: Social Policy in Development Contexts* (Cambridge: Cambridge University Press, 2004).

29. Jeremy Seekings, "A Comparative Analysis of Welfare Regimes in the South: The Social Origins of Social Assistance Outside of the Established Democracies," in *Divide and Deal: The Politics of Distribution in Democracies*, ed. Ian Shapiro, Peter Swenson, and Daniella Donno (New York: NYU Press, 2008).

30. World Bank, *World Development Report 2000/2001: Attacking Poverty* (New York: Oxford University Press, 2000); and World Bank,

World Development Report 2004: Making Services Work for Poor People (New York: Oxford University Press, 2003).

31. Franceska Bastagli, "From Social Safety Net to Social Policy? The Role of Conditional Cash Transfers in Welfare State Development in Latin America" (Working Paper 60, International Policy Center for Inclusive Growth, UNDP, Brazil, 2009).

32. David Brady, *Rich Democracies, Poor People* (New York: Oxford University Press, 2009).

33. Alex Segura-Ubiergo, *The Political Economy of the Welfare State in Latin America: Globalization, Democracy, and Development* (New York: Cambridge University Press, 2007); for Turkey, the OECD database.

34. Gosta Esping-Andersen, *The Three Worlds of Welfare Capitalism* (Princeton, NJ: Princeton University Press, 1990).

35. For the fight in the World Bank over its policy orientation as the "Washington Consensus" was being challenged, see Robert Hunter Wade, "US Hegemony and the World Bank: The Fight over People and Ideas," *Review of International Political Economy* 9, no. 2 (2002).

36. UN Habitat, *The Challenge of Slums* (New York: UN Habitat, 2003).

37. Polanyi, *Great Transformation*.

38. Peter Evans, "Is an Alternative Globalization Possible?" *Politics and Society* 36, no. 2 (June 2008).

Notes to Chapter 7

1. George Cooper, *The Origin of Financial Crises* (Cambridge, UK: Polity, 2008).

2. Will Hutton and Anthony Giddens, eds., *On the Edge: Living with Global Capitalism* (London: Cape, 2000).

3. Statistical data cited throughout this chapter originate from reliable reports published in the financial press. Therefore, I do not consider it necessary to cite the sources, as they are available in the public domain.

4. Manuel Castells, *The Rise of the Network Society*, 2nd ed. (Oxford: Blackwell, 2000), chapter 2; and Hutton and Giddens, *On the Edge*.

5. Paul Volcker, "The Sea of Global Finance," in Hutton and Giddens, *On the Edge*; and Manuel Castells, "Information Technology and Global Capitalism," in Hutton and Giddens, *On the Edge*.

6. Martin Wolf, *Fixing Global Finance* (Baltimore, MD: Johns Hopkins University Press, 2008).

7. Manuel Castells, *The Internet Galaxy: Reflections on Internet, Business, and Society* (Oxford: Oxford University Press, 2001), chapter 3; and Martin Carnoy, *Sustaining Flexibility: Work, Family, and Community in the Information Age* (Cambridge, MA: Harvard University Press, 2000).

8. Kingsley Dennis and John Urry, *After the Car* (Cambridge, UK: Polity, 2009).

9. Laura Burkhalter and Manuel Castells, "Beyond the Crisis: Towards a New Urban Paradigm," *Archinect,* July 2009.

10. Amelia Arsenault and Manuel Castells, "The Structure and Dynamics of Global Multi-Media Business Networks," *International Journal of Communication* 2 (2008): 707–48.

11. Manuel Castells, "The New Public Sphere: Global Civil Society, Communication Networks and Global Governance," *Annals of the American Academy of Political and Social Science* 616, no. 1 (2008): 78–93.

12. Manuel Castells, *Communication Power* (Oxford: Oxford University Press, 2009).

13. IMF, http://www.imf.org/external/data.htm.

14. Pekka Himanen, *The Hacker Ethic and the Spirit of Informationalism* (New York: Random House, 2002).

15. This section is based on preliminary results from ongoing research on the emergence of new economic cultures in Catalonia, in collaboration with Joanna Conill, in the framework of the research program on the network society at the Internet Interdisciplinary Institute of the Open University of Catalonia. However, there are thousands of people engaged in similar practices around the world, often below the radar of economists, business leaders, and policymakers.

16. Chris Carlson, *Nowtopia: How Pirate Programmers, Outlaw Bicyclists, and Vacant-Lot Gardeners Are Inventing the Future Today* (Oakland, CA: AK Press, 2008); various authors, "Los pies en la tierra: Experiencias y reflexiones hacia un movimiento agroecologico" (Barcelona: Virus Editorial, 2006); Enric Prat, ed., *Els moviments socials a la Catalunya contemporania* (Barcelona: Biblioteca Universitat de Barcelona, 2004); Jeff Juris, *Networked Futures* (Durham, NC: Duke University Press, 2008); and Burkhalter and Castells, "Beyond the Crisis."

1. A bemused Jeffrey Alexander recalled a period-piece scene from a mid-'70s academic conference: "When Wallerstein went on to lay out 'an agenda of intellectual work for those who are seeking to understand the *world systemic transition from capitalism to socialism in which we are living,*' he literally brought the younger members of the audience to their feet." In light of the recent experience of the collapse of actually existing socialism and the retreat of the welfare state, Alexander proposed that it was time to replace if not reverse this obsolete narrative schema. Jeffrey Alexander, "Modern: Anti, Post, and Neo," *New Left Review* 1, no. 210 (1995).

2. Edward Anthony Wrigley, *Continuity, Chance and Change* (Cambridge: Cambridge University Press, 1990), 3.

3. The account I present here of a conjuncture of overproduction relies on the research and conclusions of Robert Brenner's monumental *The Boom and the Bubble* (London: Verso, 2002). For a powerful restatement and expansion of his thesis, see the interview with Seongjin Jeong in *Hankyoreh*, January 22, 2009. For purposes of this speculative exposition, I have not presented the statistical evidence for this slowdown that Brenner provides but have instead attempted to demonstrate it as the only plausible explanation for the unprecedented decades-long buildup of private and public debt.

4. Antonio Gramsci, *Further Selections from the Prison Notebooks* (Minneapolis: University of Minnesota Press, 1995), 219.

5. Moishe Postone, "History and Helplessness: Mass Mobilization and Contemporary Forms of Anticapitalism," *Public Culture* 18, no. 1 (2006): 93–110.

6. This reconstruction of Marx is indebted to a forthcoming work by Aaron Benanav, entitled *Capitalism: Long-Term Employment Trends from the 19th Century to the Present*.

7. Robert Hawthorn and Ramana Ramaswamy, "Deindustrialization: Causes and Implications" (working paper, International Monetary Fund, April 1997).

My gratitude to Julie Skurski, Genese Sodikoff, Katherine Verdery, John French, Talal Asad, Craig Calhoun, and students in my Spring 2010 Seminar at CUNY's Graduate Center, as well as to an anonymous reader from the SSRC; their suggestions about content and form have considerably improved this chapter.

1. Reinhardt Koselleck, *Futures Past: On the Semantics of Historical Time* (New York: Columbia University Press, 2004), 259. By these terms, Koselleck explores the relationship between historical experience and expectations of the future. Scholars have shown that conceptions of history and cultural cosmologies are intimately connected to each other and are historically specific; in any given society, the relationship between present and future establishes distinctive temporalities and narratives of history. Despite persuasive critiques of Eurocentrism, canonical scholarly categories tend to reproduce Western assumptions about temporality and visions of history. While in sympathy with these critiques, I deploy here the familiar trilogy of "past," "present," and "future" as it has been commonly used in studies about Latin America, as well as in Latin America itself. My use of this trilogy is largely descriptive, restricting my critical intent to making visible assumed or naturalized conceptions of history and of space/time.

2. Norberto Bobbio, *Left and Right: The Significance of a Political Distinction*, trans. Allan Cameron (Chicago: University of Chicago Press, 1996).

3. This comment reflects my own evaluation and position (and wishes) but is indebted to the fundamental work of members of a loose "decolonial" collective, or network, without a proper name or single position; for recent works on this topic by members of this collective, see the recent thoughtful texts of Arturo Escobar and Javier Sanjinés. Escobar, "Latin America at a Crossroads," *Cultural Studies* 24, no. 1 (2010): 1–65; and Sanjinés, *Rescoldos del pasado: Conflictos culturales en sociedades postcoloniales* (La Paz: PIEB, 2009).

4. Atilio A. Boron, "Globalization: A Latin American Perspective," *Estudos Sociedade e Agricultura* 11 (1998).

5. John French, "Understanding the Politics of Latin America's Plural Lefts (Chávez/Lula): Social Democracy, Populism and

Convergence on the Path to a Post-Neoliberal World," *Third World Quarterly* 30, no. 2 (2009): 362.

6. Jorge Castañeda, "A Tale of Two Lefts," *Foreign Affairs*, May–June 2006.

7. Arturo Escobar's discussion, in "Latin America at a Crossroads," of the turn to the left in Latin America focuses on these countries, in part because they seem to represent a more radical rupture from the past and a "decolonial" political project.

8. I discuss these concepts and issues in Fernando Coronil, *The Magical State: Nature, Money and Modernity in Venezuela* (Chicago: University of Chicago Press, 1997), 45–66.

9. Leonardo Avritzer, "El ascenso del Partido de los Trabajadores en Brasil," in *La nueva izquierda en América Latina: Sus orígenes y trayectoria futura*, ed. César A. Rodríguez Garavito, Patrick S. Barrett, and Daniel Chávez (Bogota: Grupo Editorial Norma, 2004), 67–96.

10. César Rodríguez Garavito and Patrick Barrett, "La utopia revivida?" in Rodríguez Garavito, Barrett, and Chávez, *La nueva izquierda*, 40.

11. Fernando Coronil, "After Empire: Rethinking Imperialism from the Americas," in *Imperial Formations and Their Discontents*, ed. Ann Stoler, Carole McGranahan, and Peter Purdue (Santa Fe, NM: School of American Research Press, 2007), 241–74.

12. Susana Rotker, *Bravo pueblo: Poder, utopia y violencia* (Caracas: Fondo Editorial La Nave Va, 2005), 85.

13. Johannes Fabian, *Time and the Other: How Anthropology Makes Its Objet* (New York: Columbia University Press, 1983).

14. Dipesh Chakrabarty, *Provincialising Europe: Postcolonial Thought and Historical Difference* (Princeton, NJ: Princeton University Press, 2000).

15. This mode of historicizing has been observed in Latin America by literary and political elites since the nineteenth century, including by such "founders" of Latin American nationalism as Simón Bolivar and José Martí. Chakrabarty has productively used the notion of the "not-yet" in his insightful critique of historicism. Ibid.

16. Claudio Lomnitz, "The Latin American Rebellion: Will the New Left Set a New Agenda?" *Boston Review*, September–October 2006.

17. I have discussed elsewhere Nicos Poulantzas's insight that nation formation involves the territorialization of a history and the historicization

of a territory. Fernando Coronil, "Beyond Occidentalism: Towards Nonimperial Geohistorical Categories," *Cultural Anthropology* 11, no. 1 (1996): 51–87.

18. While this observation is accurate for recent periods in Latin American history, it must be noted that liberal thought has also claimed the future as its own. The very notion of the "long term" was created by Alfred Marshall in his *Principles of Economics* (London: Macmillan, 1890) to identify a time when the market would adjust all factors and define normal prices; for an elaboration of this point, see the interesting discussion of the public rhetoric of macroeconomics in Jane Guyer, "Prophecy and the Near Future: Thoughts on Macroeconomic, Evangelical and Punctuated Time," *American Anthropologist* 34, no. 3 (2007): 409–21.

19. Boaventura de Sousa Santos, "Una izquierda con futuro," in Rodríguez Garavito, Barrett, and Chávez, *La nueva izquierda*, 437–57.

20. I use the notion of postcapitalism here as a rather vague term to evoke a hypothetical future society built on the foundations of capitalism but transcending its limitations.

21. José Insulza, interview with the author, University of Michigan, October 2006.

22. Santos, "Una izquierda con futuro," 438–39. Author's translation.

23. It should be noted, however, that despite Chávez's division of the population into two antagonistic groups, he conceives of the revolutionary camp as plural, made up of many social sectors, as long as they agree with the goals of the revolution as articulated by the state.

24. Marcelo Colussi, "El pobretariado: Un nuevo sujeto revolucionario?" *Revista Amauta*, 2009.

25. Marisol de la Cadena, "Indigenous Cosmopolitics in the Andes: Conceptual Reflections," *Cultural Anthropology* 25, no. 2 (2010): 334, 356.

26. Carlos de la Torre, "Correa y los Indios," *Diario Hoy*, March 6, 2010.

27. Julie Skurski and Fernando Coronil, "Country and City in a Colonial Landscape: Double Discourse and the Geopolitics of Truth in Latin America," in *View from the Border: Essays in Honor of Raymond Williams*, ed. Dennis Dworkin and Leslie Roman (New York: Routledge, 1993), 25.

28. Atilio Borón, "Globalization: A Latin American Perspective."

29. Daniel Chávez, "Del frente amplio a la nueva mayoría," in Rodríguez Garavito, Barrett, and Chávez, *La nueva izquierda*, 172. Author's translation.

30. This concept, "permanent democracy," is borrowed by Juan Carlos Monedero from Boaventura de Sousa Santos in order to develop an argument about democracy as an ever-expanding and inclusive process. Juan Carlos Monedero, *El gobierno de las palabras: Política para tiempos de confusion* (México: Fondo de Cultura Económica, 2009), 221–75. Monedero's work reflects his engagement with contemporary social theory as well as his recent experience in Venezuela as a key member of the Centro Miranda, a left think tank established under Chávez; he left this center after a rather unsuccessful attempt to develop constructive critiques of Chávez's Bolivarian "revolution" from within.

31. Santos, "Una izquierda con futuro."

32. Fidel Castro, "Reflections by Fidel Castro: [Obama] A Science Fiction Story," *Caricom News Network*, November 13, 2009, http://csmenetwork.com/2/index.php?option=com_content&view=article&id=5799:reflections-by-fidel-castro-obama-a-science-fiction-story&catid=146:opinion&Itemid=383.

33. Steven Erlander, "European Socialists Suffering Even in Downturn," *New York Times*, September 28, 2009.

34. Max Weber, "Politics as a Vocation," in *Weber: Selections in Translation*, ed. W. G. Runciman (Cambridge: Cambridge University Press, 1978), 225.

35. Alain Badiou, "The Communist Hypothesis," *New Left Review* 49 (2008).

36. Slavoj Žižek, *First as Tragedy, Then as Farce* (New York: Verso, 2009), 87–88.

37. Ibid., 86–104.

38. David Harvey, *Spaces of Hope* (Berkeley: University of California Press, 2000).

39. Javier Sanjinés, personal communication, May 1, 2010.

40. Xavier Albó, "Prólogo," in *Rescoldos del pasado: Conflictos culturales en sociedades postcoloniales*, by Javier Sanjinés (La Paz: PIEB, 2009), xiii. Author's translation.

41. Susan Buck-Morss, "The Second Time as Farce…Historical Pragmatics and the Untimely Present" (unpublished paper, 2010), 16–17.

42. David Scott, *Conscripts of Modernity: The Tragedy of Colonial Enlightenment* (Durham, NC: Duke University Press, 2004).

43. Gary Wilder, "Untimely Vision: Aimé Césaire, Decolonization, Utopia," *Public Culture* 21, no. 1 (2009): 103.

44. Karl Marx, *The 18th Brumaire of Louis Bonaparte* (New York: International Publishers, 1963), 17.

45. William Blake, *Auguries of Innocence*, lines 1–2.

46. The notion of a counterpoint between past and future is inspired by Fernando Ortiz's redemptive counterpoint between the Americas and Europe through the tropes of tobacco and sugar in *Cuban Counterpoint: Tobacco and Sugar* (Durham, NC: Duke University Press, 1995). "Poetry of the future" is my phrase drawn from Marx's argument that, unlike the bourgeois revolutions of the eighteenth century, the social revolutions of the nineteenth century must "draw their poetry from the future." Marx, *18th Brumaire*, 18.

About the Contributors

Giovanni Arrighi (1937–2009) was the George Armstrong Kelly Professor of Sociology at the Johns Hopkins University. His most recent books are *Adam Smith in Beijing: Lineages of the Twenty-first Century* (Verso) and the second edition of *The Long Twentieth Century: Money, Power and the Origins of Our Times* (Verso).

Gopal Balakrishnan is Associate Professor in the History of Consciousness Department at the University of California, Santa Cruz. He is on the editorial board of *New Left Review*. His most recent book is *Antagonistics: Capitalism and Power in an Age of War* (Verso).

Craig Calhoun is President of the Social Science Research Council and University Professor of the Social Sciences at New York University. His most recent book is *Nations Matter: Culture, History, and the Cosmopolitan Dream* (Routledge). He has also recently edited *Robert K. Merton: Sociology of Science and Sociology as Science* (Columbia University Press) and co-edited *Knowledge Matters: The Public Mission of the Research University* (Columbia University Press).

Manuel Castells is University Professor and the Wallis Annenberg Chair in Communication, Technology and Society at the University of

Southern California (USC), Los Angeles. He is also research professor at the Open University of Catalonia in Barcelona. His most recent book is *Communication Power* (Oxford University Press).

Daniel Chirot is Job and Gertrud Tamaki Professor of International Studies and Sociology at the University of Washington's Henry M. Jackson School of International Studies. His most recent work, coauthored with Clark McCauley, is *Why Not Kill Them All? The Logic and Prevention of Mass Political Murder* (Princeton University Press).

Fernando Coronil is Presidential Professor of Anthropology at the Graduate Center of the City University of New York (CUNY) and Emeritus Professor of Anthropology and History at the University of Michigan. His most recognized work is *The Magical State: Nature, Money, and Modernity in Venezuela* (University of Chicago Press).

Georgi Derluguian is Associate Professor of Sociology at Northwestern University. He is the author of *Bourdieu's Secret Admirer in the Caucasus: A World-Systems Biography* (University of Chicago Press).

Nancy Fraser is the Henry A. and Louise Loeb Professor of Political and Social Science and Professor of Philosophy at the New School in New York City. Her most recent book is *Scales of Justice: Reimagining Political Space in a Globalizing World* (Columbia University Press).

David Harvey is Distinguished Professor of Anthropology at the Graduate Center of the City University of New York (CUNY). His most recent books are *A Companion to Marx's Capital* (Verso) and *The Enigma of Capital* (Profile Books).

Caglar Keyder is Professor of Sociology at the State University of New York–Binghamton and teaches at the Ataturk Institute for Modern Turkish History at Boğaziçi University in Istanbul. Most recently he has written *Istanbul: Between the Global and the Local* (Rowman and Littlefield).

Beverly J. Silver is Professor of Sociology at the Johns Hopkins University. She is the author of *Forces of Labor: Workers' Movements and Globalization since 1870* (Cambridge University Press).

Immanuel Wallerstein is currently Senior Research Scholar at Yale University. Long recognized for his work on world-systems analysis, his most recent book is *European Universalism: The Rhetoric of Power* (New Press).

Index

Information in figures is denoted by *f*. Information in footnotes is denoted by 'n' following the page number and preceding the note number.

Adorno, Theodor, 263
Advertising, 193–194
AEA. *See* American Economic Association (AEA)
Afghanistan war, 31
Africa: natural resources in, 40; Pentecostalism in, 33
African Union, 32
Agriculture, urban, 207
Aid, international, 57
AIG. *See* American International Group (AIG)
Akerlof, George, 128
Albó, Xavier, 262
Aliber, Robert, 135
Al Jazeera television, 32

Allende, Salvador, 21, 237, 248, 251
Al Qaeda, 31
"American Dream," 265n4
American Economic Association (AEA), 124, 125
American International Group (AIG), 102, 121, 196
Amur River, 32
Anti-imperialism, 149–150
A phase, of Kondratieff cycle, 72
Arab League, 32
Argentina, 237, 238–239, 240, 242, 250
Arrighi, Giovanni, 97, 293
Asia, size of, as problem, 79–80
Asian financial crisis, 10, 123
Atlantic (magazine), 117
Austerity programs, 11, 37, 107
Automobile industry, 191
Automobiles, 129

Bachelet, Michel, 240, 248, 252, 260
Badiou, Alain, 261
Balakrishnan, Gopal, 293
Bank collapse, 113–114
Bank deregulation, 15
Bank nationalization, 197
Bank of America: foreclosures by, 14; possible collapse of, 113
Bank of International Settlements, 198
Bear Stearns, 102
Becker, Gary, 279n34
Benetton, 100
Benjamin, Walter, 262, 263
Bernanke, Ben, 92
Bias, class, 11
Black, Fischer, 23
Bloch, Ernst, 263
Bobbio, Norberto, 232
Boesky, Ivan, 22
Bolivar, Simon, 248
Bolivia, 240, 250, 253
Bonfire of the Vanities (Wolfe), 15
Borón, Atilio, 256
Brain drain, 39
Braudel, Fernand, 54, 55, 56, 57
Brazil: in global policy fold, 133; Landless Workers Movement in, 237; neoliberalism in, 237; as relatively unaffected by crisis, 11; success of, 51–52
Breto, Frei, 254
Bretton Woods Accord, 22
Bubble(s). *See also specific bubbles*: bank bailouts as, 78; creation of, 116; financialization and, 173; ignorance of cycle of, 27; "long," 25–30; neoliberalism and, 26–27;

newspapers and, 116; overview of, 25; in United States, 26
Buck-Morss, Susan, 262
Budget deficits, global, 199
Business Cycles (Schumpeter), 125–126
"Butterfly" effect, 85

Calhoun, Craig, 293
California, 107
Capital: assemblage of initial, 92–93; as circulation, 90; deregulation and flow of, 187–188; endless accumulation of, 71; finance, 56–57; growth and, 90; historical perspective on, 211–215; human, in Russia, 39; labor market and, 93–94; limits on, 90, 211–215; Marx's formula of, 57–58, 273n6; net flow of, from rising to declining economic areas, 63; overabundance of, 57; production, 90; technology and, 96–97; venture, 24; virtualization of, 188; wages and, 93
Capitalism: complexity in evolution of, 62; contradiction of, 214; credit in, 163; cyclic nature of, 56–57; demand and, 98–101; effective demand and, 98–101; evolutionary patterns of, 61*f*; fossil-fuel, 224–225; global informational, 185–186; imperialism and, 176; left alternative to, 108–112; order and, 73; postindustrial, 228–229; replacement system for, 84–85; Smith on end of, 215–216; state, 218; viability of, 83; victory of, 236
Capitalist cycle, 163

Capitalist perestroika, 199–206
Capital (Marx), 90
Caracazo, 239
Cárdenas, Cuauhtemoc, 248
Cárdenas, Lázaro, 248
Cardoso, Henrique, 237, 244
Carrefour, 99–100
Castañeda, Jorge, 240, 241
Castells, Manuel, 293
Castro, Fidel, 237, 260
Castro, Raul, 237
Catalonia, 286n15
Causes, of financial crisis, 116–122
CDOs. *See* Collateralized debt obligations (CDOs)
Chakrabarty, Dipesh, 246
Change, crisis and, 123–129
Chaos and Governance in the Modern World System (Silver & Arrighi), 65–66
Chase Bank, foreclosures by, 14
Chávez, Hugo, 52, 240, 241, 248, 251–252, 254, 257
Chechnya, 34
"Chicago Boys," 21, 238–239
Chicago School, 128, 279n34
Chile: *Concertación* in, 231, 252; material conditions in, 243; Pinochet in, 231; revolutionary model in, 251; in 1970s, 21
China: in Asian regional politics, 32; borrowing from, 200–201; Cultural Revolution in, 76; *danwei* in, 37–38; discontent in, 79; entanglement of, with dollar, 79; financialization's benefits to, 17; as future world state, 65;

global income distribution and, 170; in global policy fold, 133; growth rates in, 106; Keynesian actions of, 105–106; neoliberalism and, 222–223; opium wars in, 99; prospects for, as material expansion center, 65; as relatively unaffected by crisis, 11; rise of, 29, 221–224; stimulus package in, 105, 181, 200; strikes in, 106; U.S. investment in, by multinational corporations, 63; U.S. Treasury bonds in, 63, 79
Chirot, Daniel, 294
Christianity, changes in, 33
Circulation, capital as, 90
Citigroup, 113, 197
Civilization and Capitalism (Braudel), 56
Civil publicity, 148
Civil society, 147–148
Class balances, 161
Class bias, 11
Climate change, 191–192
Cold War, 21, 27
Collateralized debt obligations (CDOs), 120. *See also* Mortgage-backed securities
Collective goods, 161
College of Central Banks, 197
Colombia, 253, 257
Colonialism, 99, 153–154. *See also* Decolonization
Communal living, 207
Communications systems, 193–194
Communism, 109
Communist Manifesto (Marx & Engels), 174

Community banking, 208

Competition: perfect, 71; underconsumption and, 165

Complexity: in evolution of world capitalism, 62; social, 66

Computers, 131

Concertación, 231, 252

Confusion, about future, 53

Congo, 40

Conservatism, rise of, 77–78

Consumer cooperatives, 206

Consumer credit, 163

Consumption. *See also* Underconsumption: credit and, 163; debt and, 83, 172; in Fordism, 169; investment and, 160, 167; mass personal, 129; production and, 167; savings rates and, 202; state legitimacy and, 166

Containerization, 226

Cooperatives, 206–207

Coronil, Fernando, 38, 294

Correa, Rafael, 240

Costs: externalization of, 67, 82; managerial, 81–82; personnel, 81; prices and, 83; of production, types of, 80; of taxation, 83

Counterparty risk, 17

Countrywide (mortgage company), 102

"Creative accounting," 16

Credit. *See also* Debt: in capitalist cycle, 163; consumption and, 163; easy, end of, 186; income inequality and, 172; production capacity and, 164; as proportion of real production, 163; reduction of, 204; underconsumption and, 164, 172; value and, 164

Credit-default swaps, 16, 188

Credit ratings, 119

Crisis. *See also* Financial crisis: class-relations models of, 165; environmental, 191–192; income distribution and, 168; management institutions, 194–195; opportunity and, 41–42; in Polanyi, 138–139; technological cycles and, 129–132; as term, 9–10; world-changing power of, 123–129

Critical theory, 137

Cuba, 237, 248, 251, 260

Cultural Revolution, Chinese, 76

Cycles, 56–57, 71

Danwei, 37–38

Da Silva, Luis Inácio Lula, 51, 240, 244, 248, 257

Debord, Guy, 100

Debt. *See also* Credit: consumption and, 83, 172; effective demand and, 100; of financial institutions, 188; to GDP ratio, U.S., 172; increase in, 172; U.S. household, 190; of U.S., 104

Debt crises, financial expansions and, 58

Decolonization, 20–21, 154

Decommodification of needs, 180

Deficits, global budget, 199

De Groot, Bert, 126

De la Cadena, Marisol, 255

De la Rúa, Fernando, 239

De la Torre, Carlos, 255

Demand, 98–101, 164–165, 187, 201–202

Deng Xiaoping, 267n17

Deregulation: of banks, 15; as factor in crisis, 187–188

Derivatives: assets in, 16; definition of, 16; in 1970s, 23; technology and, 188

Derluguian, Georgi, 294

Determinism, 85

Development: decolonization and (*See* Decolonization); international Keynesianism and, 175

Dimon, Jamie, 134

Disembedded markets, 140–144

Dollar: Chinese entanglement in, 79; as reserve currency, 78

Domination, 149–150

Dot-com bubble, 10, 24–25, 116, 118, 162

Downturns, "normal," 70–74

Dubai World, 108

Dutch East India Company, 62

Dutch Republic: in evolutionary patterns of world capitalism, 61*f*; financialization in, 57; Genoa *vs.*, 60; in Marx, 59

Dynamics of Global Crisis (Wallerstein), 69

Easy credit, end of, 186

Economist (magazine), 117

Economy, financialization of, 10–11

Ecuador, 250, 253

Effective demand, 98–101, 164

Electronics bubble, 131

Emancipation, 144–146; domination

and, 149–150; from hierarchical protections, 151–152; from misframed protections, 152–154

Embedded liberalism, 154

Embedded markets, 141

Employment: self-, 179; social democracy and, 177

Engels, Friedrich, 174, 212

Enigma of Capital, The: And the Crises of Capitalism (Harvey), 89–90

Entrepreneurship, 201

Environmental crisis, 191–192

Equilibrium, lack of pressure to return to, 85

Erlander, Steven, 260

Ethics: embedded markets and, 147; norms and, 148–149

Europe, Islam in, 33–34

Exchange rates, in 1970s, 22

Expansion, material, 54

Externalization: of costs, 67, 82; of infrastructure, 82; of renewing resources, 82

Extremism, 34

Fabian, Johannes, 246

Falkand Islands, 22

Fannie Mae, 13–14, 102, 119, 121, 266n5

Farming, urban, 207

Fascism, 135

Federal Reserve Board, 197

Feminism, 149, 151–152

Finance capital, 56–57

Finance industry: bubbles and, 25; debt in, 188; growth of, 162–163; growth of speculation in, 15–16;

importance of, growth in, 18; losses of, 190–191; profits in, 189; rise of, 25–26; systemic *vs.* individual responsibility of, 43–44; in U.S., 162–163

Financial crisis. *See also* Crisis: causes of, 116–122; crisis aspect of, 9–10; development of, 187; global aspect of, 11; importance of, 10–11; multidimensionality of, 191–196; overview of, 9; uneven geographical development of, 102–108

Financialization, 9–10; bubbles and, 173; counterparty risk and, 17; export trade and, 17; in Genoa, 57; history of, 17, 57; incentive for, 172–173; inequality and, 23–24; manufacturing decline and, 23, 57; Marxist theory and, 57–58; neoliberalism and, 47; in Netherlands, 57; in 1970s, 20–21; Ponzi schemes and, 173; profit and, 24; as response to previous crises, 47; rise of, 162–163; social movements and, 66; technology and, 188

Financial regulator, global, 197–198

Financial repression, 93

Forbes (magazine), 171

Fordism, 169

Fordism-Keynesianism, 57

Foreclosures, hasty initiation of, 14

Fossil-fuel capitalism, 224–225

FoxConn, 106

Franses, Philip Hans, 126

Fraser, Nancy, 294

Fraud, 115

Freddie Mac, 13–14, 102, 119, 266n5

Free will, 85

French, John, 238

Friedman, Milton, 22, 113, 128

Friedman, Thomas, 110

Frisch, Ragnar, 124

Fukuyama, Francis, 236

Future: confusion over, 53; hope for, 37–38

Futures, 188

G8, 103

G20, 103

Galbraith, John Kenneth, 128

Gandhi, Mohandas, 67

Gap (clothing chain), 100

Garn-St. Germain Act, 190

Gender hierarchy, 151

General Electric, 118

General Motors, 106, 196

Genoa: Dutch Republic *vs.,* 60; in evolutionary patterns of world capitalism, 61*f*; financialization in, 57

Geopolitical cycles, 73–74

Giuliani, Rudy, 91

Global aspect, of financial crisis, 11

Global financial crisis. *See* Financial crisis

Global financial regulator, 197–198

Global governance, 169

Global income distribution, 161, 170

Global informational capitalism, 185–186

Global institutions, material expansion and, 58–59

Globalization, 70; crisis of, 160; narrative of, 213–214; poverty and,

159; production and, 168; wages and, 167–168

Global South, welfare states in, 179–180

Global warming, 191–192

G7 meetings, expansion of, 64

Governance, global, 169

Gramsci, Antonio, 218

Great Depression, 57, 65, 123, 127–129, 135

Great Transformation, The (Polanyi), 138–150

Greece, 37, 107, 108

Greed, as insufficient explanation, 44

Growth rate: in China, 106; demand and, 99; global, 90; ultimate limits on, 109; unsustainable, 90–91

Grundrisse, The (Marx), 90

Guarantees, popular movements pushing for, 83

Hansen, Alvin, 124, 125

Harvey, David, 262, 294

Hawken, Paul, 110

Hayek, Friedrich, 124

Health care, 180

"Hedge finance," 120

Hegemonic transition, 59

Hierarchical protections, 151–152

Himanen, Pekka, 205

Historical perspective, on capital, 211–215

Historicism, 212

Hobsbawm, Eric, 53

Hobson, J. A., 176

Holland. *See* Netherlands

Honda, 106

Hoover, Herbert, 129

Hope, for future, 37–38

Household consumer electronics, 129

Household debt, U.S., 190

Households, patriarchal, 192–193

Housing prices: belief in rise of, 14; effects of fall in, 121–122

Human capital, in Russia, 39

Hypo Real Estate, 197

Icahn, Carl, 23, 24

IMF. *See* International Monetary Fund (IMF)

Imperialism, 99, 176

Income distribution. *See also* Wage(s): China as factor in, 170; crisis and, 168; effective demand and, 164; global, 161, 170; measurement of, 170–171; neoliberalism and, 169–170; population in calculation of, 171; production and, 164; social democracy and, 176–177; social expenditures and, 181; underconsumption and, 168; in U.S., 170; worsening of, 170

Income redistribution, 176, 180–181

Independence. *See* Decolonization

India: in global policy fold, 133; as relatively unaffected by crisis, 11

Individual responsibility, systemic *vs.*, 43–44

Industrial Revolution, 129

Inequality: amid plenty, 35; collective goods and, 161; rise in, financialization and, 23–24; social welfare and, 34–41; stimulus packages and, 176

Informational capitalism, global, 185–186

"Information turbulences," 188

Infrastructure, externalization of, 82

Initial capital, 92–93

Innovation: invention *vs.*, 72; needed surge in, 201

Institutions, global, material expansion and, 58–59

Insurance, securitized, 188

International aid, 57

International Keynesianism, 175

International Monetary Fund (IMF): decolonization and, 154; strengthening of, 198; on systemic risk, 89

Invention, innovation *vs.*, 72

Iranian Revolution, 22

Iraq War, 31, 189

Ireland, 107

Islam: in Europe, 33–34; extremism in, 34; migration and, 33; renewal of, 33

J. P. Morgan Chase, 122, 134

Jameson, Frederic, 211–212

Japan, bubble in, 123

Johnson, Simon, 117

Journalistic narratives, of crisis, 44

Kant, Immanuel, 261

Kautsky, Karl, 212

Kerala, 108

Keyder, Caglar, 294

Keynes, John Maynard, 116, 128

Keynesianism: in China, 105–106; Fordism-, 57; international, 175; military, 219

Killinger, Kerry, 115, 134, 276n3

Kindleberger, Charles, 116–117, 128

Kirchner, Nestor, 240, 248

Klein, Naomi, 206

Kondratieff, Nikolai, 124, 125

Kondratieff waves, 71

Krugman, Paul, 117–118, 131–132

Kuznets cycles, 126

Kydland, Finn E., 127

Labor: flow of, 81; neoliberalism and, 166; organized, 94; process, 97–98; state interventions with, 165–166; supply of low-wage, 178; underconsumption and, 167; unskilled, costs of, 81

Labor market, 93–94

Landless Workers Movement (MST), 237, 253

Latin America. *See also specific countries*: debt crisis in, 1980s, 58; elite legitimacy in, 245; future of Left in, 244–259; Leftist foothold in, 51; material conditions in, 242–244; natural resources in, 39–40; neoliberalism in, 238–239; "shock treatments" in, 238–239; socialism in, 237

Lebanon, 107–108

Left, 232–235; emergence of, 235–244; future of, 244–259; material conditions and, 242–244; political conditions and, 241–242

Legitimacy, state, consumption and, 166

Lehman Brothers, 17, 102, 122, 190–191

Liberalism: dominance of, 77; embedded, 154
Liberia, 40
Limits: on capital, 211–215; on growth, 109; in Marx, 90; on profit, 91
Liquidity: in Marxist theory, 58; mortgage lending increase and, 15; in response to crisis, 11; use of newfound, 15–16; vulnerability and, 17–18
Lloyds Banking Group, 197
Lomnitz, Claudio, 248
"London Consensus," 196
London School of Economics, 89
"Long bubble," 25–30
"Long century." *See* Systemic cycle of accumulation (SCA)
Long Term Capital Management, 266n9
Lucas, Robert E., 127, 279n34
Lugo, Fernando, 240
Lula. *See* Da Silva, Luis Inácio Lula
Luxembourg, Rosa, 99, 174

Madoff, Bernard, 115, 277n15
Management, of crises, 194–195
Managerial costs, 81–82
Manias, Panics, and Crashes (Kindleberger), 116–117
Mankiw, N. Gregory, 127
Manufacturing, financialization and decline of, 23, 57
Marx, Karl, 57–58, 89, 109–110, 116, 122, 174, 212
Marxism, 215
MAS. *See* Movement Toward Socialism (MAS)

Mass media, 193–194
Mass personal consumption, 129
Material expansion: China as future center of, 65; of global economy, 54; global institutions and, 58–59; hegemony and, 65; social barriers to, 65–66
Mathematical models, 188
Means of production, 94–95
Media, 193–194
Merchant-capitalist organizations, 99–100
Meritocracy, 86
Merkel, Angela, 260
Merrill Lynch, 118, 122
Merton, Robert C., 23, 266n9
Mexico, 237, 239, 251, 253
Migration, urban, 177
Milanovic, Branko, 283n15
Military Keynesianism, 219
Military power: declining importance of, 63–64; potential *vs.* used, 74
Milken, Michael, 22–23
Minsky, Hyman, 120
Misframed protections, 152–154
Mismatches of scale, 152–154
Mitchell, Wesley, 124
Models: mathematical, 188; risk, 121
Monedero, Juan Carlos, 291n30
Monetary Control Act, 190
Monopoly: profit and, 72; as self-liquidating, 72
Moody's, 119
Morales, Evo, 52, 240, 248
Mortgage-backed securities: as balance sheet collateral, 14–15; creation of, 14; Fannie Mae and

Freddie Mac in, 119; as Ponzi scheme, 119; ratings of, 119; risk and, 14; role of, in financial system, 14–15; in speculative bubble, 118–119; in spread of crisis, 102

Mortgages: "American Dream" and, 265n4; in leadup to crisis, 13–14; NINJA, 120; promise of sale or refinance in selling of, 114–115; "red-lining" of, 265n4; risk models on, 121; securitization of, 14; speed of issuing, 14; subprime, 14, 114–115; variable-interest, 118–119

Movement Toward Socialism (MAS), 253

MST. *See* Landless Workers Movement (MST)

Mujica, José, 240, 254, 256

Multiculturalism, 149

Multidimensionality, 191–196

Multinational corporations: capitalism in United States and, 61–62; investment in China by, 63

NAFTA. *See* North American Free Trade Agreement (NAFTA)

Napoleonic Wars, 73

Narratives, of crisis, 44

Nationalism, 135

Nationalization, of corporations, 196–197

Natural resources: in Africa, 40; demand for, 40; dependence on, 39–40; in Latin America, 39–40; in Russia, 30–31, 39

Nature, scarcities in, 94–95

Neoliberalism: apologist view of,

169–170; bubbles and, 26–27; Chinese ascendancy and, 222–223; collateral damage with, 36; crisis of, 236–241; critical theory and, 137; financialization and, 47; income distribution and, 169–170; Latin American rejection of, 231; Obama and, 239–240; as old concept, 139; opposition to, 238; privatization and, 161; reform and, 132; rise of, in 1970s, 22; 1970s and, 217; "shock treatments," 238–239; working class and, 166

Netherlands: in evolutionary patterns of world capitalism, 61*f*; financialization in, 57; Genoa *vs.*, 60; in Marx, 59

Network society, 185–186, 191–192

New Deal, 266n5

New Left, 150

Newspapers, 116

New York Times (newspaper), 43, 117–118, 172, 260

Nicaragua, 237

Nietzsche, Friedrich, 212

Nike, 100

1987 stock market crash, 123

1970s: decolonization in, 20–21; downturn in, as precursor, 216–221; exchange rates in, 22; financialization in, rise of, 20–21; neoliberalism's roots in, 22, 217; OPEC actions in, 69; recession in, 20, 22

1960s, 21

1968, world revolution of, 74–77

NINJA loans, 120

Nocera, Joe, 43

"Normal" downturns, 70–74
Norms: ethics and, 148–149; regulation and, 147
North American Free Trade Agreement (NAFTA), 239
Northern Rock Bank, 16, 102
North Korea, 32

Obama, Barack, 239–240
O'Connor, James, 95
Old Left, 75–76
Olympics, 100
OPEC. *See* Organization of the Petroleum Exporting Countries (OPEC)
Opportunity, crisis and, 41–42
Options, 188
Organization of the Petroleum Exporting Countries (OPEC), 69
Organized labor, 94
Ortega, Daniel, 240

Paraguay, 240, 242
Parity, participatory, 149–150
Participatory parity, 149–150
Partido Revolucinario Institucional (PRI), 251
Patriarchy, 192–193
Paulson, Henry, 92
Peer-to-peer cultural sharing, 208
Pentecostalism, 33
Perestroika, capitalist, 199–206
Pérez, Carlos Andrés, 239
Perfect competition, 71
Personal consumption, mass, 129
Personnel costs, 81
Pharmaceuticals, 208

Philips, Kevin, 26
Piñera, Sebastián, 252, 258
Pinochet, Augusto, 231, 243
Piqueteros, 237, 253
Polanyi, Karl, 138–150
Ponzi, Charles, 277n15
"Ponzi finance," 120
Ponzi scheme: bubbles and, 173; mortgage-backed securities as, 119
Population, in income distribution calculation, 171
Portugal, 107
Post-Fordism, 63
Postindustrial capitalism, 228–229
Postmodernism, 212
Postwar boom, 20
Poverty: as endemic, 38; globalization and, 159; policies combating, 182; welfare states and, 180
Power: cost externalization and, 67; financial expansions and, 58; material expansion and, 65; rises to, 73
Prescott, Edward C., 127
PRI. *See* Partido Revolucinario Institucional (PRI)
Price(s): determination, 80, 83; housing: belief in rise of, 14; effects of fall in, 121–122
Prigogine, Ilya, 85
Primitive accumulation, 59
Privatization, of public services, 161
Producer cooperatives, 206–207
Production: consumption and, 167; credit and, 163; in Fordism, 169; geographical extension of, 168; globalization and, 168; income and, 164; means of, 94–95

Production capital, 90

Production costs, types of, 80

Productivity: needed surge in, 201; stimulus and, 105; U.S., 189

Product life-cycles, 100

Profit: demand and, 167; in financial services industry, 189; increasing focus on, 24; limits on, 91; monopoly and, 72; order and, 73; perfect competition and, 71; prices and, 83; rise in, 117

Profit-squeeze model, 165

Project for a New American Century, 53, 63

Property, borrowing on value of, 190

Protection, social, 140–144, 181

Public health, 208

Publicity, civil, 148

Public transfers, 179

Public universities, 36–37

Purchasing capacity, credit and, 164

Pyramid scheme: bubbles and, 173; mortgage-backed securities as, 119

Queen Elizabeth, 89

Radicalism, in 1960s, 21

Rating agencies, 119

R&D. *See* Research-and-development (R&D)

Reagan, Ronald, 22

Real-estate borrowing, 190

Recurrence, 56–59

Redistribution, income, 176, 180–181

"Red-lining," 265n4

Reform, question of, 133–135

Regional blocks, 32

Regulation: capital flow and, 187–188; class balance and, 168; global governance and, 169; global informational capitalism and, 186; nonstate institutions in history of, 147; norms and, 147; in Polanyi, 139; question of, 133–135; speculation and, 128–129

Reinhart, Carmen, 117

Religion: extremism in, 34; persistence of, 33

Remedial policies, 196–199

Rentier class, 95

Repression: financial, 93; wage, 94

Research-and-development (R&D), 201

Reserve currency, 78

Responses, to financial crisis, 11

Responsibility, systemic *vs.* individual, 43–44

Right: Left *vs.*, 232–235; rise of, 77–78

Risk: counterparty, 17; erroneous calculation of, 121; models, 121; mortgage-backed securities and, 14, 119; spread of, 189; systemic: ignorance of, 89; IMF on, 89; in Marx, 89

Rogoff, Kenneth, 117

Rogues, crisis as fault of, 43–44

Rostow, Walt, 125

Rotker, Susan, 245

Roussef, Dilma, 240

Russia: development pattern in, 39; in global policy fold, 133; human capital in, 39; natural resources in, 30–31, 39

Rust Belt, 36

Samuelson, Paul, 124
Sandinistas, 237, 251
Sanjinés, Javier, 262
Sarkozy, Nicolas, 260
Sassen, Saskia, 18
Savings and loan scandal, 124
Savings rates: rising, as problem, 201–202; U.S., 190
SCA. *See* Systemic cycle of accumulation (SCA)
Scale, mismatches of, 152–154
Scaramucci, Anthony, 43, 44
Scarcities, 94–95
Scholes, Myron, 23, 267n9
Schumpeter, Joseph, 124, 125–126, 219
Scott, David, 262–263
Seattle Downtown Rotary Club, 134
"Second American Century," 53
Securitization, 14, 118, 188, 189. *See also* Mortgage-backed securities
Self-employment, 179
"Self-regulating market," 139, 141
September 11 attacks, 27, 31, 91
Service sectors, 227
70s. *See* 1970s
Shiller, Robert, 116, 128
Silver, Beverly, J., 294
Sittlichkeit, 147
60s. *See* 1960s
Slums, 177
Smith, Adam, 215–216
Smoot-Hawley tariff, 129
Social assistance, growing demand for, 179
Social change, in Marx, 109–110
Social complexity, 66

Social democracy, 176–177
Social-democratic parties, 75–76
Social expenditures, 180–181
Socialism, 109, 235
Socialist bloc, 75
Social policy, 181–182
Social protection, 140–144, 181
Social wage, 166, 181
Social welfare, inequality and, 34–41
Society: civil, 147–148; as locus of domination, 150; network, 185–186, 191–192; in Polanyi, 146–149
Society of the Spectacle, The (Debord), 100
Solomou, Solomos, 126
Sousa Santos, Bonaventura, 249
South, Global, welfare states in, 179–180
South of the Border (film), 241
Soviet Union, collapse of, 27, 30
Spaces of Hope (Harvey), 262
Spain, 107, 200, 286n15
Speculation: in dot-com bubble, 25; frenzy of, 115; growth of, 15–16; in Kondratieff B periods, 78; mortgage-backed securities in, 118–119; newfound liquidity in, 15; regulation and, 128–129
"Speculative finance," 120
Spengler, Oswald, 212
"Spirit of Davos strategy," 86
"Spirit of Port Allegre strategy," 86
"Stagflation," 96
Standard and Poor's, 119
State capitalism, 218
State guarantees, 83

State legitimacy, consumption and, 166

Stationary state, 225–229

Stiglitz, Joseph, 135

Stimulus package(s): Chinese, 105, 181, 200; duration of crisis and, 202–203; inequality and, 176; U.S., 104

Stone, Oliver, 241

Strikes, in China, 106

Structural crisis, 84–85

Subprime mortgages, 14, 114–115

Subsidies, drop in, 159

Sudan, 40

Summers, Lawrence, 127

Swaps, credit-default, 16

Systemic cycle(s) of accumulation (SCA): anomalies in, 63–68; definition of, 55; evolution of, 60–63, 61f; identification of historic, 55; recurrence in, 56–59

Systemic responsibility, individual vs., 43–44

Systemic risk: ignorance of, 89; IMF on, 89; in Marx, 89

Taiwan, 32

Tariff, Smoot-Hawley, 129

TARP. See Troubled Asset Relief Program (TARP)

Taxation: levels of, 83; raising, 199–200; value and, 166

Technological cycles, 129–132

Technological epochs, 126

Technology, global financialization and, 188

Terrorism, 27, 31

Tet offensive, 76

Thatcher, Margaret, 22, 70

Third Way, 252

Thirty Years' War, 73

Three-layer economy, 205

Time (magazine), 113

Toynbee, Arnold, 212

Toyota, 106

Traders, 15–16

"Transfers," 179, 180

Transportation systems, 207–208

Treasury bonds: Asian purchase of, 63; Chinese purchase of, 79; Iraq War and, 189

Trinberger, Jan, 124

Triumphalism, 76

Troubled Asset Relief Program (TARP), 16, 106

Tupamaros, 254

Underconsumption. See also Consumption: credit and, 164–165, 172; demand and, 165; income distribution and, 168; income redistribution and, 176; labor and, 167

Underemployment, 187

Unemployment: problem of, 202; as result of crisis, 187

United Kingdom: in evolutionary patterns of world capitalism, 61f; material expansion centered in, 61

United Nations Development Program, 67

United States: belief in continuing dominance of, 53; Bretton Woods Accord, pull out from, 22;

capital flow into, before financial crisis, 174; credit-market debt to GDP ratio in, 172; crisis as end of hegemony of, 55; debt of, 104; as debtor nation, 63, 64*f*; in evolutionary patterns of world capitalism, 61–62, 61*f*; financial sector growth in, 162–163; hegemonic height of, 71; income distribution in, 170; military resource concentration in, 63; productivity in, 189; Rust Belt decline in, 36; savings rates in, 190; stability maintenance by, 75; stimulus package in, 104; Vietnam War and, 21, 22, 74, 76; waning dominance of, 19, 30, 31, 53–54; wealth distribution in, changing, 23–24

Universal health care, 180
Universalism, 86
Universities, public, 36–37
University of Chicago, 128
Unskilled labor, cost of, 81
Urban farming, 207
Urban migration, 177
Uruguay, 240, 242, 256
Use-value economy, 206–209

Value: credit and, 164; taxation and, 166
Variable-interest loan, 118–119
Vásquez, Tabaré, 240, 248
Venezuela, 40, 239, 240, 250, 252, 257
Venture capital, 24
Vietnam syndrome, 74
Vietnam War, 21, 22, 74, 76
Virtualization, of capital, 188 .

Voluntary associations, 208
Volunteer-based social services, 208
Von Hayek, Friedrich, 22

Wage(s). *See also* Income distribution: fall in, 189; globalization and, 167–168; low-cost labor and, 178; social, 166, 181; stagnation of, 189
Wage repression, 94
Wallerstein, Immanuel, 295
Wall Street (film), 23
Walmart, 99–100
WaMu (bank), 113–114, 121–122, 124, 134
War on Terror, 31
"Washington Consensus," 51, 196, 236
Weber, Max, 261
Welfare states: capacities of, 35–36; as continuing, 159–160; in Global South, 179–180; poverty and, 180; as stagnant, 161
Wilder, Gary, 263
Williamson, John, 236
Winockas, Michel, 260
Wolfe, Tom, 15
Wollstonecraft, Mary, 151
World Bank: attention shift of, 180; strengthening of, 198
World revolution of 1968, 74–77
World Social Forum, 237, 251
World state, 61*f*, 62, 64–65
World Trade Organization (WTO), decolonization and, 154
World War I, 73, 129
World War II, 73, 129, 135
Wrigley, E. A., 216

WTO. *See* World Trade Organization (WTO)

Xinjiang, 34

Yom Kippur War, 22

Zapatistas, 237, 239, 251